Bob Garratt

Building Intelligent Boards

Bob Garratt

Building Intelligent Boards

A New Perspective on Corporate Governance

DE GRUYTER

ISBN 978-3-11-223133-3
ISBN 978-3-11-223134-0 (PDF)
ISBN 978-3-11-223135-7 (EPUB)
DOI https://doi.org/10.1515/9783112231340

Library of Congress Control Number: 2026934613

Bibliographic information published by the Deutsche Nationalbibliothek
The Deutsche Nationalbibliothek lists this publication in the Deutsche Nationalbibliografie; detailed bibliographic data are available on the internet at http://dnb.dnb.de.

De Gruyter and Walter de Gruyter GmbH are part of De Gruyter Brill.
www.degruyterbrill.com

Questions about General Product Safety Regulation:
productsafety@degruyterbrill.com

Cover illustration: Janet McCallum Design/www.janetmccallumdesign.co.uk

To Sally Diane Garratt
1945 – 2023

My lifelong partner, friend, and thoughtful critic. An astute observer, a natural social anthropologist with an acute sense of the absurd, and a collector of 'interesting' people internationally. In a very busy world, she always made time for others and knew how to throw very good parties. Her spirit was sitting at my shoulder ensuring her careful overview throughout the writing of this book.

To Peter Garratt
1948 – 2020

My dear brother, civil engineer, sailor, rugby player, cheerful contrarian, and publicly professed social sceptic. Yet despite his seeming grumpiness he was always on hand to help anyone in real need in the community. He seemed amazed that folk respected him for this.

Endorsements

"In Building Intelligent Boards, Bob Garratt tears off the respectable mask of corporate governance to reveal what insiders have long whispered but never dared publish — that the people running our most powerful institutions are, by an overwhelming majority, winging it. Bob demolishes myths ranging from shareholder ownership to the superior role of the CEO and director liability. This is the rare business book that reads like a whistleblower's confession and a manifesto at once, delivering the uncomfortable truth that the rot starts at the very top, written by someone who has sat in numerous boardrooms in many countries and watched emperors parade go by without a stitch."

Professor Michael Mainelli, Chairman, Z/Yen Group; President, London Chamber of Commerce & Industry; Lord Mayor of London 2023–2024

"In an environment of growing complexity and institutional pressure, this book challenges the myths that continue to diminish the importance of corporate governance. By reframing governance as a professional discipline and offering a clear pathway to stronger board capability, it provides timely guidance for building more effective and resilient organisations."

Coral Ingley, Independent Director

"The darkest hours are before the dawn, as they say. As we navigate these profound times, we rely on torch bearers to move us forwards in the right direction. Bob has always been a forefront torch bearer for good governance – in my view THE most important area to focus our transformational efforts. In this timely work, Building Intelligent Boards reminds us of some basics and gives us advanced tools to do the work needed. Bob shows us that this isn't about creating something entirely new – instead about recovering the original intention of the law, the best of human capacity and anchoring to the moral codes we can still see all around us... if we dare to look beyond profit."

Dr Victoria Hurth, author of Beyond Profit: Purpose-Driven leadership for a Well-being Economy

"Garratt's Classic How-To-Book *Building Intelligent Boards*, is a must read for current and aspiring Directors and for those Executives who report to them. Intelligent Boards details with precision and clarity the complexities and conflicts, regulatory, human and the operational requirements, of Board Members' accountabilities, providing Garratt's Learning Board Model for their implementation."

Dr Denise Fleming AM

 | https://doi.org/10.1515/9783112231340-202

"A brilliant read that belongs in every boardroom. Prof Bob Garratt expertly weaves enduring corporate governance challenges into the realities of modern volatility, calling for critical thinkers capable of leading human organisations with wisdom and foresight. At CCGI, this is precisely the standard of board leadership we seek to cultivate across our region."

Kamla Rampersad de Silva, Chief Executive Officer, Caribbean Corporate Governance Institute

"Good governance today needs new agenda items: IT governance and cybersecurity, risks and opportunities of climate change, different inputs to outcomes, sustainability in a company's supply chain and working on a double materiality basis. Any significant matter that influences a stakeholder should now be disclosed. From his long experience Bob Garratt addresses these issues head-on and honestly to challenge the next generation of directors."

Professor Mervyn King, 5 King Reports, South Africa

"A timely blueprint for learning boards and professional directors — practical, direct, and aligned with what society increasingly expects of boards, and what global governance standards and practices seek to embed."

Carolynn J. Chalmers, Carolynn, CEO, Good Governance Academy

"In this book, Bob Garratt continues his important work to demystify corporate governance. He provides the language and the concepts that the next generation of directors will need to be informed, competent and ultimately professional."

Daniel Malan, Director: Trinity Corporate Governance Lab, Trinity College Dublin

"Building Intelligent Boards by Bob Garratt is a powerful wake-up call for modern leadership. With clarity, conviction, and deep practical insight, Garratt transforms corporate governance from a dusty obligation into the beating heart of organisational success. This book is bold, timely, and essential reading for anyone serious about steering institutions with wisdom, integrity, and purpose."

Janice Caplan, Former Vice President Chartered Institute for People and Development

A Note on Terminology

I use the word 'Chairman' throughout this book for two reasons. First, it is a legal term that has lasted as part of the Common Law for centuries across the 56 Commonwealth countries. No country has yet found it necessary to adapt their legislation. Second, many of my clients are women. Most have an objection to be called the common alternative – 'chair'. This has been pointed out by strong women saying 'I am a powerful person in my own right. I am not an inanimate object for sitting on'. I respect their wishes.

 | https://doi.org/10.1515/9783112231340-203

Author's Foreword

This book explores the little-known world of 'corporate governance'. It is a mystery to the public and worryingly unknown to many directors, boards, and politicians. Rather than accept corporate governance as the fundamental legal framework for their key role in their organisation, most nominal directors view it simply as an irritating minor additional task – nice to do if only we had time. This book argues that by so believing they are avoiding their legal and professional duties; to steer their organisation through increasingly complex and difficult times and simultaneously to keep it under prudent control. I argue that to deliver these two key roles the next generation of directors will not have the option of avoidance. They will need to adopt a radically new and holistic perspective of their dual roles to cope with continuous change in their external and internal worlds. This is way beyond the current understanding of the roles of directors and boards. Without these changes our institutions will continue to erode. By adopting them, we shall develop mature and professional boards capable of delivering the purpose of their organisation.

 | https://doi.org/10.1515/9783112231340-204

Contents

Endorsements — VII

A Note on Terminology — IX

Author's Foreword — XI

Acknowledgements — XVII

Part I: **Recognising Corporate Governance**

Chapter 1
Corporate Governance Now: An Overview — 3
References — **10**

Chapter 2
Demystifying Corporate Governance — 11
Reframing Corporate Governance — **14**
The Four Stages of Board Maturity — **16**
Common Myths About Corporate Governance — **19**
Government and Corporate Governance — **29**
References — **34**

Chapter 3
Resisting Corporate Governance – Dated Directors And Grudgingly Compliant Directors — 35
Accidental Directors – Level 1 Board Maturity — **35**
Key Questions for The Accidental Director — **39**
Common Issues for Accidental Directors — **41**
Grudgingly Compliant Directors – Level Two Board Maturity — **56**
References — **70**

Part II: **Implementing Effective Corporate Governance**

Chapter 4
The Learning Board: Level Three Board Maturity — 75
Developing Board Intelligence — **76**
The Learning Board Framework — **91**
References — **105**

Chapter 5
Level Four Board Maturity: The Board as a Professional Team — 107
Building the Board Team — **109**
Developing Board Policy As A Team — **118**
Developing Team Board Strategy — **122**
References — **141**

Chapter 6
Issues Blocking an Integrated Learning System for Effective Corporate Governance — 142
The Five Key Players — **143**
A More Systems-based Approach to Corporate Governance — **144**
Recognising the Unresolved Questions for the Five Stakeholder Groups — **144**
Seven Unresolved Questions for Legislators — **145**
Five Unresolved Questions for Future Directors — **147**
Two Unresolved Questions for Stakeholders — **148**
Four Unresolved Questions for Financial Stakeholders — **149**
Four Unresolved Questions for Operational 'Internal' Stakeholders — **152**
Three Unresolved Questions for Environmental and Community Stakeholders — **153**
Four Unresolved Questions for Regulators — **155**
Unresolved Issues if the Public is to Oversee Effective Corporate Governance — **156**
Integrating The Five Main Players — **157**
Improving Our Rate of Public Learning — **157**
How Can Companies and the Public Combine to Integrate a Learning Approach Nationally and Internationally? — **158**
To Design a Constructive Future You Must Understand the Past: 1776 and all that — **159**
The Modern Context — **161**
The 2007 – 2010 Western Financial Crisis — **162**
Are there Alternatives? — **163**
A Proposal for National Standing Commissions on the Effectiveness of Corporate Governance — **164**
References — **165**

Chapter 7
The Challenge to Next Generation Directors to Create an Ecosystem for Developing Effective Corporate Governance — 166
The Challenge for Next Generation Directors — **166**
The Board of Directors — **166**
Signs of Spring — **167**
Reasons to be Cheerful but Aware — **169**
Ubuntu — **170**
References — **171**

Index — 173

Acknowledgements

This book is the result of reviewing hundreds of my board consultancy and board assessment projects in over thirty countries. But it is not a single effort. I worked for fifty years with my late marital and business partner, Sally, who added greatly to my insight into board behaviours and eccentricities, whilst patiently tolerating my own.

The Covid-19 pandemic of 2020-22 had a major impact on my writing. It restricted drastically my many travels yet expanded my diversity of experiences and thoughts. It stopped dead my jet-setting and forced me, within a week, into accepting such new technologies of Zoom and Teams. It proved that humans, even me, *are* infinitely adaptable. I was back 'on' five continents electronically in days. But instead of just handling face-to-face, or small group sessions, I was able surprisingly to tap into and help develop much larger groups to grow ideas and good practice co-operatively and internationally around corporate governance issues. I gained great new insights and constructive criticism in parts of the world like the Arabian Gulf, South Africa, and the Caribbean where demand for effective corporate governance is growing rapidly and creatively well beyond existing Western mindsets.

A remarkable parallel to this technological phenomenon was the emergence of many powerful women driving these developments. The work of Jane Valls at the Gulf Co-operation Council's Board Development Institute, and of Kamla Rampersad DeSilva at the Caribbean Corporate Governance Institute, is notable. They have spun off global self-help networks including Women in Corporate Governance, The International Learning Network, Institutes of Directors of Small Nations, and are now looking at the development of Small Smart States.

During 2020 – 2024 I have been helped, criticised, and fact-checked by an informal, international, and remarkably diverse group of energised colleagues, many of them female. They were very keen to help this 'founding father' and I am equally keen to acknowledge them in return.

Gill Atkins	England UK
Liz Barber	England UK
Janice Caplan	England UK
Ronaele Dathorne-Bayrd	Barbados
Carolynn Chalmers	South Africa
Denise Fleming	Australia
Victoria Hurth	England UK
Coral Ingley	New Zealand
Kate Jolly	Scotland UK
Alexandra Lajoux	US
Nandi Mandela	South Africa
Janet McCallum	England UK

 | https://doi.org/10.1515/9783112231340-206

Coralie Palmer	Wales UK
Kamla Rampersad DeSilva	Trinidad
Nathalie Romang	France
Thina Siwendu	South Africa
Jane Valls	United Arab Emirates
Charlotte Valeur	Jersey, and Denmark

This is not to deny the men. I have had continuous critical support during the last three turbulent years from:

Peter Aylwin	Australia and UK
Peter Barrett	Hong Kong, Malta, and UK
Peter Crow	New Zealand
Peter Gorer	US
Charles Handy	England UK
David Jackson	England UK
Guy Jubb	Scotland UK
Mervyn King	South Africa
Daniel Malan	South Africa and Ireland
Mike Mainelli	US and England UK
Bob Monks	US
David Prestwich	England UK
Nigel Romano	Trinidad
Gunnar Walstam	Sweden and Switzerland
Hugh Willmott	England UK
and, over a much longer time,	
the late Sir Adrian Cadbury	England UK.

Part I: **Recognising Corporate Governance**

Chapter 1
Corporate Governance Now: An Overview

Across the world the public feel that their organisations are not well governed. But they feel helpless at doing anything to change this. They feel that those charged with being ultimately accountable for delivering total organisational effectiveness, the directors, are not competent. They are usually correct.

Yet our organisations are the apex of human development. Directors are accountable for both giving them direction to achieve their purpose; and simultaneously ensuring their prudent control. So, it is a paradox that directorship, the most important job needed to sustain and develop our human organisations, is often given to those with the least training to fulfil these duties.

Arguments rage over whether our current directoral incompetence and organisational ineffectiveness are caused mainly by conspiracy, cock-up, or pure ignorance. There is evidence of a toxic mixture of all, depending on the country. However, I would argue that the dominant factor in organisational ineffectiveness is the directors' ignorance of their legal role and public accountabilities. Few directors have had any specific training for directing or for delivering 'effective corporate governance'. Globally most people neither know nor care what the phrase 'corporate governance' means. Yet this mutual ignorance and silence have become self-sustaining, blocking much useful information flowing between the board, its external world and, just as importantly, the potentially rich information flows between staff and managers within the organisation that usually cannot be shared upwards. For example, at a personal level the public are extremely vocal about the current collapse of anything resembling customer service, while they are pestered non-stop by the offending business for online 'feedback', which they then ignore.

A common language and learning process is needed now for the next generation of directors to break this mutually debilitating cycle to create more humane organisations. I think that even in more stable times the current generation of directors have failed in this respect. It is now up to the next generation to create a more professional future role for directors to cope with the much more turbulent times ahead. But how?

'Corporate Governance' concerns the effectiveness of a board of directors in implementing their organisation's current purpose and ensuring its future health while keeping it under prudent control. In 1776 Adam Smith viewed this as a strong moral duty for directors when he published the book that became the touchstone of modern capitalism – *An Inquiry Into the Nature and Causes of The Wealth Of Nations*. Often quoted but seldom read, the book has a strong focus on the need for 'moral sentiment' in business leadership. This is a surprise to many. This duty has been underplayed by economists for centuries. It is now being noted by a growing number of next generation directors. This duty still holds despite many detractors insisting that business has no reason to deal in morals. It means directors being held legally accountable for giv-

 | https://doi.org/10.1515/9783112231340-001

ing their businesses wise direction into that increasingly complex and uncertain future. Simultaneously, they are also publicly accountable for ensuring that they use rapid learning systems to guarantee the prudent control of their organisation. By doing both they deliver their purpose within the law. This is an intellectual and emotional challenge for which few existing directors are prepared. They, and the new generation of directors, must learn to rise to the challenges of such complexity. It is a huge task that affects the operational effectiveness and sustainability of all human organisations. Unless they learn to meet it, directors present, and future simply cannot do their duty.

In this book I stick tightly to the long-established Common Law concerning director and board accountabilities. It puzzles me why, having spent decades passing this legislation, few politicians know their law and seem to care little about implementing it. Even fewer seem to want to learn from it: but I do. I feel that it is a key to creating more human organisations. I frame my learning using my deep interests in history, words, design, and human creativity.

That our current approach to understanding and practising corporate governance has run aground is shown by the global public's increasing anger at the lack of effective direction shown by their leaders – directors, politicians, regulators, civil servants, state-owned enterprises, fund managers, non-governmental organisations, health service providers, and not-for-profits. I argue that the emerging next generation of directors cannot avoid having to resolve such demanding issues of economic, environmental, and social complexity that a total reset of the meaning, values, and practice of 'corporate governance' is needed urgently. It will be demanded of them. Such problems are well beyond the current 'business' boundaries of finance, supply chains, and management alone. Neither are the issues resolved by simply focussing on such narrowly abstract fields as Diversity, Equality, and Inclusion, or ESG, noble as the original thoughts behind them were.

Our current leaders are confused and wrong-footed by the simultaneous converging and competing demands that are insoluble within today's political and administrative mindsets. I argue for the reframing and professionalisation of directoral mindsets, rising above current managerial, financial, and party-political blinkered thinking. The current forms of 'corporate governance' fail, as all parties involved are embarrassed by refusing publicly to acknowledge their ignorance and lack of training. Directors fear the looming unknowns if such knowledge gaps are exposed and acknowledged, while most of the world exists in a state of Fear of Missing Out, directors are usually in a state of Fear of Finding Out. I see this book as the antidote – a mixture of demystification plus a design for a new future.

Directors dread the seemingly dire consequences of opening to public debate this Pandora's box. It is a case of corporate Emperor's Clothes. But there are too few small children pointing out the blindingly obvious. This continuing silence and lack of direction erode the cohesiveness of our communities. The silence is especially visible between the decision-makers and their staff. It must be broken. At least customers can make their views known by what they buy or do not. Citizens subject to local and national government, public services and quangos have no such immediate recourse.

The term corporate governance first appears in book form with the publication of Bob Tricker's 1984 eponymous work. From an early and energising start by the UK in 1992, and rapidly by South Africa in the heady days of the Nelson Mandela government, the global approach to developing corporate governance faltered within a decade and has eroded all too rapidly. It is important to note that such movements were started by professional institutes and private individuals, not governments. Forty years ago, many directors were aware of their need to change. But state bureaucracy rapidly saw a chance of establishing its grip on this new and powerful field and the idea of imposing politically inspired codes and regulations flourished. Instead of encouraging thoughtful, ethical, and humanity-enhancing entrepreneurial actions in our organisations, led by competent directors, the movement has been captured by legislators, bureaucrats, and Human Resources Officers, aided by short-term trading greed. These have smothered it in a web of unnecessary codes, rules, financial obfuscations, unethical values, and misunderstood cultural jargon.

This ossification and erosion of effective corporate governance is at a time when broader, more flexible, and deeper thinking and actions are needed globally to ensure our human existence. Massive conflicting environmental, societal, political, and economic pressures are converging on unprepared boards. These demand thinking and constructive actions way beyond most directors' current competences or expectations. They transcend the previously accepted 'corporate governance' boundaries as measured ultimately merely by financial performance – 'the bottom line'. They challenge future boards of directors to broaden their perspectives to think and act by simultaneously integrating their entrepreneurial purpose with their environmental, social, economic and ethical decisions, and learning from their combined impacts. This goes way beyond the current financial and regulatory fixation.

We can build a viable future for corporate governance as the essential underpinning of our future human institutions by demystifying the present mess, and showing ways to develop more mature, competent, wiser and decent boards. This distils the essence of corporate governance effectiveness – the ability to simultaneously show the way ahead, and ensure prudent control of, our organisations. Directing is becoming a distinctly demanding professional job that needs continuous learning. It is not 'management'. Nor is it a comfortable payoff to an active managerial career.

Directing is quite different from managing – intellectually and operationally. To highlight this, I describe four levels of assessing future board maturity in Chapter Three. Accepting these levels of board maturity breaks the current corrupting corporate silence and focuses future boards, investors, legislators, and regulators' oversight on assessing and criticising a board's current level of maturity. This heavy lifting must now pass to the next generation of directors. They are the ones who will have to deliver their purpose in a messy world, featuring pressures such as Net Zero, significant climate change, mass migration, monetary instability, and much else beyond.

My background is of architectural education design (combining science, art, technology, nature, and practice) and organisational development, I am considered a strange outsider by the financially fixated. I am proud to be so labelled. I remain perplexed as to why so many people in the currently stalled 'corporate governance' sector stay focused only on growing more codes, rules, regulation, and financial complexities. Where is their imagination, and the necessary broader perspective? Out of necessity, many parts of the world are having to move beyond such obsolete mindsets. I think that at its core, effective corporate governance's future focus must be on the human entrepreneurial interactions needed to create and learn from these new 'polycrises'.

However, two major problems that I have encountered throughout my consulting career are that most folk do not distinguish between national 'government' and 'corporate 'governance': nor between corporate governance and 'management'. They assume that they must be the same. They are not. This book specifically concerns *corporate* governance – the effectiveness and efficiency of human institutions, our organisations that should bind our human cultures and civilisations together. It is the erosion of this sense of belonging about which many of the public are complaining.

However, I am increasingly optimistic about, and find growing energy from, the numbers seeking to reframe 'corporate governance'. This hope arises from disaffected current directors, the rising Next Generation, and, most importantly, from two emerging new power sources. First, the continuing rapid rise of powerful, influential women in the corporate governance field, many outside Europe and the US. They are just beginning to be recognised and celebrated properly. These include in my mind the previously under-acknowledged 'founding mothers' of the corporate governance movement, for example, Nell Minow, Anne Simpson, Barbara Judge, Christine Malins, Phillipa Foster Back, Michele Edkins, Ansie Ramalho and Charlotte Valuer.

Second, I have hope for the growing number of next generation directors, the under forty-fives, who are now reaching powerful directoral and investment positions. Many accept that, given the complex future environmental and social issues, things cannot continue in the present intellectual torpor and vacuous, finance fixation. They are seeking each other out and linking informally to help develop radical, integrated, entrepreneurial, intellectual, values-based, and investment changes for their, and our, mutual survival. There are even early signs of the growth of a 'movement'.

But there is still much opposition. Many current directors still believe that 'more of the same' must always be better. In design I was taught the reverse – that 'more' usually means less in human terms. I advocate stripping the currently expensive and overblown 'corporate governance' area back to its basics – the purpose of a board of directors, and the duties of a director. I believe that effective corporate governance is at the heart of the continuous human developmental process – the desire to help others through simultaneous entrepreneurial innovation in the areas of economic, social, and environmental development, while working hard to satisfy all stakeholders.

I advocate a 'both/and' approach to corporate governance rather than the current divisive binary 'either/or mind-set.

This book faces directors with their future role – resolving the continual paradox of having to balance human evolutionary growth whilst ensuring reasonable organisational stability and control. In the current political climate of uncertainty, leadership abdication, and corporate lawlessness, both are under threat. It is ironic that currently many directors seem directionless.

As E O Wilson famously observed:

> 'As *we enter the twenty-first century, we have created a Star Wars civilisation with Palaeolithic emotions, Medieval institutions and God-like technology . . . . We are terribly confused by the mere fact of our existence and so a danger to ourselves and others.* [1]

In this book I hope to help resolve some of those medieval institutional and governance, issues, whilst highlighting unresolved cultural, emotional, and technological problems. I want to clear a way for a much simpler yet more effective future for corporate governance. To do this well we need to apply a combination of creative human imagination and more rigorous systematic thinking about our commitment to, and assessment of, our organisational purpose and learning. This is a key leadership role for boards of directors but sadly neglected currently. However, it must be the primary role for those Next Generation boards whose survival depends on the resolution of this dilemma.

Having worked on six continents I know that effective corporate governance is achievable for the benefit of all people and their organisations – private, public, and not-for-profit. Yet I know also that it always involves director investment in *long-term learning* processes blended with humility. This includes governments and civil servants. It is not popular as it confounds their continuously short-term time horizons. Yet 'corporate governance' is something that they cannot ever be seen to be against, even if their rhetoric and support is too weak, brief, and uncommitted to learn to implement it.

But how does one start? First, by accepting publicly that many of our most important and influential organisations, from companies, government departments, quangos to charities, trusts and community enterprises, are seen to be increasingly ineffective. Second, by demystifying the common assumption that past boards understood their governance role and so must have previously given clear direction and purpose. Most did not. Third, by helping our organisational leaders to acknowledge that they are failing to respond to the changed human needs and wants of the twenty-first century. Few have succeeded in describing, let alone resolving, their fundamental governance problem. There is still a deafening silence outside and inside our organisations. This leads to an unwillingness by any side to even raise the issue in public let alone discuss it. The 'fear of finding out' currently over-rides the 'fear of missing out'.

This threatens the future of our human communities. Many people – directors, managers and staff – feel that if they remain silent on the lack of effective governance in their organisations, the issue will somehow disappear. It will not. It festers. There is much evidence (shown later in this book) that it is getting worse and creating a dangerous form of self-fulfilling organisational amnesia mixed with fact avoidance. Businesses can enter la-la land. This destroys the necessary healthy debate and active learning. And with the public frustratingly inarticulate on effective criticism the festering continues This key debate needs to occur at all levels of the company and with the stakeholders, all of whom have long-term survival needs.

This book asks first, and with only mild irony, that the politicians implement the excellent basic laws they themselves have already passed but seem to have forgotten. Fundamental to these are the Duties of a Director, and the Purpose of a Board. Second, that boards consciously live, and are seen to commit to and to live, this legislation so that society can in turn understand and monitor it. This will mean creating more case-law precedents through the courts, then disseminating these so that all can know what is right and wrong in good corporate governance practice.

It is too easy to place blame solely on the awfulness of so many current boards of directors. This is unfair as they are only a part of the current fragmented non-system of directors, owners, stakeholders, legislators, and regulators. These have no agreed process for speaking and learning regularly with and from each other of the likely and actual consequences of their often random actions. Usually, it is only when a scandal or fraud hits the media headlines that the public become aware of corporate governance issues.

My immediate priority is to help stabilise direction-giving by reducing the uncertainty of existing directors and developing the professionalism of the next-generation directors. As we encounter growing turbulence, I find our corporate leaders worryingly unsure of their ability to confidently direct their organisations. This is as true of major listed companies and family businesses as for not-for-profits, government agencies, charities, and community enterprises. Their concerns reflect deeper global issues over society's inability to agree a universal language and framework for assessing and developing leadership and governance competence, especially in times of high uncertainty.

For some four decades I have had the privilege of discussing these issues confidentially with leaders globally. The growing volume and complexity of these directoral demands, especially the immediate need to learn, develop and assess the new attitudes and competences required, seems daunting.

This book is aimed at such leaders and corporate governance practitioners who face these issues in real time. It is based on my international business and community development experience derived as both a Chairman in the UK and Hong Kong, as a jobbing international consultant, and an academic. Some academics will hate this book because it deals with the dynamics of human practice around a boardroom table rather than dry, practice-light, and economic-based theory. It hardly mentions detailed Regulations or Codes, and the growing bureaucratic underpinnings of the current academic 'corporate governance' career-building cottage industry. But that does not say a lot.

The basic entrepreneurial drive for any organisation – to maintain its future health by delivering its purpose – must remain, whether it is assessed as profit or surplus. Calculated risk-taking is the essence of entrepreneurial human development. Profit or surplus is necessary but no longer sufficient. A new and much needed social contract needs developing between organisations, their communities, and the protection of their physical and economic environments. This demands 'both/and' thinking. With the growing fashion for governments demanding 'austerity' it is worth looking at local social enterprises to see evolving both/and approaches. But it is worth remembering that entrepreneurship allows for failure as learning.

New performance criteria are appearing, of which 'ESG' is a faltering passing example. These indicate how future directoral competences will be measured. Such new social demands are now found in emerging legislation in a growing number of countries well beyond the 'developed world'. They appear frequently over social media as indicators of ineffectiveness of the current governance status quo.

Many directors admit privately, and investors know increasingly, that they and their companies are ill-prepared to cope with the new demands. They include such emergent concepts as, for example, 'stakeholders' 'sustainability', 'stewardship', 'zero carbon', 'biodiversity', 'climate change', 'artificial intelligence', 'money laundering' and 'modern slavery' issues. These are converging to force a new social compact with business. But directors also feel increasingly that these new demands are well beyond their current areas of knowledge or comfort. I know of no board that can claim to have succeeded in integrating these new disciplines fully into their board agenda. Yet they acknowledge increasingly that something must be done quickly to avoid the erosion and implosion of our societal stabilising mechanisms – the governance of our human institutions.

As part of my contribution to the resolution of these fundamental human governance issues this book suggests that directors and the public need to understand four sequential stages of board and director maturity development:

- Level One: Accidental Directors
- Level Two: Grudgingly Compliant Directors
- Level Three: The Learning Board
- Level Four: The Professional Board

I have derived these titles from my experiences of developing generational board changes. Levels One and Two describe the current majority of registered directors globally. I label these the 'Dated Directors'. This is the current directors' default setting; muddling through puzzled, unwillingly and ineffectively. I label Levels Three and Four the Future Directors – those who know that they must face the coming changes or perish.

As shown in my previous books [1] (and [2] I seek to redefine and assess the concept of future 'board performance'. I start by arguing that most directors are not consciously incompetent but unconsciously ignorant of their legal duties; and have little motivation to learn them – yet. It is then a major and liberating step towards directoral professionalism for directors to recognise and accept that there is a great deal they need to learn, and that they must re-budget and prioritise their time to keep on learning throughout the time they are directors. It's at this point that they become a team member of a Learning Board – Level Three; which finally opens the way to becoming a Level Four accredited Professional Director.

At the end of the book, I encourage readers to think about ways they, from their current positions, can combine to make practical efforts to help resolve our human corporate governance problems and to create a more positive future for us all.

References

[1] Edward O. Wilson, The Social Conquest of Earth, Harvard University Press, 2012

[2] Bob Garratt, The Fish Rots From The Head: Developing Effective Directors, Profile Books, London, 1996, 2003, 2010

[3] Bob Garratt, Stop The Rot: Reframing Governance for Directors and Politicians, Routledge Books, Abingdon and New York, 2017

Chapter 2
Demystifying Corporate Governance

This book focuses on boards and directors, not managers. Across the world the widely held public perception of directors is that they do not deliver their job title; they rarely give effective direction. In my long consulting and teaching experience this is painfully accurate. Many directors tell me privately that that do not really know what they should be doing. This is unsurprising because they are rarely trained. So this chapter is devoted to going back to basics, ground clearing, and demystifying the many public myths that exist globally about directing. Why do I bother? Because I believe that this is an area of structural importance for the continuation of civil society. It still puzzles me why so many folk are ignorant of it, or consciously avoid it.

For many decades we have existed with the dangerous myth that on being appointed a director it follows automatically that the chosen individual is competent. New directors are aware that they are unprepared but are usually frightened to explore their lack of competence, even with fellow board members, for fear of being found out. The public are not encouraged to explore this myth. So, both groups often yield to, and then suffer, the consequences of powerful, narcissistic individuals running a company as if they have total ownership of it. Legally they do not. Happily, the age of the individual, seemingly all-knowing, all-seeing, ego-centric, 'Heroic CEO' is dying; but slowly and painfully. So, how do we develop the Next Generation of the world's future direction-givers – appointed, elected or dynastic – to avoid such mistakes?

Few current directors are trained to rise above the world of management and finance – the limits of their current experience usually crudely defined as 'the business world'. Most actively avoid entering the new and complex world of professional direction-giving because this demands the skills and attitudes to monitor the continuously changing external world in order to set and reset direction, and simultaneously to prudently oversee the internal, operational world of their business. Few directors feel competent to do either let alone both, individually or collectively. They argue that they have neither the skills nor inclination. Yet the law demands that they must deliver both.

This conflicts with the rising public expectation of current and future directors that they demonstrate such competence. Directors are paid as the only players in their organisations accountable for identifying and resolving these fast-growing multiple dilemmas by balancing economic, environmental, and social issues. Few were expecting to be faced with continuous 'polycrises'.

Current politicians, the legislators for corporate governance, have shown that they cannot resolve these multiple crises effectively by using their existing political frameworks. I argue that such resolution is always beyond the power of politicians and will evolve only through the continuous learning and sharing of decision-making

 | https://doi.org/10.1515/9783112231340-002

by boards internationally. Sharing these across society will demonstrate how thoughtful strategic decisions improve their entrepreneurship whilst designing their future impacts on the environment, social, and political economy.

This demands a very different set of intellectual and critical thinking skills to those that are currently available. It needs the commitment of boards to learn jointly and humbly with their many stakeholders to deliver their organisation's Purpose. The rapid growth of social media means that future boards' competence will be under closer public scrutiny, criticism, and assessment. They will no longer be allowed to mark their own homework.

A board's ultimate purpose is legally to ensure their company's healthy future and to play their part, however small, in creating a sustainable world. Many current directors are baffled by such 'waffly' demands, even if they are being developed and passed as law. Many will fail to meet them. These demands upturn the old mindsets of what boards do. But for the Next Generation of directors this challenge is the very essence of their crucial and exciting new careers – learning to become a professional director and being accredited as such. This involves directors seeking personal learning and development processes and accepting both individual and group responsibilities for their directoral risk-taking decisions.

In turn, this requires developing the attitudes to, and honing their skills of, 'business judgement' – the essence of entrepreneurship. Ultimately, this can only be learned by implementing and testing the consequences of their decisions in real time, rather than just talking and dispassionately observing them. Risks must always be taken by directors, and failures will occur. The law allows that some organisations will not be successful. That is why in civil law the areas of company administration, and liquidation, were developed. It is not unlawful to fail. However, it is criminal to fail fraudulently or corruptly. What is currently unclear is how proven directoral incompetence will be dealt with by the courts in future.

Most directors are not stupid, uncaring, nor egocentric, despite frequent media characterisation as such. Most are good-hearted and willing to 'give back' through their work to their society, although often in some vaguely unspecified way. But many have been selected or elected to a directoral position well beyond their level of directoral knowledge, skill or comfort. The legal job title 'director of the board' sounds impressive, the status is high and publicly visible; but the payment is rarely large and the legal liabilities, both corporate and personal, are daunting once understood. When it is accepted, it is too late to avoid personal liability. Therefore, personal reputations and fortunes risk being trashed. Yet so many folk still aspire to seek the title as their ultimate career goal. This is an unwise wish. Unless directorship is seen as the start of a new and challenging career, the majority will end in discomfort, disillusionment, and failure.

Globally, it is common that on appointment directors are given a large pile of legal documents concerning their roles and duties. This pile is so intimidating that it is rarely studied deeply. It is usually followed by a quick briefing from the Company

Secretary or Legal Counsel, and sometimes the Chairman. New directors are rarely tested on their understanding of that to which they have committed. They are then asked to sign their assent, to register, to assume their legal role. They often feel honoured to do so – and the seduction of the title is complete.

Such 'Registered Directors' rarely understand the depth of the commitments they are making. If they are lucky, they will have a short time with the Chairman about the sort of behaviours and values expected of them. These should be focused on the future health of the company. But they can be highly personal, seeking loyalty only to the Chairman, and some owners. This is not their legal duty, which should be concerning their independence of thought prior to decision-making to promote the health of the business.

Then it is usually a matter of hope and chance as to how they exercise their duties. There may be strong national laws specifying their role, but few countries bother to enforce them strictly. Consequently, public examples of effective directors and boards are rare. It is often only in times of crisis – fraud, maladministration or liquidation – that an individual director's lack of understanding of the directoral role emerges. By then it is much too late for the stakeholders to take redress without crippling litigation on both sides.

Directors, stakeholders, and legislators contribute to this festering problem. There is so little general knowledge about the roles and duties of a director that it is hard to hold them to account. The public rarely know which questions to ask. Even the legislators, who passed the laws originally, rarely know what they contain, despite often voicing very strong views about them. I have experienced this personally when asking a mixed group of UK MPs and Peers to name even half of the seven duties of a director, and the six subsets of the roles of a Board of directors, they had passed under the 2008 Companies Act 2006. None could.

Therefore, it is always worth asking legislators and senior civil servants to name these national legally espoused duties of a director, and the role of a board. In my experience their lack of knowledge is embarrassing, alarming and depressing. Yet the key essence of corporate governance is contained in just one-and-a-half pages of Sections 171 and 172 of the Companies Act, in the case of the UK. The public and the legislators collude unconsciously by assuming that each must know enough to be able to answer. Such answers are often a bluff. Yet when found wanting, their unwillingness to admit this lack of basic knowledge reinforces strongly the continuing silence that blocks the development of effective corporate governance. On such shifting sands an unsafe structure is then built. I want to make it simpler for directors to be able to ask focused questions of their direction-givers and know how to evaluate the answers.

Reframing Corporate Governance

Before going deeply into the legal structure of directorships and the public myths about them, it is worth pausing to understand the broader history of the words currently used and abused.

The meaning and process of 'governance' has always been deeply important to human society and has existed in its present form in the Western world for some 3,500 years. From the ancient Greek *kubernetes* it has evolved through Latin and Old French to modern English. Its stable meaning throughout is 'the steersman' – the person who gives direction to a ship. This is still as valid a description of current board role as it was in the distant past. Today's challenge for directors is to be much more aware of the physical and social environments, and economic contexts into which their enterprise is venturing. and to be held accountable for it.

Yet from the start the word *kubernetes* had an important and parallel second meaning – the control mechanisms that ensure that the desired direction is achieved – the feedback processes from the steering. This second meaning was lost for many centuries, but it has re-emerged in the 21st century through the modern term *cybernetics* and its consequence – systems thinking. This parallel use is remarkably close to the ancient original meaning, and yet very leading-edge. For me the integrated practice of 'corporate governance' describes the board of directors simultaneously balancing both steering the way ahead and ensuring the rapid feedback on progress to ensure the prudent control of the whole organisation. This is a primary legal role of the board of directors. It is not 'management'. Frequently managers do not even have legal definitions of, and little public accountability for, their roles. By contrast Registered Directors are always bound by such laws. This explains the need for re-establishing the supremacy of the board's role.

Given the rethinking occurring globally, directors have an emerging role: the need to balance three types of capital simultaneously – Finance, Physical, and Human – to create an effective enterprise. This is a massive change of mindset for most directors. These three capitals define the new ecological niches within which any human organisation, especially businesses, must learn to survive and thrive. The ethical and broad resource allocation choices made by the board between these three capitals will define both its 'business brain' and 'the conscience' of the firm.

Corporate governance can no longer be led by a simple over-focus on mere Management, Finance, the C-Suite, Codes, Rules, Regulation and Compliance. These may be necessary but are never sufficient. Many countries, led often by ignorant politicians, are in danger of developing ineffective corporate governance systems by such over-regulation. Once the regulators, legislators, and the cottage industry of corporate governance 'experts', over-specify 'corporate governance' they lose the essence of entrepreneurship, public and private, risk-taking, and business effectiveness.

However, there is a growing amount of good news. I always look for the dynamics of serious change at the periphery of current received wisdom. It is noticeable that successful businesses usually take the longer-term view for their survival even if it means suffering immediate financial pain. They incorporate financial, environmental, and social into their strategic thinking. This widens their directoral perspective, leading to a longer-term, more values-based, ethical, stance. The paradox for boards is that while coping with instant uncertainties they must still try to think decades ahead to design a future fit for their next generations. This contrasts with, for example, the disruptive influences of the immediate gratification of short-term traders masquerading as 'shareholders' and 'investors'. Future directors will need long-term investment criteria well beyond the current social media driven fads. But they know that at their core is the integration of those three types of capital. It is their motto and flag. This is the framework with which I test their future effectiveness.

As an example, Family Offices intrigue me as possible role models for long-term governance effectiveness. Their very purpose is the long-term survival of the family wealth. They are the icebergs that silently drive much of modern business development, yet 90% of them are below public view. Their combined wealth is bigger than the GDP of many countries. Combined they can invest in trillions of dollars rather than billions. The good news is that there is now an informal 'next generation' of 35 – 45-year-olds who will have growing influence over the investment decisions of their Family Offices. These 'NextGens' seem driven by noticeably more integrated and balanced views than the departing Baby Boomers over the ethical deployment of the three capitals and their consequent entrepreneurial, environmental and social impacts.

Much of their thinking is at the opposite end of the scale from the failing advocates of Shareholder Supremacy. Paradoxically, these NextGens reflect quietly similar values to the often noisier, yet unfocused general public concerns about the future of our human society. There is no doubt in my mind of the need to create more integrated corporate governance in our private, public and not-for-profit organisations, if we are to reach the common goal of more balanced human survival and development.

The rebalancing of the board's priority away from mere financial capital allocation has been noticeable during the space and time for human reflection created by Covid-19. The classic economic models are already changing. In 2020 the New York Stock Exchange's Standard and Poor's ratings showed that of the top US corporations only 20% of their wealth was held in tangible assets. 80% were formed of 'intangible assets' – with particular and growing demand from investors on the clarity of boards' competence for delivering business purpose, strategic thinking and accountability, credibility of regular reporting, generation of intellectual property, robustness of their future supply chains, and their environmental impact through their careful usage of scarce and polluting physical resources; and the social impact on the societies in which they operate including their human rights record. Each director will not have to be a Renaissance being to achieve this, but the sum of the directors must strive for this. Any of the existing directors who fail will need to be deselected rapidly.

However, there is a shadow side to such growing enthusiasm to clarify directoral competence. It is noticeable in the US, UK and Europe that party politics is intervening and turning what could be nuanced improvements into binary opposites – for example, being in favour of, or opposed to, so-called 'woke' policies. Such infantilising of corporate governance is highly damaging to all concerned. My worry is that with major parties polarising arguments and consequences that they do not understand, then backing this with dangerous regulation, this will demean the future meaning and importance of 'effective corporate governance'. It is in danger of becoming just a slogan at a time when, taken seriously, it could be of huge benefit to the way human institutions work

The Four Stages of Board Maturity

The quality and competence of boards is determined by the selection or election of each director. I have seen very few rigorous, integrated board processes for selection, induction, development, regular assessment, and deselection of directors. Few boards or stakeholders invest much time, thought, or cash in these vital processes. Budgets for such rarely even exist. Even odder is that such board development budgets are often controlled by senior executives, not the directors themselves. These executives may have a vested interest in ensuring that the directors are weak. The idea of assessing continuing board competence through testing their quality of care, skill and diligent delivery is usually treated as a fantasy. This is very odd considering the paramount legal role that boards are charged to play in our institutions.

These are professional roles and should be treated as such. One would not expect a doctor or airline pilot to be able to pay a maximum of a £50 registration fee and automatically be able to perform surgery or fly a plane. Yet this is precisely what we allow of directors – to create a company and run it simply by buying the title of 'director'. This is a nonsense. As there is no national competence regulation of this vital process, the old IT maxim of 'garbage in, garbage out' still applies.

The Four Stages

To clarify the current director developmental mess, I devised for my clients and students a simple four-level hierarchy for categorising levels of directoral maturity. This has worked well over some ten years and allowed much deeper discussions around boardroom tables as how to professionalise each board. It has enabled many boards and directors to move beyond their current muddling along to establish higher levels of professionalism and strive for their full corporate governance role.

I call those boards at Level One and Level Two maturity 'Dated Directors'. They represent an older model of a board that is now well past its 'use by' date. I call Level

Three and Level Four maturity boards 'Professional Directors', striving to create a more integrated future for their organisation and humanity.

I describe each level briefly here, and go into greater detail in Chapters Three, Four and Five:

Level One Boards: Accidental Directors

I find this the global default position for over 90 per cent of 'directors'. Most are genuinely surprised and shocked to find that the title has legal meaning and personal consequences. They are characterised by having ignorance of the legal roles of both a director and a board, plus an indifference to this lacuna. This is often caused by a lack of any directoral induction, assessment, or development processes being offered on their registration. Combined with this is an emotional temperature around the boardroom table which I describe as 'country club' – once you are a member you are not expected to challenge the existing thinking or power base. You will be given good food and drink and will meet in pleasant venues that signal your status. But you will not be expected to challenge seriously the status quo, even in a crisis. You will often be labelled by the public as a 'trophy director'.

Level Two Boards: Grudgingly Compliant Directors

These are usually uncomfortable and grumpy boards because their directors have a slowly awakening sense of what is now demanded of them legally and will be in future. However, they know that they are not prepared for this, feel that they may have been sold a pup on their career progression ladder, and cannot see why they should spend their time seeking competence. So, they blame the outside impositions by legislators and regulators for their discomfort. They are proud to seek only minimum compliance as their stand against 'growing bureaucracy'. They rarely see directing as a 'proper job'.

Level Three Board: The Learning Board

These directors have reached an inflection point and are now committed to accepting their full legal roles within a civil society. They are working towards directing becoming 'a proper job', well beyond managing. They now need to understand how they must combine entrepreneurship with the environmental and social consequences of their board decisions, and to be held accountable for these. To succeed they must invest time and money in new personal and team development processes and accept regular assessment of their developing professional roles.

Level Four Boards – The Professional Board

Let me stress that by 'professional' I do not advocate more codes, regulation and over-frequent bureaucratic assessments. I picture a board that is staffed by directors who are focused on implementing their publicly avowed purpose and are determined to learn continuously how to get there.

Such boards have fully funded selection, induction, development, annual assessment and deselection processes. These are open to stakeholder scrutiny. They measure their entrepreneurial success by their combined economic, environmental, and social impacts.

To understand corporate governance, some essential ground clearing is needed. I have reviewed some 40 years of my experiences in educating directors into their basic roles and duties, highlighting legal and ethical biases which have been accepted but which can be so easily avoided. These have so often led directors to unnecessarily painful, financial, and emotional consequences, sometimes involving whole families.

The problem I meet globally is the very public existence of so many easily accepted myths about directors, shareholders, stakeholders, and the law concerning corporate governance. These are common currency across the public, directors, politicians, stakeholders and regulators. Combined, they have blocked the development of effective boards. Problems are then compounded because there is currently no common language, nor agreed briefing scripts, for directors, owners, legislators, regulators, nor stakeholders, that allows any regular debate to reframe our institutions.

Throughout the 1980s and 1990s The UK was seen often as a world leader in developing good practice in corporate governance, following the publication of '*The Cadbury Report Into the Financial Aspects of Corporate Governance*' (1). But the UK is now becoming an 'also ran', despite having launched the world's first Chartered Director accreditation programme which was then left to trundle along at too low a level. It still has the world's best courts for testing good practice in the field. Oddly, UK politicians and regulators are surprisingly ignorant of their own laws and very timid at wanting to apply these to create legal precedents. They simply do not understand 'business', while holding strong opinions about it. So, new ideas and initiatives are beginning to emerge from nations, especially in the Gulf and the Caribbean, now facing environmental, societal, and accountability changes so extreme that they realise they must find novel solutions to survive.

As examples, the six nations of the Gulf Co-operation Council and the nine nations of the Caribbean Corporate Governance Institute, strongly influenced by Common Law, are making progress experimenting beyond the Cadbury boundaries. Both regions, for example through the Gulf Co-operation Council's Board Development Institute, are developing graded systems of assessing directoral competence. These move from the awarding of Certificates, through Diplomas and end in the award of practice-tested Chartered Director status – the current epitome of professionalism.

For me a nagging personal mystery is how the Communist Party of China will deliver their declared intention of creating effective 'corporate governance'. Although they will deny it, their nascent corporate governance law has been markedly influenced by the existing Common Law basis of Hong Kong. But now they want to develop 'corporate governance with Chinese characteristics'. This sounds to me worryingly like compliance with the directives of the Communist party of China.

There is much to play for, and not just in China. The 2025 King Five Code in South Africa is a continuing model of thoughtful code development despite the turbulence in the country. The United Nations is making very slow progress as is the European Union. Their soon to be published frameworks are well worth reading to understand the new boundaries that may influence and ring fence future board decision making. But I am very concerned that they will rely on 'more of the same' – adding regulations and codes and losing focus on entrepreneurship. However, I am cheered by the trend amongst many small nations who want to break from multinational legal dominance to begin sharing their learning to create more Smart Small States, such as Botswana, Qatar, Estonia, Trinidad, Armenia, Jamaica and Jordan [1].

Common Myths About Corporate Governance

I have listed below 16 of the most common myths that I have found block the growth of effective corporate governance. I give refutations to each. These are based specifically on the Duties of a Director, and The Purpose of a Board, taken from the UK's respected 2006 Companies Act. This is derived from some 150 years of corporate evolution and testing based on the legal precedents created under the Common Law. Its writ goes well beyond the UK. It is persuasive throughout the 56 Commonwealth countries, and to a great extent the US, although the US sets an unreliable precedent because of the current legislative stand-off between various states, the political parties, and the Federal government. This is described in more detail at the end of this chapter. It is wise to consider the current US as a basket case regarding effective corporate governance.

Worldwide, I consistently find a cluster of common myths. Some show plain ignorance. Others are defensive blockers used by existing corporate power players to demean or destroy the importance of the corporate governance role. In the current polycrisis, there is everything to play for by killing these dangerous myths. This is not a definitive list: there are many other myths found around the world. I have simply listed here the most common ones that I encounter.

1. The word 'director' has no special meaning at law; it is optional.
This is untrue in Common Law. If a person 'holds themselves out to be' or 'purports to be' a director, when they are not legally registered under the relevant Company Law or Ordinance, this is unlawful. Many HR departments do not understand this. Some

use the title 'director' like confetti especially if they want to give 'promotions' without due payment. US corporations are highly prone to this. There are criminal and civil penalties for misleading the public in this way. Yet so far there have been few prosecutions as politicians and prosecutors seem uninterested and have not been pressured by the public to do so.

When legally registered as a director it is necessary in the 56 Commonwealth countries to commit to the roles, duties, and responsibilities of a director under the UK's 2006 Companies Act, especially Section 171 on the Duties of a Director, and Section 172 on the Role of a Board of Directors. However, there are very few legal precedents for assessing directoral understanding or competence.

2. Shareholders own the Business.

This is the most widely held and dangerous myth globally. Under Common Law nobody owns a business. This bald statement is often met with incredulity by directors, politicians and the public alike. It sounds so counterintuitive to common assumptions that it needs careful explanation. Under Common Law development over some 150 years, legislation has consciously created the concept of 'the company' as a 'legal fiction'. A nationally registered company is created as a *separate* legal personality, a person in its own right, distinct from its shareholders and directors. The Registered Directors are the company's direction-giving and steering mechanism – its guiding agents. They are not owners but have been granted powers by the shareholder votes to direct and ensure prudent control of the company during their term of office. As a separate legal entity, the company can agree contracts in its own name, signed by the directors. Neither the executives nor the shareholders have these rights. This is true of privately run companies as well as listed firms – a founding family's members may own a majority of shares in the company, but they do not *own* the company.

However, whilst directors have a primary loyalty to the future health of the company, they have also duties to the shareholders. These are rights given them through the purchase of a 'share'. This physical or electronic statement gives them the voting power and some rights subject to the percentage of shares that they hold. Such 'rights' include for example, the right to any dividend stream declared by the directors, plus the right to exercise their voice and vote at AGMs or EGMs, and finally the right to any residual assets at the liquidation of the business. But shareholders do not 'own' the business. This fact sits in contradiction to the dominant, and wrong, common US assumption of 'shareholder supremacy'. Shareholders are not supreme. Their powers to influence corporate direction will become more diffuse in future with the rise of the legal power of other stakeholders as the company's wider environmental and societal duties become law. This is still a very messy area, and few politicians are willing to tackle the issues. I was told by a venerable US investor 'Bob, there are no votes for either party in disturbing this rat's nest'.

The legal fact that no one owns a business demands a lot of mental agility from directors, regulators, fund managers, venture capitalists, stakeholders, the public, and even legislators. The directors are legally bound to hold the business as entrepreneurial agents to create a healthy future for the company. They act as temporary stewards for the length of their contracts, and during that time the directors are supreme. Many do not realise their powers and defer meekly to shareholders and the Chief Executive. Some shareholders seek to make a quick killing by trading the shares rather than having any consideration of the long-term health of the business. The opposing dynamics cause issues for most boards.

The legal fact that no one owns a company is a running sore that politicians have tried unsuccessfully to resolve since the UK's messy 1896 Salomon's Judgement. The myth is so strong that it still takes a lot to accept. The shareholders, and now some stakeholders, have the power to influence the directors based on the weight of their shareholdings, but ultimately the current mess is partly resolved at law by its insistence that directors must be seen to use their *independent* judgement on the future health of the company, not the wishes of factions of the shareholders, even if they elected the director. I deal with this in more detail in Chapter Three when discussing Level One businesses and their liabilities.

What is important to stress here is that under Common Law shareholders have **no** rights to do the following:

- Manage the business of the company
- Possess the company's assets
- Use the company's assets
- Access the income of the company
- Take on any duty or responsibility to the company
- Deliver any representative shareholder duty to their ultimate beneficiaries

Many shareholders hate these facts and prefer the common myths.

3. Shareholders control the business.

Wrong. Given the paragraph above, this is impossible. On appointment as a director, it comes as a shock to many shareholders that, at the very moment of their appointment to a board, a directors' primary loyalty must switch permanently from obeying the orders of those who had appointed them to using their independent judgement to prioritise a healthy future for the company itself. This fundamental pillar of company law is surprisingly little known.

In addition, directors must use their independence of thought to be seen to take careful, skilful, and diligent decisions about the company's future. They must learn their new role competently. Few have the time and the budget to do so. It is unlawful for them to act as agents of others. This creates confusion in many directors when they are put on to boards by, for example, fund managers, venture capitalists, public enterprise, or as a director of a subsidiary company. The law demanding 'independence of thought' is clear but few like to obey it. The board, and individual director's focus must be on creating that long-term organisational health as reflected in its continuing success for the benefit of its members as a whole as stated under Section 172 of the UK's 2006 Companies Act. Until now 'members' were assumed just to mean shareholders. But the world, and the meaning, has moved on. Stakeholder groupings are gaining new powers as part of the wider ecological business system.

4. 'Stakeholders' are an unnecessary invention imposed on hard-pressed companies.

The concept of the company existing free of its society and physical environment, able to exercise its free will in any way it wants, has been challenged increasingly since the start of the 20th century. Previously the over-riding size of Big Business in free markets, with their natural urge to create monopolies, was recognised as being unhealthy for society, but with a few exceptions it was not illegal. One hundred years later it is increasingly apparent that a company only lives within the changing dynamics of the total, ecological, system which supports it. If it becomes too large, too monopolistic, and without societal licence, it can become a danger to itself and others. The 'polycrisis' has arrived and is creating a new business ecology with more comprehensive values.

Growing legislation of environmental protection, and social equality and sustainability, are forcing change to the previously assumed limits of a board's decision making. For example, in a growing number of countries it is now mandatory for a board to consider and record their thinking on environmental impact assessments, community impacts, workers' rights, modern slavery, sexual and racial discrimination, and other aspects of social justice that have become part of the 'rights-based', civil society context. Few companies have rushed to implement these. However, the next generation of directors will increasingly be held legally accountable for them, watched by social media. This is the likely framework in which boards will be judged. It sounds remarkably like society seeking to reinforce Adam Smith's earlier warning in 1776 against companies and professions seeking to come together as 'conspiracies against the laity'.

5. 'Directors' are just older managers put out to grass. They have few powers.

Directors have a distinct and superior legal role to managers. Registered Directors are bounded by a mass of legislation. Managers rarely are. Being a director is not necessarily age related. Although most directors tend to be older, this is not a legal requirement. I argue for diversity in age for a balanced board of directors. I argue further for diversity of opinion on future boards. This will deliver a much wider range of ideas and experience for making wiser decisions on possible futures.

Moreover, Directors need to agree a clear set of written '*Reserved Powers For The Board*' which state their ultimate powers for Policy Making, Strategic Thinking and Decision Taking in contrast to the managerial roles. Few do so, and managers often then take these powers by default. This leaves many boards open to Michael Grade's infamous accusation that 'boards of directors are like bidets. No-one really knows what they are for, but we assume they must add a bit of class'.

6. Directing and Corporate Governance are too complex and sophisticated for the public to understand. They should be left for politicians, regulators, and directors to develop alone.
I wrote this 'demystifying' part of the book to counter this nonsense. Politicians, regulators and directors are those I find most baffled by directors' legal roles. But until the public have a clear grasp of both the roles of a director, the Purpose of a board, and the necessary assessments of their competences, they cannot hold boards to account. The current mess will continue and fester.

7. You are only a director when you are attending a board meeting or a board committee meeting.
Wrong. A registered director is on duty and personally liable 24/7 for 365 days of the year. It is a continuous responsibility. There is no time off when accountability can be avoided. In addition, you are jointly and severally liable for your and your fellow directors' decisions and actions until your resignation or termination. Even then you can be held accountable for board decisions taken during your time as a director.

8. There are many different classes of director.
Wrong. This is one of the greatest myths globally and the US has really muddied the water here. In Common Law countries the term 'director' is a single designation. You are either a registered director or you are not. At law there are no differentiators like 'executive director', 'non-executive director', nor 'independent director'. A director is a director; with all the consequent liabilities. Even legislators and regulators get this wrong frequently. So, for example, the UK banking legislation, as distinct from Company Law, often uses these other designations wrongly as do many venture capitalists. These other designators have not been tested yet in the courts. I argue that they are likely to fail.

The US has made matters worse by showering the title 'director' at executive level and senior management levels. In many US companies a 'director' is an executive level below that of 'Vice President' – whatever that may mean legally.

9. Chief Executives run businesses.
Wrong. It is a common assumption that Chief Executives must run businesses, if only because of their job title. To the public and the media, they can seem all powerful and are often treated as folk heroes, or fools. This assumption may seem behaviourally correct but is legally wrong. If it is seen as true, it means that the board is not doing their duty. The board of directors are the ultimate decision-takers. A 'Chief Executive' is not even a legal member of a board, only the top of the managerial hierarchy. To become a board member they will have to commit to being a registered director. At this point they become a 'Managing Director'. Few seem to know this.

10. Directors add no value.
Directors are the only group in a business legally charged explicitly with the total oversight and prudent control of the business including its civil society impact (Figure 1 shows this relationship graphically). Increasingly the Board is charged to act not

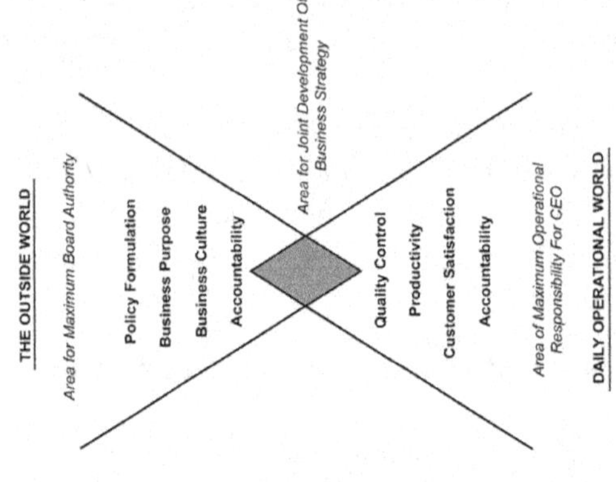

Figure 1: Areas of Influence.

only as 'The Brain of the Firm' but equally 'The Conscience of the Firm'. They are the balancing mechanism between steering the way ahead and ensuring control of the feedback flows from the operations side. They are the central processor of the total business intelligence flows. It is the quality of this directoral learning and decision-making that determines the flow of future wealth and ultimately the survival of the business. This is where they add value.

11. People appointed or selected as directors must know all they need to know or they would not have been appointed
Wrong. Just look around you at the present public distrust of so many boards – public, private, and not-for-profit. There are legal role specifications for directors, but there are no publicly agreed continuing performance specifications, except under criminal law when any infringement is usually too late to change. Anyone can be registered as a director on registering a company, provided they have no criminal record. In most countries there is no check on whether a registered director is a 'suitable person' for that society. There is no initial check on their knowledge, skills, ethics, or diligence. Nor is there any expectation that directors must be open to development and new learning. Neither is there a national or internationally agreed level of accreditation – yet. It is just beginning to appear in a few countries.

12. All that matters on appointment is that directors have 'Experience'
This is one of the oldest and most persistent myths about directing. 'Experience' is too vague a term. In most cases new directors simply import their previous managerial and specialist experience to a board and hope that this will be sufficient. It is not. But if most directors think this way and merely recycle purely managerial experiences, then it will have negative and long-term effects on the future health of the business. Many new directors are only comfortable in their previous specialist role and do not wish to launch themselves into a new career stage. If such combined board 'experience' is too similar, if it is not sufficiently diverse, and the directors focus their attention only internally by micro-managing the managers, then they will kill their business.

13. Directors have neither the time nor inclination to train and be assessed
The public perception of directors being 'pale, male and stale', meeting a few times a year for a good dinner, and having a 'board meeting' where assent is the default mode, is still too close for comfort. In an increasingly turbulent world this image helps fuel the public fury at cases of gross corporate misgovernance scandals such as the UK's Post Office, Blood Transfusion, and water companies scandals.

I note approvingly that some Next Generation directors accept the concept of directing being a profession for which training, development, competence assessment and accreditation are necessary. For example, the concept of the Chartered Director was accepted by the UK's Privy Council on behalf of the Institute of Directors because there was an activist group within it trying to create a Chartered Director scheme. It had a promising start but then faltered. It still turns out a few dozen accredited directors a year. It is not well-resourced, publicised, nor has it been taken up by the political parties as a key to growing a robust economy. So, the expected national impact on the quality and quantity of future directors has not happened.

There is a growing renaissance, not just in the UK, but, for example, in South Africa, Australia, New Zealand, the six countries of the Gulf Co-operation Council and the nine nations of the Caribbean. The next generation seem more accepting of professionalisation as a necessity. What is noticeable is that many participants now pay for themselves rather than be supported by their companies or governments. They know making that commitment as future directors, to a 24/7 role, and to their continuous learning, is valuable personally and nationally. On the one hand I find such self-motivation reassuringly healthy. On the other hand I find the lack of buy-in by current corporations worrying.

However, there is a shadow side to such growing professionalism. This is rich ground for the bureaucrats to set up over-blown rules, regulations, and codes to impose on such directors. Unless we are nuanced in such growth we will yet again create a self-serving cottage industry for pointless accreditation.

14. Politicians create governance legislation which they must understand fully and continue to monitor and learn from its full implementation

Wrong. Politicians rarely know the details of the company law or ordinances that they and their predecessors have passed. They certainly do not track them, test them, nor live them. Their focus is on the immediate politics and short-term rhetoric before the next election. Their timeframe is in contradiction to the business needs of long-term strategic thinking. In 2021 during a break after the Covid-19 lockdown I was able to address briefly a joint voluntary meeting at The UK's Houses of Parliament – around 100 Peers and MPs. These had expressed an interest in the future of effective corporate governance. To start I asked how many in the room could give me three of the seven duties of a director, or two of the six Purposes of a board, reminding them that they had passed these as law in 2006. No one could give even half an answer to either question. I was shocked. They were embarrassed. Later only six expressed a wish to learn how to rectify the situation.

These six came forward afterwards to say that they too were shocked but that I must understand that they had all entered Parliament well after 2006. They were offered no encouragement to learn about any existing legislation, and certainly not the Companies Act, especially the corporate governance aspects. They were beginning to realise that this is crucial to creating effective institutions. They had no induction, training, or assessment on the key issues. However, they felt that they were forced to behave publicly as if they did know and had to express strong opinions despite little knowledge. They said that they now realised that they were mere cannon fodder for their political parties and asked for private briefings to help fill in their lack of knowledge. These were provided but only to a very small number. I have found similar ignorance amongst the politicians in all the countries in which I have worked. They too hold strong personal views with very little knowledge and so subscribe easily to, and can reinforce, the many myths that I outline in this chapter.

Sadly, I have found similar issues with Regulators. They appear expert at telling directors to be compliant without much testing of what this means in practice, why Codes were developed, or even what the basic law is that they are trying to regulate. Many of those I have met have never practised corporate governance and often see their job as simply being mechanical administrators of the system, however, ineffective. There is no national accreditation or assessment of such regulators. And most do not expect their regulatory role to be central to their career.

15. Regulators are skilled and helpful in their interpretation of existing law and practice

Corporate governance regulation is in its infancy. It has grown with little intellectual, integrative, or practical oversight. It is based on a loose patchwork of incidents and scandals with a partial understanding of the law. This triggers short-term political responses rather than carefully considered systems-based design. These expedient responses have been turned into Regulations and Codes of Practice driven, written and administered mainly by civil servants and non-practitioners. Hence their tendency is to default to obeying the letter of the Code, however inappropriate for the circumstances. Little learning is encouraged. I say more about the alternative 'principles-based approach' in section 16 below.

Regulatory practice involves too much time focusing on those 'easy' short-term and financially-based outputs and numbers-based – reporting and audit. It gives little importance to the human, and more 'difficult' yet crucial inputs of director selection, induction, competence development, assessment and deselection. These seem unfathomable to the administrative mind.

Regulators are not trained nor assessed on any agreed national or international standard that the public can understand and criticise constructively. Current regulators are more like football referees who take decisions without explanation, despite VAR [video-assisted refereeing]. It is hard for them to learn effectively.

I argue strongly that what is needed is more the approach of rugby referees. These run with the game in real-time, giving immediate warnings to the players and explaining the reasons for their decisions. In this way players and referees can learn continuously. Disagreements over decisions are rare. I want the same mindset developed for the regulators of boards of directors. But who will be the referee for future boards? There is a need for an independent officer, an internal, real-time referee sitting with the board. That post exists in part already – the Company Secretary – but is often seen as powerless and undervalued. How shall we increase significantly the power of this independent referee role without losing entrepreneurship?

16. The US Leads the World in Effective Corporate Governance

Wrong. I see the US as a looming basket case in terms of effective corporate governance. This is shown through its national constitutional weaknesses. The US has little Federal (national) legislation in this area. The over-blown Sarbanes-Oxley Act is one of the few examples. Driven by good intentions on better financial disclosure it has become a bureaucratic burden on companies. The other Federal law used is the Securities Exchange Act of 1934. The US uses the basis of Common Law in that it places a Duty of Care and a Duty of Loyalty on its directors and uses the concept of the company as a separate legal personality but these are the domain of state law.

Therefore, most US corporate governance legislation is fragmented because it is developed by individual states. These can be in open competition to create the most business-friendly laws to attract company registrations and so tax dollars. Races to the bottom are increasing now aided by President Trump and his declared fight against the eastern establishment's 'swamp' including the players in company law and corporate governance.

An example is the State of Delaware which admits that its small size means that it cannot deliver the services demanded by its citizens without this major source of tax income. Ironically, it had been seen as an example of how to strike a balance between basic corporate governance and the need to maximise tax income. It now seems intent on destroying what shareholder protection laws it had. Its legislators had at least created a basic framework in which a majority of US corporations could register. But it seems to have started self-destruction when in June 2024 it passed legislation that jettisoned the state's long-respected laws that protected all investors. It now proposes to allow company management to strike secret side deals with large shareholders that bypass the board on governance questions that had previously been reserved for the directors (sic). This will have grave consequences for many forms of investors worldwide. It demonstrates the growing split in US political and business thinking, with many of the Silicon Valley 'Magnificent Seven' corporations re-registering in states such as Texas where they can have even wider ability to 'move fast and break things' with few legal consequences for minority shareholders and the wider community.

Many US states still follow misguided mantras about 'shareholder supremacy' and so encourage over-powerful CEOs to influence the decisions of their 'independent' directors and weak boards. Currently there is little chance of such US boards developing the competence and diversity to ensure the long-term future health of their companies.

It gets worse because the US's over-focus on that myth of 'shareholder supremacy'. US Chief Executives are often given absolute power and rewarded outrageously only on the doubtful metric of the short-term rise in their company's share price. In the short-term this can always be manipulated, and environmental and social impacts be downgraded or 'washed'. Isolation from environmental and social impacts are shielded also from international reality by the way in which such legislation is enacted and enforced in the US. What is unforgiveable to me is that, in most US states, directors can sit on the boards of competitors, which blows the notions of independence of thought and declarations of interest completely out of the water.

Common law generally is based on the pragmatic testing of each piece of legislation by the courts to create a historical string of precedents. This gives rise to a 'principles-based' approach to corporate governance which allows the law to evolve through testing and common sense. US company law has taken a different approach. It relies on a 'rules-based' approach where you can do what you like unless there is a rule to stop it. While this seems a free-wheeling, Wild West approach, it can now often create the opposite effect. It can encourage bureaucracy through the reporting systems. Legislators and regulators issue a growing number of edicts to block the liberties taken in the 'free market'. This is costly in terms of cash and time to both sides. It creates a continuing field day for lawyers. It has become politically divisive so there is little national demand for over-arching national, federal, legislation. Indeed, growing anarchy in US corporate governance seems to be the case.

And it gets even worse because US arrogance over its 'soft' imperial world power is shown by the demand for 'extra-territoriality' whenever its shadow reaches an overseas company. When an overseas company is deemed to need to report to the US authorities (however minor the activity), it automatically becomes liable to obeying the full US governance and reporting laws. This exports weak US corporate governance practice worldwide while creating costly bureaucratic demands. It is especially ironic that this is happening at a time when the US government is keen to become more isolationist.

Government and Corporate Governance

Ever the optimist, I am reassured by the growing Next Generation of directors who think we should demand something much better. I see this especially regarding significant reforms needed in, for example, director competence, board responsibility-taking, strategic thinking, accounting and audit practice, rewards linked to performance by Chief Executives, addressing the under-reward of employees, and the issues of fraud and corruption, and of environmental and social impacts on the sustainability of our human systems.

Which means there is one more piece of demystifying to complete. Throughout this book I try to use the term 'government' to refer to the regional and national direction-giving and administration of a total population within a defined geographic area. I use the term 'governance' to refer to our individual institutions, the corporate legal entities, whether private public, hybrid or not-for-profit. These are legally charged to both give direction to their organisation and to keep it under prudent control.

However, the words 'government' and 'governance' are often muddled and abused in the minds of many. So, here I shall share how I clarify this confusion, starting with the legislators who create the field within which the two gubernatorial deliverables are developed.

I am still baffled as to why governments, whether elected or selected, find delivering their roles so difficult. They are expected by their public to protect, shape, and develop their societies through direction-giving and prudent control. My experience of such government covers many Western democracies, Communist China, various autocracies in Africa and Asia, the Arabian Gulf, and the democratic islands of the Caribbean. I find often their rhetoric strong yet their delivery very patchy. It fluctuates frequently along party political lines. I often feel that their behaviours look as though they are trying to sculpt the Venus De Milo with a butter knife. It is messy and unedifying. I deal with this more in Chapter Six.

The unstated fact is that on attaining power so many legislators feel lost, untrained, and frightened of immediate public exposure. They do not have a model of competence for government. Indeed, few legislators around the world have any training at all for governing a country. So, they try to bluff about their inadequacies through public relations and unwisely try to manage an overwhelming 24-hour 'news' agenda. In a time of mass multi-media outlets and little agreement or prioritising of what is 'news', as distinct from entertainment or muck racking, this is a tactic bound to result in failure and public disillusion.

I remember a long, personal, and reflective private conversation with an African Prime Minister. He did not know the basic Company laws of his country and was pleasantly surprised to find how advanced they were – at least on paper. However, he admitted that he had no idea how to implement them to deliver his publicly espoused drive for economic growth and against corruption, that helped him win an election. Nor could he see a way of selling his ideas to his disgruntled citizens. There was no common language to do so, and he did not want to appear weak. He used all the right words, but not necessarily in the right order. He floundered for three years and then was voted out. He was replaced by someone facing exactly the same national issues, and with the same lack of humility to be seen to learn publicly. Ultimately, it is these uncertain legislators who define their country's future energy, options, and optimism though their approach to government competence. In future, can they show the humility to be seen to learn co-operatively for the national interest? They do have the power to amend and develop governmental and corporate governance laws. Yet few rate the stability generated by such a balanced approach as a national priority.

There is much public disenchantment over the lack of effective government in both liberal and authoritarian governments, and in all political parties. It would take a separate book to analyse the failings and solutions needed to resolve them. We have now reached a tipping point where we have the freedom, the opportunity, and the space to experiment with remodelling at least the *corporate* governance of our organisations – public, private, and not-for-profit – to show how those organisations with a clear Purpose can stabilise their societies and so show government how to think and behave in future.

This argument is counter to a current political trend that says that post-Covid, only a concentration of centralised national government can see us out of the current economic, environmental, and community mess. Given the rise of effective small, smart, states, like Singapore, Switzerland, Norway, Estonia, Qatar, Botswana, and especially Denmark, this is patent nonsense. Yet it is seductive to a public desperate for effective, competent government.

What would it look like if these principles were put into practice? Any effective national government promises to protect its citizens from outside interference and deliver three basic services to its citizens:

Implementation

This takes place through directly or indirectly employed labour. It starts with the defence of the nation's borders and moves on to delivering the promised economic, environmental and community benefits.

Procurement

This is from suppliers in the private, public and not-for-profit sectors to ensure delivery of cost-effective and corruption-free services and goods.

Regulation

This is effected through the judiciary in regulated services covering criminal and civil law, and the impartial oversight of service standards and delivery.

It is this focus on governmental implementation rather than the spouting of political rhetoric that interests me. Much public criticism highlights the many disconnects between the legislature, executive, and judiciary in ensuring seamless and corruption-free action. Again, it is a sign of the times that this seems to interest the public and the media only if there is scandal attached, as with the UK Post Office, which involved the prosecution, and in some cases imprisonment, of hundreds of law-abiding sub-postmasters wrongly accused of theft when the actual cause was an error-strewn accounting system which the institution covered up. A public inquiry has taken place, although the full report has not been published at the time of writing [2]. The structural governance issues and necessary learning processes are rarely mentioned even in major scandals – indeed, in the Post Office Inquiry the quality of corporate governance has hardly been mentioned.

'Twas ever thus. It is a lifelong issue for human systems of government, a human failing, as a quick historical scan reveals:

1726, Jonathan Swift in *Gulliver's Travels* has the King of Brobdingnag proclaim:

whoever could make two ears of corn, or blades of grass, grow upon a spot of ground where only one grew before, would deserve better of mankind, and do more essential service to his country, than the whole race of politicians put together.

In 1902 Winston Churchill stated '*A politician needs the ability to foretell what is going to happen tomorrow, next week, and next year. And the ability to explain afterwards why it did not happen'.*

In 1925 Frederick Lewis Donaldson said in a sermon at Westminster Abbey

'The Seven Social Sins are: Wealth without Work, Pleasure without Conscience, Knowledge without Character, Commerce without Morality, Science without Humanity, Worship without Sacrifice, and Politics without Principle'.

And in 1980 Douglas Adams said in *The Restaurant At the End of The Universe*

'It is a well-known fact that those people who most want to rule people are, ipso facto, those least suited to it . . . . . . anyone who is capable of getting themselves made President should on no account be allowed to do the job'.

So, in a cynical and disenchanted governmental world how can we develop effective corporate governance? Demystification is a good start. Daylight is a natural disinfectant. Experience shows that it will not be through a 'big bang' piece of legislation or in adding yet more regulatory Codes, but through the humbler and more nuanced development of continuous learning systems between the five main players – directors, stakeholders, legislators, regulators, and the public.

The ancient question of whether senior civil servants are mere short-term agents for delivering governmental policies and initiatives, or play a clear role as an

experienced reviewing and balancing force to ensure the effective implementation of national stability and governmental services, remains unresolved. Sadly, in my experience neither politicians nor senior civil servants are willing to be seen to *learn* publicly from their strategies and the implementation of their plans. Indeed, several politicians and senior civil servants have accused me privately of 'destabilising the confidence of the British public' by even mentioning their obvious ignorance. This would mean their admitting mistakes which their opponents would jump on. But learning is only built on thoughtful reflections of mistakes. Hence the government and governance silence continues.

I suggest removing two current blockages to the implementation of proposed legislation and towards better government and governance. First, that political implementation plans are made public so that external monitoring is transparent. Many senior civil servants, and their parliamentary advisors and secretaries have had the equivalent of an Oxbridge Philosophy, Politics, and Economics degree, and have been seduced into thinking that the tracking and implementation of policy is not their responsibility. Continuous learning is seen as well below their pay grade. They need to be held more openly responsible for the implementation of their strategies and plans.

Second, legislators rarely know the laws, current and past, passed in their name. Get them to learn and live them. I urge citizens to learn to keep asking any politician in public to name the seven duties of a director, or the six aspects of a board's purpose, under the UK's Companies Act of 2006, or its equivalent. They are doing well if they can name even two. Do remember that the answers are contained within just one-and-a-half pages of the 2006 Act. They are the foundation stones and central pillars of effective corporate governance. Yet so few know them.

This ignorance is a key component of the silence and confusion around corporate governance. It is compounded by the high rate of churn in governmental and civil service jobs. 'Superior' intellect is prized over operational experience and priority is given to 'fast track' graduates where a degree automatically rates higher than time-served experience on the job. This is central given the ideological obsession of higher education humanities. High-level posts are seen as frequently interchangeable without the need for training or assessment. In many civil services it is normal to change posts every three years. Management skills are also prioritised above on-the-job experience. This allows little time for effective learning. Indeed, at the time of their maximum experiential learning a person is moved to an area about which they know little and must start all over again. They are expected to master their brief instantly and with effortless superiority. And then to advise their Ministers. This is madness.

Matters are made worse as such new leaders are exposed immediately to 24-hour media questioning on their 'responsibilities'. Even in ministries devoted to business, economic development, and commercial law I have found the levels of subject knowledge of the legal foundations woefully lacking. I remain shocked. Because these are the very people who form legislation and regulate our current national corporate governance system.

From the end of the Cultural Revolution I was in China and I was fascinated by the top mandarins' love of the BBC TV long-running series *Yes Minister*. They found it very funny, and painfully true. The constant battle between the wordplay of the public-facing minister and the machinations of the invisible senior civil servants with their own agenda of retaining true power was seen as fundamentally human. It is a global phenomenon.

Matters are then compounded as it is highly fashionable amongst politicians to want to emulate the US Presidential model. Ironically, this is frequently quoted as 'more democratic' even though there is little of such in the current failing US government non-system. Here an elected administration will typically sack the existing civil service and install their own. The loss of learning and experience is devastating. Yet world-defining decisions are taken rapidly by the incomers. By the end of their first administration the politicians are beginning to learn how to implement their policies at a time when they may well be deselected by the electorate. Here a 'democratic system' seems to be one of continuous short-termism designed against delivering in the national interest. Yet many nations seem keen to emulate it.

No corporation nor national government is currently proposing such a comprehensive embrace of effective corporate governance. Yet they will need to do so, if they aspire to create sustainable, healthy and long-lived, effective human institutions.

References

[1] Armen Sarkissian, The Small States Club, Hurst Publishers, London, 2023
[2] The Post Office Horizon IT Inquiry, see www.postofficehorizoninquiry.org.uk

Chapter 3
Resisting Corporate Governance – Dated Directors And Grudgingly Compliant Directors

The people I describe as 'Dated Directors' are remainers from previous, easier and less accountable eras. Such directors are typically found in Boards of Level 1 and 2 maturity. Level 1 directors frequently do not realise that they are registered directors, and when they do become aware, feel that it was an accident that they ever accepted registration. Often, they hope that they can slip away quietly, and no one will notice. Their legal position is tougher than that, because for any decisions taken by the board during their directorship they will be held jointly and severally accountable.

Level Two board maturity comprises those registered directors who recognise that they *are* legally committed, and usually resent it; sometimes bitterly. They may realise that they have accepted what they now regard as a glittering poisoned chalice. They then strive to do the minimum possible to comply with the law and spend energy on protecting their previous decisions rather than concentrating on the future health of the company they direct. They are rarely a ray of sunshine around the boardroom table.

Accidental Directors – Level 1 Board Maturity

The days when simply 'being a director' ensured social status, the comfortable end of a managerial career, and few personal obligations to deliver the role or responsibilities of a 'director' are fast dying. Now with rising public expectations of proven directoral competence and accountability, boards needing rapid responses to environmental and social changes and their consequences to their business strategy, and with increasing legal pressures in many countries, boards must reframe directoral responsibilities. This is increasingly true around fraud and corruption laws in many countries. These pressures combine to make the role of next generation directors sharply different from the present. The spotlight is now on Directing becoming a distinct, crucial, and professional job. But how do we get there?

Globally many directors are stuck at Level One Accidental Director and remain blissfully ignorant. Those few who do understand their personal responsibilities are often frustrated because, while they know what they should be doing, few others around the boardroom take the board or directoral roles seriously. I found it difficult to set the right 'tone' for this chapter. On the one hand I wanted to warn the vast number of unaware directors of their legal directoral responsibilities and liabilities that they have assumed consciously or unconsciously, and of the professional and emotional dangers involved. Yet I did not want to cause panic or despondency because there are ways out.

 | https://doi.org/10.1515/9783112231340-003

On the other hand, I wanted to stress that directing, as distinct from managing, is so heavily bounded both by law and much deeper social responsibilities, that understanding these clearly defined boundaries means being careful, skilful, and diligent in delivering them. This is the key to breaking away from accidental status and starting to become a professional director. You will be the judge of my success.

'I think I am in trouble. I never realised that I was legally a director. Help me!'

This is the most frequent plea I hear when I am consulted about a 'governance' problem. It astonishes me that around the world so many people do not realise they are legally registered as directors, or that such registration has deep legal and personal significance. Perhaps it should not continue to astonish me as this is a regular source of my consultancy fees, but it does. And it worries me greatly that this still is the international default position for so many 'directors'.

These are the 'Accidental Directors'. Getting them to understand their basic condition, plus encouraging even small immediate improvements in their knowledge and behaviours, can have marked beneficial effects on the quality of their corporate governance and the comfort of their personal lives. Many have been placed in, or volunteered to be in, a position that exposes them to responsibilities and liabilities for which they are not prepared.

The reasons are a mix of ignorance of Common Law, a feeling of doing good or of improving their status by becoming a director, and a feeling that their legal commitment will not be taken seriously by the courts or the public. This is not surprising. Often on being asked to sign up as a 'registered director' they first feel flattered at being asked and then they are commonly reassured by more senior directors or charity trustees by the weasel words 'do not worry, it doesn't mean anything personally, and we will always give you protection'. Ultimately, neither part of this statement can be true in law.

What many Accidental Directors do not realise is that their condition is found widely in so many individual directors. This general air of ignorance is explained in the tour of corporate governance history in Chapter Five. From the start corporate governance has been overly focused on finance, large corporations and their shareholders, plus reporting and audit issues. This perspective flows from the rapid and unquestioning acceptance by governance practitioners, the professions, legislators, and the better informed of the general public of the near sanctity of the *1992 Cadbury Report on The Financial Aspects of Corporate Governance* [1]. I still find it held in reverence in so many countries.

Yet it is not holy writ, but only a partial descriptor of much deeper governance issues. I worked on developing 'action learning' with Sir Adrian in the 1980s – the application of diverse brains on real-time issues to resolve seemingly intractable problems. More on this in Chapter Four. In a personal letter to me in 2015 at the end of his life, Sir Adrian Cadbury regretted that 'finance' had to be in his Report's title. This was because the sponsors of the report were the then London International Stock Exchange and the Institute of Chartered Accountants of England and Wales – the financial power brokers. Sir Adrian knew that *Corporate Governance* must mean so much more. He said that it had to start with entrepreneurship and include, therefore, the company's impacts on the financial, physical, environmental, and social worlds.

But politicians, regulators, stock exchanges, fund managers, auditors and accountants loved the over-focus on finance because these aspects are so easily assessable by numbers only. This made 'corporate governance' part of their comfort zone. It kept 'difficult' areas like entrepreneurial risk-taking and failure, climate change, stakeholder demands, social impact, and the ability to design a future very different from today's as low priorities around the boardroom table. An establishment desire for a 'compliance' focus through simplistic metrics outweighed intellectual rigour from the start. Wittingly or unwittingly, many claimed the Cadbury Report had 'solved' the issue of corporate governance. It had not even started in most of the issues that are germane.

It did popularise the phrase 'corporate governance', but this was rapidly abused by many power players to give whatever limited meaning they wished for it. By so doing they helped create the international public perception that 'corporate governance' equals, and is led always by, big finance. Therefore, the majority of smaller forms of legal entity must conform to these big boys' needs. This has meant that for family businesses, not-for-profits, charities, state-owned enterprises, health authorities, civil servants, mutuals and co-operatives, regulatory 'compliance' has forced them to distort their broader perception of more inclusive corporate governance to fit this big finance version. Hundreds of corporations and many countries copied or created rapidly their own version of the Cadbury Report. They did not attempt to deal with the 'missing half' – the entrepreneurial, environmental, and social impact contracts made by organisations with their communities. Post-Covid and with growing public criticism, this missing half is becoming glaringly obvious.

Before going into more detailed analyses of the plight of Accidental Directors let me clarify my position on the roles of directors and their boards. The inputs for effective corporate governance rely on complementing the board's entrepreneurial ideas on markets, products and services with their assessment of their environmental and social impacts, and accountabilities, within a fast-changing world. To this must be added the quality of policy formulation and foresight, strategic thinking around the boardroom table, and with the management, the board's ability to monitor quickly and accurately the results of their day-to-day business operations. There is a need for both better quality and regular internal *and* external reporting of a business' performance. This spotlights the future board's role as The Brain of The Firm.

There is now a growing ethical element demanded publicly, as the interconnectedness of board decisions to the external world is open to much more scrutiny through social media. Such pressure is not the voice of the public, but it does force the issue of: What is the Conscience of the Firm? Financial results will always be a necessary yet crude measure to assess total 'performance', but they are no longer the only metrics now demanded. New and more inclusive risk assessment and reporting regulations based on, for example, ISO 37000 and PAS 808 are beginning to appear and look promising. They are closer to a sustainable eco-system approach. As this movement is key for the next generation of directors, I shall investigate them in Chapters 4 and 5. Both business and ethical judgements by the board will be subject to wider scrutiny in future. Most existing boards have not yet faced up to this challenging future role. Most Accidental Directors are blissfully ignorant of all of this.

This is important in redefining the future meaning of corporate governance, as some 95% of enterprises around the world are not part of 'big business'. They are not listed on a stock exchange, nor ever will be. They are not directly subject to their national Codes but are to the basic Company Law. They comprise that remarkably diverse and largely invisible majority of human organisations; a mixture of small family businesses, large Family Offices, mutuals, not-for-profits, state-owned enterprises, co-operatives, mutuals, partnerships, and B-Corps. These often have only a hazy understanding of the company laws that surround them and the key roles of the directors who are meant to steer them.

Accidental Directors are often ignorant of the expectations of the complex and challenging world they have entered. It is only when things go badly wrong that they face the possibility of a civil or criminal action as a Board member and individual director. They are suddenly faced with their dire legal situation and such possibilities as administration, liquidation, or even personal bankruptcy with the legal and financial consequences. But ignorance is no defence at law. Even worse, they have often entered this world as good-hearted folk wanting to help family, friends, community or charity. But they can find themselves trapped in Level One maturity boards. It feels a terrible fate from their well-intentioned agreement to register. Sadly, the small business, community-based, and charity worlds have many of these folk.

Initially it can feel a great honour for an individual to be asked to become a director, especially in the listed company and the charity worlds. But this is not always the case. Sometimes the role can be an imposition forced on one by a Head Office, a venture capitalist, a spun-out governmental body, a state-owned enterprise, a very bossy friend, or a senior family member. Accidental directors rarely figure in the thinking of politicians or regulators when framing their laws. They exist in a liminal world below the public horizon; puzzled and searching for the right questions to ask about their role from people in superior power positions on the board. At the end of this chapter, I have described typical problems for Accidental Directors drawn from too many painful experiences presented to me for consultation.

The need to register nationally as a director is often rationalised and downplayed by chairmen, senior executives, civil servants, politicians and HR departments as 'just an administrative necessity' without any likely real enforcement or personal impact on the individual concerned. This shows their level of ignorance of company law. They feel that registration has no real meaning. The unquestioning employee who registers meekly as a director is often told that they must sign because 'someone has to do this to keep the paperwork legal'. An employee is likely to be simultaneously flattered and worried by such a statement. They are likely to yield to the higher power and so be unlikely to reject such a demand. In this circumstance saying 'no' can be seen as a career-limiting opportunity. They have become an Accidental Director. This imposition is fundamentally wrong ethically yet happens so often in the private, public and charities sectors.

Key Questions for The Accidental Director

The developmental stages of a director's maturity flow from selection through induction, professional training, personal development, regular assessment, and deselection. Before signing up as a registered director it is wise to ask four simple questions:

1. Will there be a Mutual Observation period?
Do the selectors take the appointment to this challenging new role seriously enough for both parties to check their utility and compatibility?

I advocate a formal six-month Mutual Observation and Induction contractual period for any proposed, or imposed, new legal director. After this there will be a mutual assessment of their suitability for the role on that specific board. This is a key part of their induction process. This will allow them to continue or leave without social stigma. As status and ego are always an issue for directors, this needs discreet handling. In this way new directors are not subject to a sink-or-swim immersion.

Being in a Mutual Observation and Induction period allows them more easily to ask 'intelligently naïve' questions as they feel their way into the board. They do not then face a common worry that directors must keep silent around the boardroom table for at least a year before they can 'learn the ropes' without looking stupid. Even better, a formal contractual induction process to learn the legal, intellectual, ethical and behavioural aspects of their new role is then accepted as essential by all parties. This process is rarely considered, or budgeted for, in most boards.

2. What does registration as a director actually mean?
The need to register nationally as a director is often rationalised by chairmen, senior executives, civil servants, politicians and HR departments as 'just an administrative necessity – to keep the paperwork legal', showing their level of ignorance of company law. They feel that registration has no real meaning. An employee, simultaneously flattered and worried, yields to the higher power as they seek to maintain their career. They have become an Accidental Director.

Chairmen, and their agents as selectors, dismiss too easily this issue with a vague 'don't worry we will always protect you' statement. This is untrue. They cannot protect you from your personal exercise of, for example, 'care, skill and diligence', especially 'independence of thought', or being held accountable for fraud and corruption under the 2006 Companies Act when devising the policy and strategy for a business;

nor their need to declare their personal interests in any action. Matters are made worse in some countries by the growing number of social and environmental laws that surround such decisions.

Accidental Directors asked to register are in a dilemma. On the one hand if they say 'no' to their bosses, this may be a career-limiting. If they say 'yes' without understanding fully their obligations, they may be exposed in the media and the courts as failing in their duties. They need some form of protection way beyond an incorrect and simplistic idea that directors can be totally protected by a Directors' Liability insurance. They cannot. Directors and Officers Liability insurances have very limited scope.

I see frequent examples of this dilemma in family businesses, in state-owned enterprises and agencies, and when venture capitalists have the right to nominate a director to a board. It can also involve friends and family and is seen frequently in charities and not-for-profits where goodhearted people can be trapped by equally well-meaning folk trying to do good without understanding the laws that bind them. Registering as a director is not merely an administrative matter but a very personal legal commitment. It is ironic that the very legislators who create these laws are so bad at understanding, implementing or obeying them. They often see themselves as above them, or at least that they are optional for them.

Being an Accidental Director needs careful briefing before making a commitment. You have maximum exposure to the decisions taken by the other board members but little protection because of your low level of the relevant directoral knowledge, ethics and skills. Registering as a director can on occasion give you a privileged tax status, but in many of the cases I see people accept the role for free. For example, as in 'just signing up' as a director of a subsidiary company of a main board without asking for a legal induction, a director's fee or insurance.

3. Will the company invest in training me to directoral competence?
Directing is a fundamentally different role from being a manager or a subject specialist. How will you ensure my directoral competence development? An under-performing board will not only sink the company but could damage your career and civil reputation. This is where a mutual commitment to an induction process, a probationary period, a personal development programme and guaranteed regular assessment are key. How will I be assessed? is a crucial question.

4. Am I Insured?
It is rare for an Accidental Director to consider any form of professional and personal liability insurance cover. If the superiors seeking to appoint them also have little knowledge of this area, then they are likely to reassure falsely by saying 'do not worry you will have liability insurance cover'. This is often a half-truth at best. Most of such insurance schemes are of the Directors and Officer's Liability Insurance type (the 'officer' is the Company Secretary or registered general counsel). However, the majority of Directors' and Officers' Liability Insurance policies only cover legally reg-

istered directors. A 'shadow' director, attending meetings and taking part in decisions without being formally registered, may still be held legally accountable for decisions, as discussed in the following section Common Issues. Even then such cover is not absolute but only for legal costs in actions brought against them, and, worryingly, only if they acted lawfully. Remember that ignorance is not an excuse at law. Sadly, many Accidental Directors tend to act without knowing the law. In these circumstances they are likely to face the force of any consequential costs of their actions, if found unlawful or criminal. Their personal wealth is not then protected.

This is why I argue for the probationary period as a director so that an individual can assess the quality and professionalism of the board they are joining, and the board can size them up equally. Mutual trust is vital on a board. Then, at the point of agreed registration, they sign a declaration that they have read and understood the Purpose of A Board (Section 172) and Duties of A Director (Section 171) of the UK's Companies Act 2006, and commit to them. It would be even better that they passed a basic examination in these areas as a start to their professional development such as having passed the entry-level Certificate process of a Chartered Director programme, but this is still rare. It is not demanded currently but is being considered by a few non-Western countries. Remember that from their registering as a director the law insists that the individual's primary loyalty must switch away from those selecting or electing them to the company itself as a separate legal personality. This astonishes many new directors. Some refuse to believe this law. The consequence of this concept takes time to learn. But some Accidental Directors can never bring themselves to say 'no' to their selector. It is not part of their culture.

Common Issues for Accidental Directors

I have listed below typical problems that Accidental Directors find themselves facing. My frustration is that I find them repeating frequently across all types of organisations and countries.

1. Start-ups and Spin-outs

Although most Directors that I see internationally are unconsciously Accidental Directors, not all are. Some Level One, non-Accidental Directors are consciously motivated by passion, ambition, and status. They are bound up, for example, in the heady and wild enthusiasm of start-ups and early-growth companies. There is usually so much focus on developing the new product or service that any 'legal niceties' are not known, put aside, or forgotten in the excitement. The idea that good corporate governance must be designed in from the start is rarely understood. This is why so many start-ups and spin-outs crash. I have seen it happen so many times.

Failing to understand and live by the Duties of a Director, the Purpose of a Board, and not knowing that a Director is a director 24/7, seem guarantees of failure. In the late 1990s at Imperial College, London, working with the redoubtable Professor Sue Birley, we offered all the 5,500 faculty the ability to spin-out companies. There was a good take up. Every potential director was offered free training by Imperial to basic directoral competence as a key part of ensuring their and their company's survival. Many flourished and still exist. A few are on the FTSE AIM, 250 or Nasdaq. The Imperial College spinout portfolio on its website listed around 80 successful companies by 2025 (Ref). This initiative was a wise investment by the college to start with a robust corporate governance-based design that avoided the potential embarrassment of creating hundreds of Accidental Directors.

2. Playing the Role of A 'Shadow Director'

Shadow Directors are potentially sinister persons often intent on manipulating Accidental Directors to their own ends. They are not registered officially as a director yet by regularly attending and participating in board meetings they seek to influence the board's decision-making. They often want to be the power behind the throne but without immediate accountability. They may be a family member, a source of funding, a politician, a bureaucrat or a friend. The irony is that they rarely realise that by participating in board decisions they open themselves to legal liability and court scrutiny, but without even the basic protection of liability insurance. This can become obvious if the decision-making goes wrong. The courts will hold them to the same level of responsibility and accountability as a registered board member.

They can be especially dangerous to a business if they espouse a particular cause or bias that does not mesh with the existing directors' strategy and values. This can be caused, for example, by family members or nominated fund managers. Often, they do not feel that showing care, skill and diligence, or applying independent judgement in favour of the company, applies to them. They feel that their primary loyalty is elsewhere. It is not. They are often dominant personalities who do not want to hear such messages.

What can be done to counter their influence? If board members do allow them unchallenged to attend meetings and speak to the issues, then their influence can be malign. So good boardroom practice is to always have the Company Secretary, or Legal Counsel, record all persons in the room at the time of a debate and decision-taking, who spoke for and voted for and against a proposition.

3. Becoming a Director of a Subsidiary Company

Being 'offered' a directorship in a wholly owned company usually means being told that you are to become a 'director' in a subsidiary company of a larger entity. This is common at the top of corporate life. It can be seen by those seeking power and status as a notable upward career step, signalling recognition of that person's worth and potential. As a serious career change away from management, it can open the opportunity to learn the fields of policy-making and foresight, strategic thinking, higher-level supervision of management, and Board accountability.

But it can be frustrating, as many subsidiary Boards, especially overseas ones, are not treated by main Boards as separate legal entities with a consequent need for independent judgement. Too often they are treated as just another operational department led by subservient executives beholden to head office.

Tension between head office and overseas subsidiaries is highlighted with increasing clarity internationally as more independent nations assert their legal autonomy and consequent directoral demands. They want local boards registered in their country and then to follow their law. They wish their national policies to be reflected in the thinking of local subsidiary boards. Few main boards are comfortable acknowledging publicly that these issues even exist. Yet with the growing focus on, and cross-border legislation emerging in, for example the environmental and social fields, this development is strengthening.

Many main Boards do not consider subsidiary boards as 'real' boards despite their legal existence. They see them more as irritating necessities that get in the way of the politics of main Board's resource allocation. They are rarely considered to have the power to inform and influence upwards to the main Board and its decisions. There are strong signs that main Boards will need to take a more diplomatic approach to such subsidiary boards as they gain increasing legal powers at the national level, and much better political and local economic intelligence. This development is causing subsidiary Board directors to have to move beyond their passive, often comfortable, country club roles as local Accidental Directors.

This growing tension between international-based corporations and their local boards will not go away. It is exacerbated for US companies by their insistence on applying the US Federal policy of 'extra-territoriality' insisting on US board's legal dominance, but other Western and Chinese corporations are facing similar issues. Old-style corporate colonialism is grudgingly conceding more national power to subsidiary boards, although it can be a painful process for both sides. A few Western business folk and politicians are realising what Adam Smith had warned in 1776, that although the-then new corporate joint-stock entities would improve world trade massively, they would have increased economic domination through their four 'unlimited powers' – unlimited size, unlimited life, unlimited licence and consequently unlimited power. The current fightback against these 'four unlimiteds' from the smaller national governments is a germane issue, and will be key for the next generation of directors. To enforce their local laws, some governments are beginning to threaten to remove the multi-nationals' 'licence to operate' in their countries, or to restrict them to very short life if they do not co-operate. Do keep a watch on the rise of Smart Small States and their efforts to reframe future corporate governance in relation to the old colonials.

4. Being Nominated As A Director By Venture Capitalists Or Fund Managers

I am delighted to report increasing problems for venture capitalists, and fund managers, in this area. They have frequently behaved as if corporate governance laws do not apply to them. They do. But as these laws have been so rarely enforced, they feel that they can act with impunity. Venture capitalists' business models are often designed in opposition to the values of effective corporate governance, especially concerning the maintenance and development of the long-term health of the business. If an investor wants to get out in four years or less, then the timespans are often contradictory to long-term viability. In this way they have become the generators of many of the wrong sort of Accidental Directors.

Their business model tends to go for very short-term investments, load up the business with debt by which to overpay themselves and their short-term shareholders, and greatly increase the risk appetite of the business. This is not a way of 'ensuring the long-term health of a business' as required by company law. The registered directors they place on a board are not encouraged to have any corporate governance training, nor independence of thought, but are encouraged to focus on the short-term needs of the investor only. They will be long gone before the usually dire consequences of their brief 'investment' flurry are manifest. We are seeing this strongly in the behaviour of the boards of the UK's water monopolies as they are investigated by the national regulators. So, nominees for directorships are often mere cyphers for the investors rather than true board members. They tend to intervene only when instructed to do so when their boss's short-term interest is threatened.

This is fundamentally wrong, even unlawful, on two counts. First, the UK's Common Law is crystal clear on nominee directors and has been since 1953:

> *Or take a nominee director, that is a director of a company who is nominated by a large shareholder to represent his interests. There is nothing wrong in that. It is done every day. Nothing wrong that is, so long as the director is left free to exercise his best judgement in the interests of the company he serves. But if he is put on terms that he is bound to act in the affairs of the company in accordance with the direction of his patron, it is beyond doubt unlawful.* [2].

When I quote this to nominee directors, they often turn pale. A complex mixture of disbelief, horror and fear crosses their face. They immediately say that this was never explained to them on nomination and registration as a director. This may be true, but they still are at risk of being unlawful. If things go wrong, and they often do in high-risk companies, then they can face personal liability issues.

The second count is of refusing to be registered as a director but sitting in on a board and, therefore, acting as a shadow director. This applies to many other types of owners who wish to distance themselves from Company Law – to be the shadowy eminences grises influencing board decisions without obvious authority or accountability. As I have mentioned shadow directors earlier in this chapter, here I shall simply reinforce my concerns over venture capitalists and their worrying habit of regularly planting 'shadow directors'.

5. Fund Managers as Registered Directors

Fund managers can find themselves in similar positions to venture capitalists. If they are registered directors, however unwittingly, and their fund has a right to influence a board decision through a vote, or by them being nominated as a board member, they risk being treated by other board members either as a shadow director or an Accidental Director. The problem is made worse by some fund managers wanting to exert influence on Board decisions without wishing to accept their director role.

I have talked with fund managers responsible to their client for a portfolio of, say, 4,000 different shareholders, put in impossible positions. Perhaps some 50 of their portfolio are important, active and are reasonably monitored by them. These are the ones likely to get attention as their performance pays the fund manager's quarterly bonuses. But what happens to the 3,950 companies in the other part of their portfolio? I have had fund managers whisper to me that such client companies are lucky even to get their portfolio's annual statements read in full during a year, let alone analysed – for which they are paid. Some say that they have budgeted a total of just 30 minutes a year for each such client. What this says of the ethical basis of charging their client is open to serious debate. If they also influence a company's decisions on such a slim information base, they are a danger to effective corporate governance. They could be seen to be operating more on a whim. When fund managers are also registered directors of many different companies, they are doubly dangerous as they will not have the time or inclination to train as a professional director in any of them. They can have decision power without accountability in each company. Ironically, they often are relatively non-influential in the hierarchy of their home base. There they are frequently rated as just above middle managers. So many see their nominated director role as simply reporting back to a higher authority to await orders. I argue that this is against the well-established Denning Judgement, which confirmed that a Board member cannot act purely as a representative of an appointing party, and that each director is bound by the legal duties to exercise independence of thought, personal care, skill and diligence.

6. Belonging to a Family Firm

All family firms are different. Their history, culture and mix of personalities form the unique emotional temperature in which family firms make decisions about their future. Power within and between generations is always an issue. Many family members become Accidental Directors without realising it. Some feel trapped by always subsuming their personal priorities to the wider family needs. In the long term this can create frustration and depression. Others feel they want little to do with the business part of which they 'own', yet many still want a guaranteed annual cash flow from it. There is a common belief by such people that modern corporate governance practice is irrelevant because family duties will always have a higher priority than any skilful directoral competence.

Typically, a family business will comprise a founding father or mother who will be the Chairman of the main board. What started as, for example, a basic trading company extends its activities over time to acquire others, move into manufacturing or service delivery and, if successful, over the generations become a Family Office with its own investment banking operation and a philanthropic wing. Subsidiaries may be created, or a Holding Board which the founding mother or father will chair. 'The Children' will have various nominated functional and directoral roles for which few may have any professional experience. So, their inputs and outputs are mixed. If the business expands sufficiently, uncles and aunties and then nieces and nephews may expect to join and dilute the share base. But whatever the business expansion, the central power of 'the big man' or 'big woman' usually overshadows all final decision-making.

Culturally it can be an exciting environment because the family answers only to itself for its decisions and, in theory, must think long-term to protect the interests of future generations. But often it can be felt to be stifling, particularly if 'the dear octopus' of the extended family dominates all decision-making. Then any notion of a director's independence of thought, and the importance of the development of the duties of care, skill and diligence, are easily lost. They will tend to operate as Level One boards full of Accidental Directors without any thoughtful regular strategy review processes.

In family companies *the first generation* are typically the most entrepreneurial. They are the founders with the great idea, or they have seized a golden opportunity. They put maximum energy into the 'take-off' phase and nurture carefully its rapid advance. They define the original product, service, brand and culture. If they have a functional board at all, it is typically Level One-style, an anarchic group of good folk capable of unwittingly doing wrong things. They are often oblivious to the fact that they are legal directors, about which they have little interest.

It is *the second generation* who recognise that the creative chaos of the first generation cannot go on forever without sinking the company. They strive to resolve the idiosyncrasies of the first generations' growth and seek rationalisation by establishing more systems in its daily operations. They spend time managing the ever-widening ownership base as more family members and a few trusted outsiders are brought into the minimalist corporate governance system. These are often given shares. These may dilute the original shareholder base. They realise also that they must now be seen by the wider world to have at least minimal levels of corporate governance compliance. But they are usually grudgingly compliant in accepting the implications. I develop this argument later in this chapter.

It is *the third generation* who are often the ultimate disruptors and company killers, wittingly or unwittingly. Typically, they are less committed to the founders' ideas and values, have less energy to sustain the company, but still want 'their' proportion of the wealth generated. They are Accidental Directors in that they know little of their duties and the basic company law, but think they have an automatic right to be directors through family membership, and certainly a say over what is rightly theirs.

There can be a level of arrogance about them and their 'rights'. This means that they often resent even the suggestion of them needing to progress to Level Two board compliance, development, and learning. They have no intention of becoming professional directors. This leads to a degradation of the viability of the business's future health. Their commitment to the business can be highly variable. When the inevitable fights for succession meet the business needs for both expansionary funding and directoral competence, then emotional turbulence can reign in the extended family. This is particularly true if the third generation have been promised a guaranteed annual income with no directoral duties, or obligation to contribute to the company other than to be trophy directors.

A common fallacy that I see within such families, especially currently in the Arabian Gulf and South-East Asia, is that much of this generational turmoil over the lack of effective corporate governance can be resolved simply by an IPO or an M&A. This 'externalises' the family issue, and the anticipated cascade of cash expected to flow automatically will resolve all other issues. It is also expected to resolve all family problems by tilting the governance burden towards the appointment of more professional managers, company secretaries auditors and accountants because these will be demanded by new external investors.

Due Diligence is a corporate governance issue that is rarely discussed by the family until much too late in the funding or refunding process. For example, IPOs are frequently assumed to offer 'free' money to the family shareholders for a slice of their equity. Crudely, this is correct, but the route to such wealth is more complex and demanding than many expect. Usually the biggest stumbling block, and deal breaker, is that IPOs and M&As must undergo the deep exploration process demanded by stock exchanges and other public regulators called 'due diligence'. This is basic fact-checking on all elements of the public offer, including the cultural and organisational fit. It exposes to potential investors the hard truths of the ownership, finances and internal workings of the business. As many families have secrets and debatable decisions taken many years ago this is often a culturally turbulent and emotionally difficult period for many families. It can open old wounds.

Matters are made worse internationally as IPO analysis is now entering a more sophisticated phase. What used to be treated as a quick two-to-three week process at the end of the prolonged financial and legal hassling before a listing, has extended into probing deeper into family holdings and relationships, the competence of often Accidental Directors, the robustness and quantity of their reporting systems, and the quality of the operational management. From the IPO investors and regulators' viewpoint this makes sense. So many IPOs have foundered shortly after launch on directoral, cultural, managerial, and cultural incompatibilities combined with the incompleteness of their reporting systems. This new complexity sits uneasily with the previous simplistic, easily assumed, primacy of just assessing the financial fit. From the family point of view, it raises larger and difficult questions as to whether they have the range of competences to run an IPO and, if not, how they will professionalise their corporate governance compliance to assure the wider market trust in the family's future. A number of families withdraw at this stage. They rarely want to face public humiliation through publicising the often-embarrassing facts and feuds unearthed during an even superficial due diligence process.

What can help them? First, by consciously planning to install the basic disciplines of Level Two Directors by training competent directors and managers; and then agreeing as a family to refocus their energies on ensuring the family's future wealth by becoming a truly Level Three Learning Board.

7. Becoming a Director of a Not-For-Profit Organisation

It is usual for people asked to become a director of a not-for-profit organisation, often a charity, to take this both as a great honour and a social duty. Most people like to 'give back' to their community. It is even better if this pro-bono offer has the double reward bonus of increasing their social status. I note that Post-Covid there are a growing number of people who wish to participate willingly. But do they know what they are getting in to?

Many do not realise that not-for-profits and charities are legal entities under the Companies Act and must, just like registered companies, abide by its laws and regulations. Indeed, many worried directors who come to see me when they have hit trouble are concerned that they had been told, or had wrongly assumed, that they need not worry about the Companies Act, and that the Charities Act would give them all the personal liability protection they need. It does not. The Charities Act is separate and specific legislation dealing mainly with the roles of Trustees, a distinct legal category from directors, although many must be both. The Companies Act is not optional.

Not-for-profits and charities tend to be very values-driven with strong purposes and sometimes messianic leaders. Over time they can suffer from 'Founder syndrome', in which the charisma and values of the founder dominate the culture and influence major decisions. They also frequently downgrade the concept of generating mere financial surplus, particularly if thought of as 'profit', to their lowest priority. However, this does not exempt them from having to make an annual surplus legally to remain liquid and solvent, and to act always in a business-like manner. This is where things can become difficult for accidental directors and board members. If the majority of the board are strong advocates of the good cause, they often spend little time designing the control and feedback mechanics of the administration, its finances and especially its cashflow. A lack of cashflow kills any organisation, especially charities. I know of no charity whose logo is 'cash is king'. I know of many where it would have been a great saviour, especially as in the age of social media it is now fashionable to create immediately a charity for any cause.

Many charitable boards assume that the mere presence of a lawyer and an accountant on a board exempts the other members from their directoral liability. It does not. They still need to be careful, skilful, and diligent; have their primary loyalty to the charity as an entity, show independence of thought when taking board decisions; and avoid conflicts of interests. It surprises me how so many good-hearted folks only realise that there is a professional aspect to their role when it is too late to avoid a crash and their consequent liabilities. I outline below two examples of how these dilemmas can play out very damagingly in real time.

I know from 40 years' experience that it is always dangerous to use current issues as examples. Humans are always creating new dramas and scandals and repeating corporate governance mistakes. Below I describe three current UK scandals live on broadcast and social media:

1. The first is the Post Office scandal, which was only really addressed when the public were informed – by a dramatised series account on TV, aired in January 2024, following the start of the public inquiry. The drama of many innocent post masters and post mistresses being sacked and sometimes jailed was a tragedy. The failure of the IT system overseeing each post office's accounting process was rarely investigated in depth and independently via the board. That it was rarely questioned by the board despite the issue lasting over a decade was remarkably lax. Whether it was unlawful has yet to be tested. The originating issue has been before the courts and large compensation sums are being negotiated, but grudgingly. Two aspects stand out to me. First, the Board's seeming indifference to a long running sore. Second, it is noticeable that the prosecution case hardly mentioned corporate governance. I find this another example of those with power not using the corporate governance legal framework to seek justice on behalf of the less powerful.
2. The second is the behaviour of the monopoly water companies since their nationalisation in the late 1980s. They are charged with ensuring a pure drinking water supply, disposing safely of sewage, and maintaining and reinvesting in the maintenance of their systems. Britain still has good quality drinking water but there is growing outrage at the rising water pollution incidents that affect the rivers and streams that support the local eco-systems. The business model seems to be to load up with debt, pay generously shareholders and executives, but not Boards, and do as little as possible to avoid pollution and the maintenance of the water system. Their corporate governance is complicated by the messy connections between the environmental ministry, and Ofwat, the regulator (during the writing of this book the Government announced the abolition of Ofwat and other regulators, and the proposed creation of a new regulator with wider powers). In all the public outpouring of protest against the water companies, little is made of the weak corporate governance within the companies, and between them and their regulators.
3. The case of nurse Sandie Peggie involves the conscious ignoring of new legislation by the executives and the board. When she was distressed by a 'transwoman doctor' – biologically intact male with no gender change certificate – getting changed in the women's changing room, Peggie was accused of transphobia by NHS Fife management and charged with serious misconduct. This was on the advice of the Lead on Equality and Human Rights, a 25-year-old woman whose 'expertise' consisted of a degree in immunology followed by two years as a Covid contact tracer. This was despite the new Supreme Court ruling that women are entitled to single-sex spaces, NHS Fife is continuing to defend its actions at an employment tribunal, at the time of writing.

> The key point for me is that in all the above cases, neither the authorities, the press nor the public used or is using the term 'corporate governance' – because it's simply not recognised that that is the issue. The issue of the board acting as the Brain and Conscience of the organisation is missing. And if it's not recognised, it can't be dealt with.

Looking back, two other examples have remained in my mind strongly. The first, Kids Company is a classic example of when big egos, strong PR, politicians rushing in to wave their view of righteousness, social media echo chambers exaggerating the views of both sides, and confused regulators combine to create total confusion.

Example 1: Kids Company

Kids Company in the UK was an example of how good-hearted directors, charity workers, public personalities and politicians ended up involving the mass media, the police, the courts, and the Charity Commission in a mess that derailed a flawed yet apparently successful charity. They did this by not appreciating fully the core elements of effective corporate governance. After years of high-profile media publicity of its effectiveness, and growing public controversy about its conduct, this charity collapsed in a media frenzy. It was sufficiently divisive in the political, charity, and corporate governance worlds, that *three* investigations into it were opened, ending in the Charity Commission Report published in February 2022. I have selected a few examples from the reports below [3–5] to illustrate how confused the understanding of effective corporate governance is in this area.

Founded in 1998 by the high-energy children's rights advocate and psychotherapist, Camilla Batmanghelidjh, Kids Company had a high media profile. It provided emotional and practical educational support for severely traumatised children in conditions of neglect, violence and poverty initially in South London. Its admirable purpose became widely supported nationally, was frequently mentioned in the media, and included such early advocates as J K Rowling, Prime Minister David Cameron, and Coldplay.

However, reports started appearing in the media of unusual behaviours such as paying for a first-class transatlantic flight for a boy to see his girlfriend, lavish handouts of designer gifts, holidays, birthday presents and housing support, leading to a general feeling of decreasing management and directoral oversight. Their business model was criticised as too dependent on the fund-raising of the charismatic founder and, like so many charities, it ran into cashflow problems especially when it expanded its operations to a wider area of London, and then to the cities of Bristol and Liverpool. It sought emergency help from the Conservative Government and with high publicity was given a much-debated £3 million grant from the Cabinet Office to be matched by private donations.

However, on the very day that the grant was made, news emerged of a police probe into allegations of sexual abuse on two of its sites following a BBC *Newsnight* investigation. An irony here was that one of the 'great and the good' trustees was Alan Yentob, a senior BBC employee. The charity's trustees convened and after much debate decided that these allegations would make further fundraising impossible and reluctantly closed the charity. The police dropped their investigation after five months having found no evidence of safeguarding failures or criminality. Later a judge, Mrs Justice Falk, ruled that had it not been for the unfounded abuse allegations, the charity might have survived. During this time directors and senior executives were under constant public scrutiny, criticism, and stress.

By then all sorts of social and political interests and opinions had been stirred and aired. The politicians then decided to investigate. Undoubtedly the founder, Batmanghelidjh, polarised public opinion, being seen either as a saint or a 'mesmerising' influence on donors, the trustees, and the government. In 2016 a committee of MPs responding to public disquiet held their own investigation through the National Audit Office [3]. They declared the cash payments to children as irresponsible and accused the board of negligence in their directoral and trustee duties, lax financial controls, exaggerating the number of children it served, and of following a reckless business model [4]. I note here that many registered companies have at times behaved in similar ways. Usually, the markets ensure that they fail quietly, but here high-profile taxpayers' money and social media were very publicly involved.

This high public profile meant that they and others were demanding also action under both the Companies Act and The Charity Act be taken against the directors/trustees. In 2017, asked by the coalition government, who were increasingly embarrassed by the divisive publicity, the company regulators brought legal proceedings via the Official Receiver seeking to ban Batmanghelidjh and the seven trustees from holding directoral/trustee roles in companies or charities for six years. By 2020 a total of 600 pages of evidence were submitted to the court to support this claim.

The High Court under Mrs Justice Falk dismissed the case. She exonerated the board of mismanagement and praised the board as 'highly impressive and dedicated individuals'. The case cost the taxpayer £9.5 million.

Even then it was not over because under a separate law The Charity Commission had begun its own investigation [5]. It made a formal finding of mismanagement relating to failures of payments to Her Majesty's Revenue and Customs, and one instance of staff wages paid one day late. It stated that the charity ran a 'high-risk business model' and was heavily reliant on the founder's ability as a fund raiser. It said that it kept insufficient levels of financial reserves although it did concede that this was not unusual in the charity sector. It questioned the seemingly high payments to a small group of children whilst accepting that the charity had the right to do so. But it also stated that 'there was no evidence of dishonesty, bad faith, or inappropriate personal gain'. They decided that no regulatory action should be taken against the trustees or executive and agreed with the High Court judgement. The issue had become such a very high-profile political football that this finding led to many red faces. But no review of the corporate governance framework in which the crisis developed was held. The process damaged unnecessarily both personal and institutional reputations, and left animosity all round. Batmanghelidjh threatened to sue. The Charity Commission is under continuing criticism for initially seeming to ignore both the judge's findings and her praise for the trustees' behaviour. Others argue that the case should never have been brought by the Official Receiver. Batmanghelidjh died in 2024.

For me this a classic example of all parties failing to understand the meaning and systems of effective corporate governance, whilst having the arrogance to assume that their interpretation of the role must be the only acceptable one.

This example is an extreme case where a good cause and people wishing to give back to their community, clashed in public with political partisanship infighting amongst the wider stakeholders including the regulators. There was an acknowledged imbalance between the directoral duties of delivering the company's Purpose by showing the way ahead and yet maintaining prudent control. My concern is that I am consulted by too many good-hearted people who have cheerfully entered the not-for-profit field without a proper briefing and without realising the personal, legal, and emotional consequences. That is why I am arguing that all directors and trustees have a mandatory six-month probationary period to test their aptitude for the role before becoming a registered director. I am reassured that so many members of the public are still willing to put themselves forward to be charity directors and trustees, but I do believe that not-for-profits have a moral and legal duty to train their directors and senior executives to much higher levels of professionalism.

To help this, in the UK, the remarkable pro-bono work over 20 years by the Worshipful Company of Management Consultants, London, in co-operation with the Centre for Charity Effectiveness at Bayes Business School, has led to a range of high-quality advice, publications and connections to help resolve this problem. Too few good-hearted people take advantage of these before launching themselves into the turbulent, high-risk, not-for-profit world.

Many of the worst corporate governance problems on which I am consulted, both nationally and internationally, arise in the public sector. Like in the charity sector there is a prevailing attitude that they are beyond the laws of corporate governance, and that their priority is always to their minister's wishes. The irony is that often it is the legislators who have passed the laws that then block effective corporate governance implementation in the public sector or state-owned businesses. This paradox is because the very politicians who pass the national laws seem neither to know what they are, nor care whether they are enforced. This is noticeably so if those laws seem to counter their current political mantras. If senior civil servants behave as though they were also above the law and demand actions from directors and boards that are likely to be unlawful if ever exposed to public scrutiny, then there is a problem. Their arrogance is often surpassed only by their ignorance. Over the last twenty years I have never found any politician or senior civil servant who can quote from memory the seven duties of a director, or the six elements of the Purpose of a Board. Yet both are contained in just two A4 pages in Section 171 and 172 of the UK's Companies Act 2006. They are the foundation stones of Corporate Governance. They are not difficult to learn. They are not difficult to live by, if you are honest and respect them. Yet some ignorant bureaucrats assume that their personal position and powers are above such mundane things. I demonstrate this below with an NHS example.

For the Accidental Director this is particularly treacherous territory. Being asked to join a charity board or joining a public sector board can be seen publicly to be a great honour, a boost to one's personal reputation. It gives a warm feeling to be able to 'give back' to your community. The offer of such a 'directorship' may be to an executive agency, or a state-owned enterprise, or a Health Trust. A regular message on being asked to join is 'not to worry over the legalities because the government will cover any personal liabilities'. This is not necessarily so. The legal position of 'directors' in the NHS, government agencies and state-owned enterprises is not fully established in the courts. Politicians are not concerned about this. But people accepting such 'directorships' should be.

'Political cover' is often promised through the 'protection' of a minister or Secretary of State. But these people change frequently and are unlikely to know, or care, what their predecessors promised. So, asking three basic questions – what are my role responsibilities, what am I personally liable for, and how much training, assessment and development shall I have for this new role? – are fundamental for any new charity or public sector director. It is worth being seen initially as questioning, awkward, difficult, or even dangerous to the status quo, when accepting any public role for which you are unprepared, and which may well involve you publicly in political controversy and financial harm. Given the dominance of social media your standing in society can become rapidly and badly damaged.

Ministers and civil servants always have pet projects which may have been part of their electoral promises. As I scan the media I notice for example, entrepreneurial 'hubs', 'launch pads', 'accelerators' 'breeders', 'generators', and 'enterprise zones' and 'magnet cities' being proposed by politicians for regrowing economies. Many are talking about saving the environment through 'rewilding', soil reactivation, water conservancy, reducing air pollution, stopping the use of fossil fuels and, of course, 'net zero' policies, and 'sustainability'. Others are more concerned with 'alleviating poverty permanently', 'minority rights', 'anti-slavery projects' and 'Equality, Diversity, and Inclusion' initiatives. A few advocate new forms of legal entities such as 'Public Benefit' or 'Community Interest' companies, although very few have taken the trouble to put effort into trying to change company law to do so. Even fewer advocate rectifying their legislative mistakes, and the consequent potential for corruption, as seen in the recent law concerning the advocacy of 'Limited Liability Partnerships'. These deliberately anonymise and obscure the ultimate ownership of a company. This continues in the UK and the Commonwealth, facilitating money laundering and modern slavery worldwide.

When appointed in the public sector, new directors are often recruited to follow a specific political initiative. However, they are usually told that for their safety 'they should apply Company Law, and especially the Corporate Governance Code', to regulate their actions. This raises two major issues. First, how can they use their 'independence of judgement' when expected to follow governmental policies which may prove to be in contradiction? This becomes a major problem if the directors' judgement on ensuring the health of the company's future is in opposition to the political will of the minister? Second, how can such a director illustrate to the courts and the public that they have exercised their 'care, skill and diligence' and independence in taking board decisions when there is no basic public benchmark, funding, or training to do so?

The moral problem for such publicly appointed directors, and for new Accidental Directors especially, is whether to attempt to use their powers under the Companies Act (that have not been fully tested in a court for a public enterprise), even if this goes against current political wishes? Or whether to bend to the political will regardless of what the law advocates? Currently I know of no easy resolution to this problem but can point out brave directors who have tried to work within the law and against political and administrative arrogance. Many of this minority have been side-lined, not had their directorships renewed, or, less frequently, sacked. Politicians cannot stand directors who oppose on such 'legal' grounds. They and their special advisors then argue that their policies were voted by the national electorate, even if there has not been time to change the relevant legislation. This is a corporate governance issue of our time.

My second long-term example focuses on the way a political imperative is translated rapidly into bureaucratic newspeak, gold-plating, and job-creation way beyond the minister's intentions. It is a long example as I have followed the intricate paths that bureaucrats love.

Example 2: NHS Foundation Trust Boards

Since its creation in 1947 The National Health Service (NHS) has been seen as the 'national religion of the UK'. It was founded with the best of intentions but was underfunded, from the start. It still over-promises through the politicians, and under-delivers through its over-complex structure and highly centralised administration. With continuous battles for resources at both the national and local constituency levels the politicians see fighting for 'their' local share of such resources as a major plank in their next re-election fight. So, the NHS is in continuous political play with only short-term objectives prioritised by those seeking power. It employs directly over one million people and although seen by most as a 'good thing' because it delivers health services free at the point of need, although of decreasing quality and scope, it is also seen as an overblown organisational monster with a shadow side culture of top-down authoritarian management style, which enforces compliance through bullying and rewarding obedience.

A dysfunctional corporate governance system was developed for the NHS Foundation (Hospital) Trusts and their Boards of Directors. In my experience corporate governance was never given serious consideration, as political imperatives were more important. These boards were meant to have increasing autonomy to best deploy their scarce resources for what they saw as the key needs of their local area. Unsurprisingly, this was seen as a major challenge to the status quo of the existing centralised powers of ministers, local politicians, and civil servants as to who 'owned' the NHS. They became very keen to stop the new Trust Boards taking the 'wrong' decisions. Then, to add confusion on confusion the government, urged on by politicians of all sides, decided that the NHS had to become 'more democratic' to be more publicly accountable. The new structure was praised in Parliament as giving new levels of 'fairness', openness' and 'diversity' to the Trusts. It did no such thing. The use of such language was Orwellian, and the implementation processes Kafkaesque. It was against all that was known about effective governance or managerial practice. It was a whim of ministers and their special advisors. It added unnecessary costs across the nation at a time of declared 'austerity'.

In 2004 I was co-director, with my colleague, Georges Selim, of an NHS England Director Development programme run through the then Cass Business School. We would initially work with some 400 Directors, 800 Finance Directors and 200 Company Secretaries within the Foundation Trusts. Our brief was that the new Trusts must learn how to work as 'proper' boards under the 2006 Companies Act laws. Having done a little work on the internal governance of the new regulator, Monitor, I asked immediately what the legal basis, and entity, was for these new boards? This created some confusion at the Department of Health. First, I was told not to ask such an impertinent question. I may be a governance guru, but this was beyond my pay grade. It was resented, especially by the young governmental special advisors who were enthusiastically sponsoring this project. When I asked for an instruction in writing they reluctantly admitted that there was no legal entity – yet. They thought the question politically unimportant.

So, a compromise was struck. We agreed to start each programme with a formal statement that what we were teaching was within the legal context of the Companies Act, especially the Duties of a Director and the Purpose of a Board, and that the new boards were expected by the NHS to abide by this 'as best they could'. We had to explain that no cover was given to them if they were forced outside the law by their bosses, and would certainly not be granted if they went outside national policy for the benefit of their local region. Confusion reigned from the start. Amazingly hundreds of the public still applied to be directors of Trust boards. Accidental Directors blossomed.

To give such directors due acknowledgement, many struggled valiantly to obey their role within the Companies Act. If, for example, they made a proposal to combine hospitals in their geographic area to improve greatly the delivery of better health for their neighbourhood, these were frequently opposed by national and local politicians fearful of losing their votes when asking their constituents to travel further for a noticeably improved level of health service. This impasse continues.

Later a higher form of madness developed with the naïve proposal from senior civil servants backed by politicians and their special advisors that to increase democracy and public accountability, the Trusts should have a *second* board of directors to run in parallel with the first – to be called the Board of Governors. The fatal design flaw and arrogance was not to see that instant hostility and competition was guaranteed between the two boards. Common sense is very rare, especially in the NHS. There was very limited public consultation and no pilot testing for this scheme. It was imposed, and the existing Trust Directors dreaded the likely clash with these new Board Governors, foreseeing the resulting confusion, lack of trust generated, and potential for continuous conflict and wastage of scarce resources. Yet few Trust Directors were willing to speak out publicly against this design. The NHS shadow culture of yielding, obedience and a fear of bullying prevailed.

When the new Board of Governors structure, designed to generate 'openness', 'fairness' and 'diversity', was launched it was greeted with astonishment by the corporate governance community, and any member of the public who had some notion of common sense. Inevitably, I asked again what the legal entity for these new Governors was but was dismissed as 'just being difficult'. No-one wanted to know because obeying their political masters and their fashionable rhetoric was the new priority.

The politicians continued to stress that this would 'improve public oversight of NHS Trusts' in two ways. First, by ensuring that the new Governors were 'more representative' of their communities than the existing directors. No evidence was given to show any lack of diversity or representation of the existing Trust Directors. My questions for such evidence went unanswered. Second, that the new Board of Governors would be given an ultimate power over the Board of Directors – they could sack the Chairman of the Trust Board. The chairman was now both the Chairman of the Trust and Governors Boards. The chances of continual conflict between the Directors and the Governors were, therefore, designed in, despite the sponsors denying this design fault. In terms of designing maximum hostility, inefficiency, conflict and wasting public money it was perverse genius.

Things did not go well from the start. The public were encouraged to apply to become a member of their local NHS Board of Governors. The advertisements stressed that no special experience was needed. Most citizens treated the appeal with indifference. However, those who did apply often had very good reason to do so. A few really wanted to help their local community. But others had an axe to grind. A striking example was in a mental health Trust. Some applicants seeking to become a Governor were the relatives of current or previous patients with outstanding grievances to settle. Some were dissatisfied previous patients, and some were from trades unions with clear party-political objectives on behalf of their members' employment, but not necessarily the patients' health. There were no publicly agreed selection criteria.

Differing and conflicting agendas were brought to the Governors' board table from the start. This made the Chairman's job very difficult as they were trying to handle simultaneously two often opposed boards. Unlike the Directors, the Governors were given no training or assessment, so the notions of 'independence of judgement' and 'care, skill and diligence' were not prominent in their oversight and decision-making processes. And as their only real power was to sack the Chairman, guess what they focussed on?

In corporate governance, and in small group psychology, it is well proven since the mid-1940s that the optimal size for a small group to learn to work together effectively is between 6 and 12 people. This has been a rule of thumb for directors over the past 50 years. Fewer than 6 does not allow sufficient diversity for the critical review of decision-making. More than 12 means that an ever-increasing amount of board time is taken in just managing the group inputs and discussions. Clarity of problem definition and problem resolution is hampered. The concept of having a maximum of 12 directors is well-tested. If civil servants had specified a maximum of 12 for the new Board of Governors, as it was for the Board of Directors, it might just have worked. But it did not. Bureaucratic inflation, and 'gold-plating' immediately started. Their natural inclination to add as many members as possible to demonstrate 'participation', 'representation' and 'equality' then took over. This created a large and destructive structure which often reverted to factional warfare. A typical Board of Governors now comprised:

- 13 elected Governor volunteers from the wider community
- 4 Service User Governors
- 2 Carer Governors
- 4 Staff Governors

Plus

- I appointed Governor from:
  - A local university
  - A local college

And

- 2 appointed Governors from:
  - The County Council
  - The local Constabularies (sic).

The total was some 30 people. Not all could attend every meeting, but all wanted their say, so meetings were long, fractious, repetitive, boring, and ineffective. A small concession was made later when the Board of Governors was retitled the' Council of Governors', but still without full legal definition of their roles. And remember that behind all of this are politicians and civil servants acting as Shadow Governors exercising power without responsibility to achieve their personal ends. This was never going to deliver effective corporate governance.

Level One board maturity is a highly frustrating state of existence. All Accidental Directors are in a stage of pre-Purgatory. To escape they need either to accept the seven duties as a director and their role as a member of a board, or to resign immediately, remembering that even then the decisions taken by their board during their stay will keep them liable.

The next step towards board maturity is to move to Level Two – Grudging Compliance. This is a form of self-imposed Purgatory, so moving through it quickly is essential. I see it as a temporary state of pain and suffering necessary before achieving the enlightenment of Levels Three and Four.

Grudgingly Compliant Directors – Level Two Board Maturity

The move from being an unknowing Accidental Director to being aware that you are a Registered Director can be a major shock. As your newly registered public role, liabilities and responsibilities become manifest, the daunting scale of the new learning demanded becomes obvious. This forces such directors to a grudging acceptance of the need to comply with the required company law. This demands a period of sometimes uncomfortable learning. I am surprised as to how many Grudgingly

Compliant directors are angrily resentful to find themselves in this position. Many feel under duress, yet few feel strong enough to demand personal training and development budgets to ensure that they can comply with the law. On the other hand, I see few boards accept the need to consciously design and fund the induction and development of each new director. Both conditions need fulfilling to escape the limbo and purgatory of Level Two board maturity.

There can also be strong pushback from those newly registered directors who either resent being put into this new and demanding role, sometimes under duress, or who feel that directing is not a separate and learnable job distinct from management or their specialist knowledge. They resent strongly being exposed to increasing regulation and public transparency. And they can be noticeably grumpy if you point out that, like it or not, once they are legally registered as a director, they must obey the law or face the consequences. Few will face the serious alternative of saying 'no' to being a director. This may hurt their immediate career prospects, but it can ease their minds.

Becoming a registered Director means being subject to the law relating to this role. This is contained in the opening paragraph of Section 171 – the Duties of a Director – and Section 172 – the Purpose of a Board – in the UK's Companies Act 2006. The synopses of both cover a total of eleven points in two pages. They are not difficult to remember. They are more difficult to live openly. Any board should ensure that they and their colleagues are assessed regularly internally, and externally by their stakeholders on their implementation of them. Then they can have the pleasure of escaping Level Two Purgatory and move quickly to the energy of becoming a Level Three Learning Board director.

Sections 171 and 172 are for me the foundation stones of future effective corporate governance. They need to be engraved on directors' hearts so they can learn to live by them 24/7 and 365 days of the year.

To ensure directors' compliance with their Civil Law *duties*, they are bound under Section 171:

- To act within their legal powers (their constitution),
- To promote the success of the company (as a separate legal entity),
- To exercise independent judgement on board decisions,
- To exercise reasonable care, skill and diligence (in problem definition and resolution) Author's parentheses.
- And in the three that deal more with Criminal Law, they are bound:
- To avoid conflicts of interest,
- Not to accept benefits from third parties,
- To declare interests in proposed transactions.

These create the ethical basis for directors and their boards. They are persuasive of the 56 Commonwealth countries. They also influence informally corporate governance law development in many other countries.

These seven Duties are then underpinned by the key one-page synopsis from Section 172 of the UK's Companies Act 2006 on the *Purpose* of a Board of Directors. It states six crucial elements for delivering the board's Purpose:

"The Board has a Duty to promote the success of the Company.

A director of a company must act in the way he considers, in good faith, would be most likely to promote the success of the company for the benefit of the members as a whole, and in so doing have regard (amongst other matters) to –

a) The likely consequences of the decision in the long term,
b) The interests of the company's employees,
c) The need to foster the company's business relationships with suppliers, customers, and others,
d) The impact on the community and the environment,
e) The desirability of the company maintaining a reputation for high standards of business conduct, and
f) The need to act fairly between the members of the company."

This was made law back in 2006 after eight long years of debate in the UK parliament. It predates by two decades the now fashionable 'ESG' approach. Who knew? Sadly, it is rarely known or espoused by current boards.

The simplicity and completeness of these two sections gives a rock-solid foundation for the development of any director or board. The problem still remains that most directors, national and international, are ignorant of them. Hence, they resist them. Even worse, the current legislators seem equally ignorant and so do little to enforce them. This allows regulators to produce increasingly unnecessary codes and rules that do not honour the spirit and content of these two key pages. However, they create the illusion of regulatory action whilst creating additional cost and time wasting for boards.

Directoral life is clearer and simpler when these two pages are viewed by a board through the lens of the fundamental values of corporate governance:

- Accountability (to the stakeholders),
- Probity (honest dealing with all parties involved),
- Transparency (in its behaviour).

Sadly, most directors do not have a personal plan to reach such clarity, and so grudgingly attempt slavish compliance with the many codes and rules. This makes them even more grumpy about their perceived pointlessness of 'corporate governance'. To escape the seemingly endless limbo of being a Level Two director it is wise to remind oneself of the definition of corporate governance stated originally in the globally influential 1992 Cadbury Code:

Corporate Governance is the system by which companies are directed and controlled. Boards of directors are responsible for the governance of their companies. The shareholder's role in governance is to appoint the directors and auditors and to satisfy themselves that an appropriate governance structure is in place. The responsibilities of the board include setting the company's strategic aims, providing the leadership to put them into effect, supervising the management of the business and reporting to shareholders on their stewardship. The board's actions are subject to laws, regulations, and the shareholders in general meetings.

This has stood the international test of time and utility for over thirty years. It does not deal directly with the shareholders' rights as investors or owners. The only criticisms I would now make are first that there is an over-emphasis on shareholders' right in an age when 'stakeholders' have growing powers. Second, that the concept of the board as 'a system' has not yet been adopted and developed rigorously by boards, regulators or politicians. In 1992 they concentrated most on the easy outputs of reporting and audit and much less on the difficult inputs of entrepreneurship, strategic thinking and operational delivery. I say more about this in Chapter Four.

Two factors combine to make Level Two directors permanently uncomfortable despite meeting their legal requirements. First, there is often a personal reluctance by new directors to be seen to need to be learning publicly a new and very different discipline away from their previous comfort zone of managerial or technical expertise. The idea that they are entering a new level of professionalism is rarely considered. This is especially true when confronted at a later stage of business life. The need to raise your eyes to interpret the dynamics of the outside world, and to expand your perspective beyond daily operational activities, can be both simultaneously exhilarating and very discomfiting. However, once achieved, it is a positive move to the necessary higher rungs on the directoral intellectual and maturity spectrum. This first requirement depends on accepting the mindset that directing is a proper job. To become effective, each director needs a personal budget for time, resources, learning and assessment. In most organisations this is dismissed as adding unnecessary costs and seen as an annoying imposition on existing over-stretched managerial or professional roles.

Second, there is an unwillingness to acknowledge and accommodate those seemingly endless legal and regulatory demands. This second factor concerns more the directors', and stakeholders' political views on legislation and regulation. In many Level Two Boards these are frequently seen as impudent blocks on their demands for absolute autonomy as directors. For example, in the US the massed ranks of business and the Republicans have deep objections to 'ESG' and 'EDI' in all its shapes and forms. It is seen as a worrying mix of unwarranted state intervention, socialism, and imposed wokery that must be resisted strongly to save the nation. This feeling is often visceral rather than logical because all human organisations need to balance rules, rights and duties for them to be effective. The sudden rush to employ fashionable phrases to show that you must be included, and then drop them for fear of being excluded, is very human.

However, there is still a strong flavour of anti-regulation bias around many Level Two boards. Their grudging compliance is despite the growing international waves of legislation, regulation as corporate governance laws expand the range of a board's deployment of Financial, Social and Environmental capitals. How can one break this negative cycle? How can a Level Two director accept their legal responsibilities and cross the bridge to become a Level Three director – one capable of playing their full part in a Learning Board? I outline below three simple processes that I have found consistently effective in helping Level Two Directors move forward.

1. A Written Contract for Services as a Director

It still amazes me how few directors have registered with the national authorities without ever having seen or signed a contract for their directoral services. Whether they are full-time or part-time, whether they are also an executive, a civil servant, or charity trustee, they need a written contract for services as a director to protect themselves, their families, and their tax status. The written contract must list their duties *as a director*, the purpose of the board of directors, and their consequent duties and liabilities, and any remuneration. This then needs complementing with an agreed time budget and their Induction, Training and Development, Annual Appraisal, and Deselection processes. This is rarely done. The consequences of boards not doing this has helped my cashflow for many decades.

I am seen as odd in many companies by my insistence that any person being registered as a legal director, who is also an employee of a company, must have *two* contracts for their work. Many directors continue with their executive or expert role. For this they need a standard Contract of Employment for their 'normal' work. Typically, this would be for 80–90% of their time. But for the critical directoral aspect of their work they need a separate contract for services as a director. This is to clarify their legal and taxation position. This allows them to make the case strongly that they must have protected time, say, 10–20%, away from 'normal' work to fulfil their legal directoral duties.

Then to fulfil their directoral work, and especially when they enter the boardroom or committee rooms, they can shed their executive role and adopt the 'independence of thought' mode that defines an effective director. This takes time to learn. They must behave and think way beyond their specialisation to deliver the future health of the total company. This mindset does take some rigorous focus, especially if it starts towards the end of a single-specialist career. Having a chairman conscious of such issues and able to coach a new director is key to moving out of Level Two board maturity.

Remember that there is no such thing as an 'Executive Director' in Company law. Nor do 'Non-Executive Director' or any other 'Non-Executive' titles exist. When used, these are examples of the ignorant and arrogant assuming they can transcend the company law and use any title that they wish, or follow fashionable but bad US practices.

The signing of a contract for services as a director is a fundamental step in the development of the individual director. It is necessary but by no means sufficient. Yet it is much more than a transient moment. It is a symbolic act. It is a personal commitment to the company and your fellow directors. Sufficiency comes through then living the accepted values and behaviours for the rest of a director's life.

2. The Directoral Commitment Ceremony

I argue strongly that on the introduction of a new director to a Board by the Chairman a small but personally significant ceremony is carried out around the boardroom table. It takes only a few minutes, but it is highly significant. The seven Duties of a Director and the six aspects of the Role of a Board are read out by the Chairman. The new director is asked to confirm in front of their fellow directors that they will undertake these to the best of their ability, and that they will pursue the purpose and long-term health of the company as their prime duty. This is an oath made before equals. It is an act of inclusion and acceptance of the joint and several liabilities as a fellow director. It is simple yet profound and ensures that due gravitas is given from the start to the new director's role. It is the first step to bonding to the board as a group of equals. It also acknowledges that there will be a necessary period during which enhanced intelligently naïve questioning will be expected of the new member. This allows them to bed in, but also allows the testing of the existing board members' previous assumptions. I say more on this in Chapter Four. For those not selected but simply assigned to a board, the very idea of a commitment ceremony will come as a shock sufficient for them to consider seriously their position and to question their nominators about how they can pursue their legal duties without being unlawful.

So few organisations understand the law concerning directorships that the ceremonies of the contract and the oath are avoided or never considered. Discomfort then follows for many new directors who can spend months or even years puzzling over precisely what they are meant to do on a board. It surprises me that internationally the formal induction of a new director is not mandated as a key duty of a Chairman. Regulators please note.

3. Time Commitment

Such an induction process builds on the issues clarified Chapter Two's *16 Myths* section. Paramount amongst these is the myth that a director is only a director when they are attending a board or committee meeting. This is a strong belief of Level Two grudgingly compliant directors. This is fundamentally wrong and why I argue that any contract for services as a director should spell out a time and money budget for attending to board duties within and without the boardroom, and for learning effective directoral performance. Once registered, a director is legally locked into the role 24/7 until the time you resign or are deselected. Your responsibilities and liabilities cannot be delegated. This stands in stark contradiction to the often-heard message from recruiters and higher authorities in companies that 'it is not a full-time commitment and should only take, say, four board meetings a year, a few committee meetings and some good dinners'.

My experience is that a single directorship even in a small company will demand a commitment of at least four hours a week, plenty of additional homework depending on the presenting issues, plus the need for continuous horizon-scanning to foresee and debate likely future issues at the Board, and a commitment to update continuously your knowledge. This is as true for not-for-profits, family businesses, and state-owned enterprises as for private companies. Some will argue that it is even more necessary for a director of a not-for-profit because the quality of the management controls, especially cashflow, is unlikely to be as good as the private sector; and the issues are more likely to be large, irregular, more time-consuming, and often political.

Expanding Level Two Board Perspectives to Escape to Level Three

Corporate Governance is the superstructure for board activities. Learning to give direction and prudent control of the total organisation are the two key processes. Both require much broadening of a director's, and boards', perspectives on the wider world. Even internally the director needs to know how to ask pertinent questions of each aspect of the many disciplines within their organisation, and how to interpret the answers. This is where the Board dashboard comes into play, showing the trend line in each sector – as explained in Chapter Five. The external broadening starts with the director's homework around the PPESTT (Political, Physical environment, Economic, Social, Technological, Trade flows) and SWOT (strengths, weaknesses, opportunities, threats) analyses, and the Board debates and implementation of policy and strategy.

Professor Mervyn King [9], the international doyen of corporate governance, has been fundamental in ensuring board accountability through reporting and audit in a growing number of countries. In these it is becoming mandatory for boards to report at least annually to their stakeholders, not just their shareholders. Such a report outlines the consequences of their board decisions on, for example:

- The continuing viability of their business model,
- The impact of the company's operations on the community,
- The impact of the company's operations on the physical environment,
- The company's business relationships with their customers,
- The company's relationships with their supply chain,
- The interests of the company's employees,
- The need to maintain the company's public reputation for good business conduct,
- The need to act fairly between members of the company.

This builds well on Section 172 of the UK's Companies Act. I note that many next generation directors accept these demands as both necessary and inevitable; information necessary to inform the public as part of their stakeholder group. It highlights the broadening perspective and the move towards more community transparency and away from the previous veil of corporate secrecy. In a few countries *auditors* are now asked to report on these questions as a separate aspect of the reporting mechanism.

To a harassed Level Two Director they can look unnecessarily onerous, but to a growingly aware group of grudging directors they are the future for corporate governance compliance: except in such autocracies as China, Iran, and Russia. The US is vacillating, especially after the June 2024 Delaware Court of Chancery decisions. There is a strong, visceral reaction against such broadening issues as 'ESG' which with 'DEI' is now characterised as a party political issue – a trend that is splitting the US business community. The widening of board perspectives is happening despite political divides. Previously it was widely assumed that as the strong dollar encouraged US companies to invest abroad the irony is that they are coming up against these new and wider national and cultural definitions of corporate governance and its annual reporting. With Trump's emphasis on tariffs and US isolationism and deregulation, this process may be delayed, but not for long.

As new nations exercise increasingly their legislative independence, directors will become involved in an intriguing power game as many such nations possess vital raw materials for future manufacture, especially copper, lithium and rare earth metals. The main weapon for these small, increasingly smart, nations is the threat of removing a US company's Licence to Operate in that country unless it obeys local laws. Against that will be the US's once all-powerful 'extra-territoriality' policy. This raises plenty of questions as to what the nature of future compliance will be, and how grudging it will stay in an increasingly uncertain and dynamic world. Directors are no longer outside national and international politics.

The 1992 Cadbury Report on The Financial Aspects of Corporate Governance (ibid) was a masterly synopsis of much that had been gathered piecemeal previously about the financial aspects of corporate governance practice. He knew it was incomplete. In later life his report has been copied as near-gospel in so many countries. His worries were twofold. First, that focusing on the financial aspects only distorted the broader meaning and application of effective corporate governance. At the time of the 2008 financial crash, it was understandable that the financial authorities saw imposing corporate governance codes as a knee-jerk response to underpin such emergency measures as quantitative easing. But they are not and never can be sufficient. There are always deeper policy, philosophical and moral issues that boards must address. This is where broadening their perspectives comes in.

What Sir Adrian saw, and on which we corresponded often, was the *entrepreneurial* energising aspects that initiates effective corporate governance. We both saw that without the motivation, drive, and the continuing energy of entrepreneurship no organisation can sustain its future health. Just sticking to codes and regulations guarantees nothing. It just risks generating more rules. We took 'entrepreneur' from its original Old French sense of a risk taker through being a 'stager of dramas' – led by the

Board. It did not matter if the drama was in the private, public or not-for-profit sectors, the drama and associated projects needed to be directed and played out from the boardroom table. Success is in achieving the company's purpose thus creating a profit or surplus whilst simultaneously giving back to its community and environment. This demanded a new mindset of a board creating and nurturing its own eco-system.

We both agreed that the past fixation on the primacy of creating 'shareholder value', especially but not exclusively in the US, had eroded effective corporate governance for over 30 years. Remember that shareholders do not own a company under Common Law. It was not true. Shareholders are not supreme under Common Law. And it had given rise to over-powerful CEOs who rode roughshod over shareholders. We saw that the growing public pressures would mean that corporate governance must broaden its scope significantly. This would happen in two ways. First, the scope of corporate governance would be widened through stakeholder demand such that all nationally registered organisations be included specifically under sections 171 and 172 of the 2006 Companies Act or their equivalent. This includes family businesses, family offices, partnerships, mutuals, NGOs, quangos, charities, state-owned enterprises and trusts.

Second, that many boards would have to change fundamentally as they dropped the cult of 'Shareholder Value'. The old metaphor of a company being an inanimate machine only for churning out profit, standing apart from the physical environment and its community, is being replaced by the more integrative, holistic, assumptions based on the values of the next generation.

This is a major challenge for Level Two directors. To move from their grudging and repetitive limbo they need to go through a form of intellectual and emotional purgatory. This purging entails accepting a more ecological model of the firm. Many existing Level Two directors resist this, at least initially. But for them the purgatory is necessary to reach Levels Three and Four of Board maturity – The Learning Board and finally the Professional Board.

I find that next generation directors' thinking is already moving closer to the Gaia model – seeing the world as a living organism within which humans and their organisations exist only in 'energy niches', or eco systems, [10]. They live only for as long as they have purpose and are sustainable within their diverse micro-system. Intellectually this means directors see the board as driving simultaneously both its rational strategic and operational purpose and its values-based c*onscience.* This combination creates the *Brain of the Firm.*

The brain, or cerebral, functions deal with the integration of those many dynamic forces operating simultaneously outside, and within, the company. The conscience functions are those values chosen, consciously or unconsciously, by the Board that reflect their priorities, opinions, attitudes behaviour, and finally their deep beliefs, to achieve their Purpose, within the social boundaries of accountability, probity and transparency. In an ever-emotional world Boards need to learn better how to fine-tune their emotional responses. There are still too many Dated, 'tin eared' boards.

Moving to Level 3 Board Maturity

Stepping back to take a wider and deeper perspective enables the arc of the corporate governance story to emerge from recent history. That story is very clearly one where only progress in Board maturity can respond effectively to the increasingly complex demands that directors must now meet. This fundamental shift means widening the board's approach to designing the company's future health.

Inconvenient though it is to writers of modern corporate history this necessity was acknowledged by some parts of Big Business back in the 1970s. Shell, now demonised by the public for its oil and gas operations, was already thinking along such lines and delivering its annual reports in terms of *People, Planet and Profits,* based on the initial thinking of John Elkington [9]. Shell was seeking to explain its complex and simultaneous future roles on all three aspects. They acknowledge that they still have not got it right but are still trying. And they do publish relatively openly. Even a quick scan of 20 years of their annual reports shows today's social and environmental issues clearly acknowledged together with early versions of appropriate targets and measures.

There were more signals in the wider media of such trends than many thought. Public awareness had already been aroused by the power of two contrasting globally viewed images. One was the social consequences of the 1973 oil price rise of 400%. Austerity, hunger, and insecurity were being played out on screen to the horror of many. The other was the beautiful, yet haunting, picture of Earthrise taken from the Moon. This reinforced strongly in the public consciousness the concept of Gaia, showing the uniqueness and fragility of the Earth, and its connectedness as a living system. This was reinforced by, for example, the popularity of Fritz Schumacher's book *Small Is Beautiful* [10] which triggered a new generation to begin to take more seriously the concepts of sustainability, natural resource management, wastage, climate change, food sustainability and species extinction. This was in direct contradiction to the then current notion that Big Business would always provide everything for everyone in future.

At that time Gaia-type thinking was often dismissed as scaremongering and socialist nonsense by many, especially the Chicago school of economists with their fixation on Shareholder Value. This always seemed a nonsense to me as in the US minority shareholders seldom had any serious rights and CEOs' behaviours and inflated egos were rarely in line with their shareholders' need, let alone global needs. It was seen by them as a binary game of winner takes all, not a collective one with stakeholder co-operation. However, the early stirrings of stakeholder capitalism were just becoming visible. It was inspiring the public, many disenchanted employees, students, social and environmental activists but it was rarely acknowledged in the board rooms.

The broader corporate response to this public shift was to go for minimal, watered-down, and grudging, compliance. Advocating Corporate Social Responsibility (CSR) became fashionable for a time. This was acknowledged in boardrooms as increasingly necessary to calm growing public criticism of what was being called 'rampant capitalism' or worse; but it proved intellectually insufficient. In many cases it was seen only as 'virtue washing' public relations. CSR reports became common at Annual General Meetings but were increasingly ridiculed as being boiler-plate statements of buzz-word-generated platitudes and wish lists. Most were good-intentioned but without hard, independently audited, comparative metrics they were not credible. Boards thinking that they will be seen as OK by doing a little 'good' was an approach that was no longer credible.

Sir Adrian Cadbury's wish to link corporate governance more firmly to entrepreneurship evolved more strongly during the early 2000s. But it was knocked off-course by the scandal of the financial crash of 2008 when the venalities of some Wall Street investment vehicles and credit rating agencies nearly toppled the world's financial system. The horrified public reactions to a business model that worked on the principle that it was OK to sell those sub-prime mortgages to naïve investors who could not pay for them, to expect massive defaults, yet still feel OK by dumping quickly the resulting financial instruments as tradeable assets, was outrageous and unethical. It still is.

In contradiction the concept that the Earth was a living entity, dynamic yet increasingly fragile, was gaining ground. This asked directors to strike new balances between their Financial, Physical, and Human capitals. This resonated with many but less so with dated directors. Indeed, the idea that each of the three capitals had 'impacts' and that these needed to be scrutinised, measured, and balanced in relation to the growing crises, became part of the general consciousness. The problem for corporates was that such new public expectations were now focusing on the implicit and expressed values of boards of directors, in the expectation that they could solve such complex issues easily.

The general public's assumption was that as these 'corporates' were most likely to have caused the crash in the first place, they were proven guilty must be held to account. The politicians were keen to agree. No board that I met at the time was prepared for this. It was taking them away from the simple focus on money-making and bottom lines and into such utterly unknown worlds as climate change, community development, diversity, modern slavery and anthropology. No wonder that they were grudging. In many cases they were increasingly angry and frightened.

Many directors knew that they could not cope with such mind-bending demands. They were particularly uncomfortable because many had long-held beliefs that business must always be separated from 'politics'. Therefore, these issues were seen as way beyond their pay grades, or intellectual capacity. Their initial responses were either denial of the issues along the lines that 'these are just not business problems', or ham-fisted attempts to resolve business issues with a quick silver bullet solution. Many thought that a version of 'washing' whether green, virtue, or HR, would be sufficient.

Only a few realised that their business model was changing forever and that directors and their boards were now considered by the public as an integral, accountable, and important part of their living Gaia system, with consequent strong liabilities and responsibilities. Major concerns over climate change, the need for carbon zero deadlines, the frugal and better use of the Earth's scarce resources, community cohesion, mass migration, and the increasing volatility of the world's financial system, could no longer be side-lined. Politics had to become part of the board's conceptual mix.

However, the analysis adopted by most corporates was 'we must do something but will do the minimum possible to sate public opinion'. But what to do? 'ESG' – Environment, Social and Governance' – then became the golden bullet, and acronym, to seemingly resolve all these issues. It had already been driven enthusiastically by the UN, many NGOs, a few governments, many environmentalists, social change advocates and, much later, a few fund managers. It was a good-hearted attempt at saving the Earth and its institutions. But it had little joined-up systems thinking within it to create a new, effective corporate governance system. The acronym ESG was often without context. The 'E' and 'S' did not easily connect to the 'G'. Like CSR it was too easy to ridicule as another well-intentioned piece of socialist claptrap. It was seen by many companies as a fashionable bolt-on, a form of more advanced virtue-signalling. Again, grudgingly compliant directors knew they had to acknowledge somehow this current fashion but hoped that it would soon pass over.

It has not passed entirely – yet. Amid energy crises, pandemics, disrupted supply chains, wars, international political instabilities, the growing rise of right-wing thinking, and the challenges to globalisation, the ESG-type pressures continue. Their advocates are attempting to reframe and redevelop the very heart of the business model, entrepreneurial judgement, and consequently corporate governance. This advocates a move well beyond finance-fixation to embracing an integrated business concept, closer to creating each business as a mini-Gaia – a fragile organism sustained only for a time in its energy niches by supportive organisms that currently need it – stakeholders, employees, the environment, the community, and finance sources.

These energies are moving constantly so a company's future health will depend on its ability to scan the horizon, sense the changes early, and be nimble enough to learn to move its scarce resources to take the opportunities as they arise. This is the new entrepreneurship. It treats the company as a living entity that is capable of withering quickly unless constantly learning and nurtured. It is the opposite to thinking of a company as an inanimate object with unlimited life, size, licence, and power. It is the driver of next generation directors.

In many nations the political and social moves in this direction for companies are reflected already in the sheer weight of changes emerging through law, codes, regulations, reports, and public inquiries. These have set alarm bells ringing in finance-fixated companies. There is a growing backlash against these trends, especially in parts of the US as seen in the bitter infighting of the 2024 election and the Trump presidential Executive Orders.

However, it is worth stepping back to take that broader perspective – the helicopter view – and consider the growing list of the current and evolving guidelines, codes, regulations and possible legislation. These highlight the inevitability of future directors having to accept these new roles and mindsets, An awareness of, and critical responsiveness to, such developments will define the board's capacity for future corporate governance compliance.

Just a few of the external international pressures affecting even the smallest companies and charities from recent history are:

2006 The UK's Companies Act
2006 UN Principles of Responsible Investing
2010 UN Global Compact – The Ten Principles
2010 UN 2030 Agenda
2015 Net Zero by 2050 Declaration
2019 EU Sustainable Finance Disclosure Requirements
2020 The Davos Manifesto 2020
2020 US Security and Exchange Commission ESG Committee Reports
2021 UK Sustainable Disclosure Proposals
2021 All annual COP Reports onwards to COP26
2022 IFRS Sustainability Disclosure Standards For Investors
2023 ISO 3700
2024 BSI PAS 808 Purpose Driven Organisations Proposals

This is only a very partial list, but it is enough to freeze most dated directors in their tracks. I argue strongly that, like it or not, the thinking behind such reports frames the context and work of the next generation directors. It is way beyond 'greenwashing' or 'values washing'. I repeat, this is the point where the board's role as 'The Brain of the Firm' begins its transformation to become *The Brain and the Conscience of the Firm.* This moves it towards becoming a Learning Board – Level Three board maturity. Such innovations as long-term financial instruments generated by performance-based green bonds, and social impact bonds, are signs of possible ways ahead for financing beyond the dated vehicles of funding by fickle, short-term, shareholder traders. It is significant that these newer developments are based on the idea of reward through long-term performance and collaboration. Shall we see the appearance of corporate governance bonds?

For still-grudging directors I note the growing international campaign pressures for more international agreements on, for example, accounting, audit, disclosure, and governance. We have not yet reached the international sunlit uplands of Mervyn King's proposed 'Globally Accepted Comprehensive Corporate Reporting System', but we are moving in that direction as more companies and nations begin to see the benefits of a major reframing of their Reporting and Audit systems. Smart Small States are particularly interested. The double drivers of climate change and the pandemic consequences have highlighted the connection between future sustainability performance and financial risks and return. They are creating a growing urgency to build a bridge to that globally necessary comprehensive reporting and learning system. How will a future board learn to cope with these pressures? That is what Chapter Four develops in detail.

Before we leave this chapter, I remind you that it is worth remembering that the original Cadbury definition of Corporate Governance is much wider than a mere set of arbitrary rules. It contains recommendations for board behaviours, values, responsibilities, and liabilities in its first three lines. These have not been sufficiently followed up and developed, because neither the politicians nor the civil-service-based regulators have much experience in such fields. They therefore over-specify their rules in their known fields to compensate for precisely this lack of experience. Fear of being found out may explain partially why they are reluctant to apply the laws they have passed. The feedback would lead to the painful but factual learning of their own lacunae.

The good news is that with weak regulatory enforcement still common this can leave much control and responsibility at the discretion of increasingly diverse boards. The bad news is that regulators and politicians do not get promoted by advocating more useful anthropological, behavioural, psychological, or ecologically 'soft' approaches to board effectiveness. To keep their jobs, they must be seen to add untested, top-down rules. This satisfies short-term focused politicians but few others.

Rather than take a systems-thinking approach to effective corporate governance, starting with the inputs from the other main players of directors, stakeholders, suppliers, consumers, and the public, there has been an increasing regulatory focus only on the outputs from the three easily measured aspects – reporting, disclosure and audit. These are necessary but by no means sufficient. What is currently defined as 'best practice' in corporate governance is rarely even 'good practice'. For example, why have we accepted an absolute rule that a Chairman should only serve a maximum of nine years in office if the business and the Chairman are healthy and effective? Or why should regulators accept and propagate so easily the term 'Non-Executive Director' when it does not appear at law? And why do they continue to say that shareholders have supreme directoral powers when this is fundamentally wrong? Such muddled thinking pervades current corporate governance and muddles compliance.

There are two basic approaches to corporate compliance. The US favours the 'Rules-based' approach. Here the rules are spelled out in great detail and, provided the company complies, they can do anything that is not specified within the national legal boundaries. It takes a lot of money, staff and time on both sides to ensure such detailed compliance. It is an industry in itself. If you are a subsidiary of a US company, or a foreign company that trades with the US, then it is highly likely that you will have to comply with their regime under their Extra-Territoriality Act, as well as the Sarbanes-Oxley Act. A significant problem with the Rules-based approach is that it allows 'mission creep'. Over time more and more elements are added to the rules to block the loopholes practitioners have created to avoid complying. And the costs go up as lawyers seek to find even newer loopholes.

The ever-growing list becomes a bureaucratic drag on companies. It also creates job opportunities. A growing number of well-paid people are brought in as Compliance Officers, Diversity Officers and so on to keep the company within the growing pile of rules. It seems to be 'The American Way'. Their politicians and regulators assume an omniscience that assumes they must know everything about human nature and so be able to draw up a definitive list. This is nonsense.

The 'Principles-based' alternative approach is more nuanced and so more tolerant of human foibles. It is found across the 56 Commonwealth countries. It is based on the notion of 'comply or explain'. It accepts the laws as they were promulgated but accepts also that all humans and organisations are different in their history, culture, personalities, and current make-up. So, it is up to a board to decide whether they will accept the full raft of regulations. If not, they must explain to their stakeholders, at least at an Annual General Meeting, why they are deviating within the wider rules. It is then up to the stakeholders, especially the shareholders, to vote on whether they agree with their board. The South Africans, for some years leaders in this approach encouraged by Nelson Mandela, have called this 'apply or explain'. I feel that the principles-based approach will be much more useful to next generation directors in the turbulent future business conditions, and much more cost-effective.

If national politicians see directors' corporate governance compliance as a purely mechanical system to be obeyed without question, then we shall continue to have many grudgingly compliant directors. Know there is something better.

Combining their financial, environmental and social impacts to implement effective corporate governance sets the new framework for future board decision-making. This is still a work in progress. But the right elements are now falling into place, even if not yet in the right balance. It is the basis on which I build the concept and practice of the Learning Board – to which we now turn in the second part of this book.

To do so we need to get into our personal helicopter to both view the entrepreneurial opportunities in this new landscape and to plan our personal development to cope with it.

References

[1] The Cadbury Report on The Financial Aspects of Corporate Governance, London, Gee and Co., 1992
[2] The Imperial College Spinout portfolio can be found at https://www.imperial.ac.uk/enterprise/about/data-and-reporting/spinout-portfolio/
[3] The Denning Judgement, Boulting vs The Association of Cinematographers, 1963, 2 Queen's Bench 606
[4] UK National Audit Office Report 29.10.2015
[5] UK Parliamentary Public Accounts Committee November 2015
[6] Charity Commission Report 10 February 2022. report

[7] Cadbury report (ibid)

[8] Mervyn King and Leigh Roberts, Doing Business In the 21st Century, International Integrated Reporting Council, London, 2013

[9] James Lovelock, Gaia: A New Look At Life On earth, Oxford Landmark, 2016

[10] John Elkington, Cannibals With Forks; The Triple Bottom Line of 21st Century Business, Capstone, Oxford, 1997

Part II: **Implementing Effective Corporate Governance**

Graphic by: Mick Kidd of Biff cartoons.

Chapter 4
The Learning Board: Level Three Board Maturity

This is the tipping point in the book where my focus becomes the development of future directors, not continued criticism of dated directors. I call them the Next Generation directors. I seek to build a bridge for this next generation to move beyond the 'codes and compliance' mindset to reach a futures-orientated style of entrepreneurship built on direction-giving through continuous learning. These are the future Professional Directors. Without them our institutions, the cement of human society, will erode.

Directing combines the thinking processes of showing the way ahead – leadership – with prudent control of their organisation. Yet surprisingly little research has been conducted on the *thinking* processes needed for effective directing. Future directors will be rewarded on their results not just from the bottom line but increasingly on those related to the quality of their wider thinking and its implementation in polycrises. Learning this combination demands continuous action learning from each director. This learning needs to combine the results of their independent judgement with co-operative action.

So, this chapter reviews my experiences of expanding the little explored *processes* of directoral thinking. Chapter Five then takes these learning processes forward to expand the thinking necessary, the *content,* to include the ethical behaviours associated with them. The combination of these two chapters leads to my view of the Professional Director.

I have advocated the concept of the Learning Board for over 30 years. It has been well received and proved helpful in developing boards internationally. But I have always been up against hostility. Previously board decision-making was often based on a binary 'yes' or 'no' to a proposal by the CEO, backed by a complex spreadsheet. Debate was usually truncated and critical questioning, let alone dissent, was often considered disloyal. The idea that the Board should budget time and skill to consciously learn how to face both a turbulent future and a determined CEO and then exercise its ultimate decision-taking power was considered dangerously radical. Oddly, it just happened to be the law.

However, with the sudden and disorientating arrival of Artificial Intelligence I am often questioned whether in future humans, especially boards, will need to think and learn at all. Are boards redundant? Are we reaching a time when leisurely stupidity is our acceptable default position because human intelligence no longer matters? Even ten years ago such a question would be considered outrageous. But as we have seen, for example, our arithmetical and wider mathematical skills are overtaken by pocket computers, our written skills being devolved to AI, our navigational skills diminished to GPS reading, all of which are now combined in our smartphones. No wonder that some are arguing that human intelligence is collapsing under that God-

 | https://doi.org/10.1515/9783112231340-004

like technology. There is mounting evidence that literacy and numeracy skills are diminishing worldwide. Will anything replace them; or are we doomed to screen-based games and gaming?

I am not so pessimistic. Currently there are increasing examples of AI not having the subtlety to juggle complex data into useable new thoughts and processes. And sometimes it can be remarkably dumb and just runs amuck. Whilst it can offer a wider range of possible actions, its predictive abilities are still limited and the human race continues to juggle contradictions and learn through human action learning and reflection. Therefore, I argue that the human race still has a long life, provided it encourages conscious and continuous learning. For new directors, the people charged with giving direction and control to their organisations, they must prioritise such 'action learning' as their prime task to deliver a healthy future for their organisation and their communities.

Developing Board Intelligence

To introduce Levels Three and Four of board maturity I use three pictures to signify the necessary changes in directoral mindsets. First, Mick Kidd's Biff cartoon of 'I wish I was deep instead of just macho' signifying the *intellectual* bridge needed to be crossed from macho management into thoughtful professionalism. Second, the book cover design symbolises a double loop of learning (more of this later in this chapter), a critical process for every board to develop. At the convergence of the operational and directoral learning loops sits the Intelligent Board. Third, at the centre of that board is the Little Owl of Athena – goddess of intelligence, wisdom, skill, craftmanship, and diligence. New directors must now develop these capabilities simultaneously – the intellectual art and craft of directing.

The most expressive word to describe this kind of nimble mental skill is the modern 'nous'. The word is an adaptation of the Ancient Greek *noos* (νόος), meaning the kind of response that was 'of the mind'. It's this modern use that translates 'having nous' as 'being streetwise'; a rare commodity for many current directors. It is closely linked with the Ancient Greek word *sophía* (σοφία) which is usually translated as 'wise', but which has a strong component of crafting skill. This aspect of σοφία as 'skill in *handicraft* and art' goes back to Homer. Most directors are oblivious to this – at their cost.

Any organisation, from simple trader to multinational corporation, needs to maintain and develop their supply of directoral nous. It demands real-time awareness of rapidly changing external and internal dynamics combined with the ability to manoeuvre scarce resources nimbly and intelligently to achieve their organisation's Purpose.

I use the dictionary definition of "intelligence" to mean *the human capacity for understanding: the ability to perceive and comprehend meaning and use it.* In an increasingly turbulent and risky world this spotlights the key board role as setting and testing a healthy direction for their business to achieve its purpose.

What distinguishes human intelligence from artificial intelligence is the human's innate ability to discern relevant information from amongst heaps of messy and confusing data often beyond the boundaries of the original problem statement. It requires the conscious development of board 'nous' – the application of critical review, rationality, and human values. Such discernment is the essence of a Learning Board.

Algorithms cannot discern. Near my house in central London were two major roundabouts through which heavy traffic flowed reasonably freely. But they were 'improved' by the roads authority who removed the roundabouts without explanation and installed complex traffic light-controlled systems. It was assumed locally that this was to help cyclists. That was only a partial answer. The undisclosed answer was that it was part of a national experiment to test the concept of driverless cars. This slowed and congested the traffic dramatically. Previously, the roundabout allowed drivers to use their nous (discretion) to filter into lanes, showing courtesy and thoughtfulness to other road users. Now they have no discretion, must always wait on the lights, and so become bad tempered when previously they could have used their nous; relying on their human judgement to keep the traffic moving. I finally found a traffic controller who explained why this had happened. 'Bloody Elon Musk, plus there are no roundabouts in the US' he said. I have removed his worst expletives. He explained that they were building more experiments in preparation for driverless cars. These have no discretion. They cannot be allowed loose to kill randomly, so their algorithms must be guaranteed to always fail safely. This is a logical impossibility. Meanwhile, humans must lose their discretionary powers. The public were never informed as to the purpose of the changes so are still baffled by them. I find this a useful metaphor to illustrate the need to preserve human nous or risk encouraging wider stupidity by following slavishly AI.

All human organisations comprise continuous flows of new data. Organisations are not algorithms. An effective organisation turns such data into usable information at all levels to resolve their problems in real time. It learns from this process rigorously. An effective board of directors creates continuous oversight of the patterns of these information flows (their 'dashboards'), then adds value by regular critical questioning, using the continuous action learning for organisational advantage. This leads to conscious foresight, thoughtful risk-taking and encouraging learning at all levels of a business. The Board is the central processor of such corporate intelligence and needs to create and value a culture for encouraging and sustaining such mutual learning. Human nous demands from boards the conscious development of the essential thinking crafts of care, skill, and diligence to cope with rapidly evolving polycrises to achieve their purpose.

Do new directors need to be proudly intellectual? Yes. But this goes against some 50 years of business school teaching where the apex achievement for students was the Master's in Business Administration (MBA) award. This was mis-sold as being universally portable into any organisation. It was not a passport to automatic expertise and skill. The dangerous notion that management is a stand-alone expertise is disastrous. The UK's NHS is a good example made worse by the importation of many specialist financial MBAs. This limits the diversity of experience noticeably, whilst diminishing the medical thinking. This is the opposite type of 'learning' to that which I advocate.

Here I see the fashionable rise and rise of Artificial Intelligence (with its rapidly evolving generative, agentic, and predictive abilities, to process masses of existing data and prompt suggestions for comparative interpretation), with the need for new generation boards to budget time and money to learn their intelligence roles as the Business Brain and Conscience. This requires expanding their intellectual ability to cope with the strategic issues arising from interpreting this growing deluge of data flows. It cannot be left simply to the AI machines, especially if we are to disprove the avowed intent of some AI purveyors 'to surpass human intelligence'. This crucial need to 'keep the human in the loop' is the antidote to the current corporate paralysis caused by the slavish acceptance of that 'God-like technology'. And it safeguards against the day that the electricity fails.

AI overseen by smart human direction can improve business performance, but lazy use of AI without human nous is not merely ineffective but can actually impair productivity. In October 2025 the *Financial Times* and *Harvard Business Review* reported findings from real businesses which revealed a growing problem of what is termed 'AI work slop', stating: 'Poor AI-generated content can result in bloated reports with mangled meanings and excessive verbiage, creating extra work for colleagues to decipher.' [ref 1] It is likely, inevitable even, that many such reports are being presented to the board.

Creating an effective Learning Board's guardian role is vital to keeping all the humans in their business in their organisational learning loop. Without acknowledging this, future boards and their organisations will wither. Yet many dated directors are intimidated by, or cynical of, even using the words 'intelligence' or 'intellectual'. That this was never part of their business education says much about the paucity of such education. Many are frightened of such words because they may be seen as 'soft', 'woke', 'smart-arsed', or even 'liberal'. However, the new generation know better and accept the necessity of developing integrated intelligence way beyond the previously comfortable and often mundane world of managerial thinking.

Dated directors are often reluctant to want to start down such a new career path. Their world expects simpler, binary answers despite the complexity of the issues faced. However, the emerging directoral challenges rarely have a binary answer. They are dependent on stating the human values and intellectual framework within which a Board formulates its own problem definition, and from which it then seeks its unique resolution – using the conscience of the firm. Initially this can seem very scary, even impossible.

New generation directors need to achieve the seemingly impossible by positioning the Board as that central processor of all intelligence for the organisation's policy formulation and strategic thinking. Then more appropriate decisions can follow at the operational levels. I will go into detail about Board problem formulation and problem resolution later in this chapter.

Learning the New Directoral Role

Fundamental to this new learning is the question of how directors develop their range of radically new *thinking* skills? This major shift demands an active commitment to new personal and board learning processes. This takes time and energy. And it is essential.

Working with boards seeking to develop this unique directoral role, I notice that Level One and Two directors always find this learning difficult at first. It takes them away from their specialist, siloed thinking and explores the range of different integrative thinking styles and skills necessary to reach Level Three maturity. Given the polycrises that boards now face, I ask how they can budget time to study the full picture to secure a broader perspective of the dynamics and shifting external fault lines affecting their business. This is where enterprise, risk appetite, the quality of their board decision-making impacts on the physical and social impacts, and how they can combine to improve corporate performance. At this stage I do not deal with financial and managerial control issues. I focus on giving practical help to develop these often missing aspects of new generation competence.

I address directly the global default assumption that no special training is needed to become a director. I argue throughout this book that the new generation of directors must learn way beyond the previously stilted intellectual limits of shareholders, management, law, and finance. The new areas now combine, for example, entrepreneurship, thoughtful risk-taking and the unpredictable combined impacts of economic, environmental, and social trends. Many directors will admit to me privately that they are ignorant of such areas and very worried about being found out when exposed to these looming demands. I point out that accepting such current ignorance is the stepping-stone into Level Three board maturity.

This takes humility and leaves some feeling even more exposed. But their salvation is then using it to their advantage. Few directors are unintelligent. Most seek strongly to understand and comprehend the confusing crises with which they are now faced. They need to release their innate 'naïve intelligence' and to learn to rely on it to seemingly naïve, fundamental questions. Naive intelligence is having the courage to ask 'what does what you have just said mean, please?' Or, less courageously, 'just remind me what the exact meaning of that phrase is, please?' In many national cultures asking such questions can be seen initially as rude and unacceptable because it questions the authority and knowledge of existing power players. I argue that without such questioning the board maintains an Unlearning Organisation.

Remember that no one around the boardroom table knows everything needed to resolve complex problems. Under Section 171 of the UK's Companies Act each director has a legal duty to question the details of any proposal put to the Board. They have a right to take careful external advice when they do not understand the content, and to record doubts in the minutes they have relating to any board decision if they are still uncertain. For example, many directors do not understand much of the technical language used by executives or other specialist directors. Most sit there in uncomfortable silence and hope no one asks their opinion. My alternative is for a new director to start with a Mutual Observation Period that *expects* the use of naïve intelligence, then follow with a Board agreement that for at least their first year it is their duty to use openly such questioning to complete their induction. When they do question frequently, I notice that this is often a great relief to those directors who had stayed silent on the issue for years. In turn they also learn to ask better questions. This encourages greater diversity of thought in board decision-making. Naive intelligence is a great asset in tackling polycrises. It keeps directors firmly in the human loop.

Remember that the full directoral role is to ensure the future health of the company whilst ensuring prudent control of its daily operations. I stress that each Board needs to agree its two or three total oversight 'dashboards' by which it can monitor visually and numerically the total weekly and monthly business performance. More of this in Chapter Five. Here I shall go beyond monitoring such operational issues and concentrate on the learning needed to think strategically and into the world of policy-making.

I note that the biggest discomfort for directors in taking these first steps is their constant worry about the amount of time they will need to spend thinking, rather than doing. That is precisely why they are paid as directors, not managers. Much of their work is not managerial. Many have become so addicted to the comfort and adrenalin rush of rapid managerial action that budgeting time to scan the external world and developing a framework to think about alternative possibilities seems intimidating.

Attempting this alone is daunting. But combining with 'colleagues in adversity' to commit to joint problem resolution is why the Board of Directors exists. I have found that the key to developing directoral competence is committing with fellow Board members to create a Learning Board that focuses on creating the business's healthy future and leaves the managers to manage.

The Parallel Development of The Director and the Board

There are two key parallel learning needs. First, the individual director's need to consciously develop their confidence in their unique range of different thinking and problem-resolution behaviours to deliver their legal duties with of care, skill, and diligence. This requires a time and money budget for each director and for the Board.

This is a step change for the new director and not all will succeed, or want to proceed. It is OK if they drop out and stick with the managerial world, provided others are willing to be developed as directors in their place. They need accept that they are facing those polycrises where the convergence from external demands, ranging from Net Zero issues to new national legislation, plus cultural pressures from the economic, social, accountability and regulatory spheres, all arrive simultaneously. Understandably most current directors are baffled as to how to proceed. To cope, their development requires an agreed, contracted, and disciplined induction, benchmarking, development, and regular assessment learning process.

Second, as they are severally liable, they need to learn how to work jointly as a valued member of a true board of directors. They need become a competent, effective, and trusting work group – growing the Business Brain and Conscience to deliver the corporate intelligence needed to ensure the future health of the business. They can no longer be a bunch of isolated egos bonded loosely by social status. Creating a Learning Board is essential.

From my research, I have tested internationally four inter-linked, directoral learning processes of thinking, problem formulation and problem resolution that are the basis of any Learning Board:
- Policy Formulation and Foresight,
- Strategic Thinking,
- Operational Oversight,
- Ensuring Full Accountability.

I shall show practical steps to build on this in Chapter Five. Many hundreds of boards have used this simple framework to start their learning journey to board intelligence. It does not matter if one's directoral role is full-time or part-time, whether you are a misnamed Executive Director or Non-Executive Director, or whether you are in the private, public, or charity sectors, the basics are the same: learning to integrate all four quarters of the Learning Board into an annual *rhythm*, with a time budget, to achieve and assess board competence, the objective is the same. New knowledge, attitudes, values, plus humility and an ethical stance, will be demanded from all.

This means developing the personal and board capacity to step back from the immediate operational problems, rising above the current organisational turbulence, and learning how to achieve longer-term policy making through improved strategic thinking. This re-establishes the historic role of the board. It is now under critical examination through the rise and rise of Artificial Intelligence. The lacunae in AI helps to highlight the very human nature of Board decisions and the risks needed to create a business's unique future. This puts Board oversight of *managerial* performance into its proper perspective. Boards will ask more discerning questions. So, the executives' ability to help develop alternative futures and new performance measures will improve greatly. Total corporate intelligence will improve across the whole organisation.

AI will cause major disruptive issues for boards on the cultural and social side of organisation, especially the loss of so many jobs in the administrative, coding, and managerial sectors. In addition, there are major ethical issues such as whether a board wishes to use an AI system which has 'scraped' (stolen) intellectual property rights without payment for their large learning models, thereby wrecking and possibly blocking future cultural and learning processes. And whether AI's massive use of energy and water is environmentally a global danger, especially as they are advocating the use of many small nuclear reactors to energise future data farms.

So Boards need to have open discussions between themselves, and with their stakeholders, to agree that a large part of their future directoral life needs to focus on the development of their corporate intelligence to create the skills to handle these crises. Even then boards can only hope that their combined intellects are sufficient to use future contradictions and ambiguities to make their risky strategic decisions better able to take the opportunities offered. This is what they will be paid for in future as Level Four Professional Directors.

PolyCrises and the ESG Wars

Does any of this matter? As I write I see examples of such combined intellectual and practice battles being played out in boardrooms and in the wider party-political world internationally. The demeaning 'wars' between the 'shareholder supremacy' brigades, proxy voting advisors, and the 'woke ESG' supporters are typical. I argue that both the shareholder supremacists and the virtue signallers of ESG are busted flushes. Their perspectives are too narrow to cope with the polycrises. The political fights waste large amounts of board resources because neither faction is listening to the other, especially in the US. This is reinforced by the massive resources deployed in the anti-social media. Politicians and governments seem unwilling to rise above the immediate fray to take a wider and deeper perspective, reframing their goals for the future benefit of all stakeholders. This puts the boards on the frontline to create a positive future. The good news is that new generation directors realise that they will have to move beyond this current dialogue of the deaf to the more nuanced problem of how to integrate future entrepreneurship whilst balancing environmental, social, and economic impacts, to deliver effective corporate governance.

The future purpose of a business is to ensure an integrated return on the three capitals used – financially, environmentally, and socially. For a business this must include generating a profit to stay alive and for a not-for-profit, generating a surplus. To deploy their always scarce resources the board needs to start by generating creative entrepreneurial ideas for products and services, releasing from their staff the learning currently trapped internally. Only then can they steer the way ahead in rough seas whilst ensuring prudent control. The end is to deliver its Purpose through effective corporate governance. To repeat a continuing theme throughout this book, the board must return to the original double meaning of *kubernetes.*

This requires director re-education. I do not mean this in terms of authoritarian Maoist, Putinesque or Trumpian imposed, closed loop, thinking frameworks; but in terms of individuals and boards voluntarily committing to reframing and broadening and deepening their thinking processes based on their unique values. This delivers both the company's Purpose and reinforces the board's conscience. I know this is possible as I have seen it happen on five continents.

In medicine it is a sign of recovering health if a patient stops looking downwards and inwards, and begins to look up, makes eye contact with others and, eventually, looks outwards beyond their immediate surroundings to be aware of what is happening to others, and finally to imagine future opportunities. I have used this metaphor many times to help a board move beyond the comfort of their operational inward focus to enjoy turning seemingly intractable continuous uncertainties into opportunities.

Even as a manager it is hard to have a complete picture of how their varied daily operations link to create a total managerial system. So, before consciously developing their levels of strategic thought and decision-taking it is essential for a Board to ask a key question: 'do we really have an operational *system*?' For example, Finance may not speak the same language as Engineering, and both often cannot really understand IT let alone HR, Marketing, PR, or AI. Confusion is often because the 'hard' areas, which have been seen as key to past business success, have lost priority to these new 'soft' areas. Even fewer managers can now make sense of the added complex demands of, for example, Diversity Champions, Equality Officers, Inclusion Officers, Money Laundering regulations, Modern Slavery Officers, Employment Tribunals, or Artificial Intelligence gurus.

I make the detailed case for agreeing integrated Board dashboards to oversee management in Chapter Five. New directors must now learn to ask those discerning questions more broadly to understand the answers from management.

The Learning Board Perspective: Seeing the Whole Picture

New directors need to develop the mental capacities to rise above the immediate to understand, comprehend, and think critically and constructively about the wider trends impacting on the future health of their business. This is often referred to as 'the helicopter view'. Such thinking needs be set within their agreed ethics, and the law.

A new director needs to learn how to balance an understanding of what is emerging from the complex murk of the world outside the company (so that effective direction can be given); with what is occurring in the internal fog of daily operations (so that prudent control is ensured). Understanding these complex corporate weather patterns and then deciding policy and strategy around the boardroom table are the essence of the board's 24/7 + 365 agenda. Developing the director's perspective means stepping back so that you can see the *whole* picture of your company and the dynamic eco-system it inhabits. Not every board member will be capable of dealing with all of this. So, the design and balance of the mix of directors to create a suitable mix is a crucial role for the Chairman.

The board's task is always to steer their company into a healthy future whilst keeping it under prudent control. But how on earth is a new director going to become comfortable with dealing with such wide and seemingly continually changing issues and events? This is especially worrying when most issues occur in fields in which the director has little expertise. To many directors it feels annoyingly like that old definition of history as 'just one damned thing after another'.

For example, for understanding these external trends priority must be to creating a board monitoring system for the regular tracking of often opposing trends in. The simplest framework I have found effective is that of PPESTT:

Political Change
Physical Environmental Change
Economic Change
Social Change
Technological Change
Trade Flows Change.

This can sound impossible to tackle for a previously single-disciplined, newly appointed director. They feel that they may have conquered one or two disciplines, but to demand knowledge of an additional six new disciplines seems outrageous. It is intimidating and often creates initial resistance. However, it is necessary for a future director to learn to ask discerning questions of all six. I deal with the required learning process at the end of this chapter. The good news is that all the other directors have the same duty. So, to remain lawful the learning must be done by the whole Board agreeing to raise its game.

To the horror of some of my academic colleagues I insist that new directors start their development by accepting that they will have to learn to use the framework of the PPESTT analysis, to focus their thinking. Some of my colleagues consider my approach so old-fashioned that they concede it might even become popular again. I know from experience that this simple PPESTT framework is robust enough to start to put boundaries around polycrises. This is the start of the broadening and deepening of most directors' thinking.

Two key messages then need stressing. First, that you cannot do it on your own. The Board is trying to allocate scarce capital resources – finance, environmental and social – to design a future that is impossible to predict accurately. Even with the combined diversity around the boardroom table they are doing well if their group decisions are right more than half of the time. Risk is always present. That is the essence of entrepreneurship. It is thoughtful risk that we seek.

Second, perfection is not possible in the directoral world. So, flexibility of thought and nimble adaptive action is key. This is 'nous' in action. I seek to help develop such broad-minded and nimble learning boards. It is why a Board exists – to give sufficient variety of views and experiences that more informed, well-debated and better-quality decisions are made in a turbulent world; and then implemented rapidly with fast learning and frequent feedback.

Diversity of thought and debate are the lifeblood of a healthy Board. This role goes far beyond formal board meetings. But not the sort of 'diversity' often specified administratively by bureaucrats and politicians with their fixed minds and tick boxes. They can specify, for example, sex, colour, specialist background, and age. But they cannot specify what they mean by 'diversity of culture' because you cannot specify the unique human characteristics of thought, behaviour and intelligence that combine to make an effective board. There is no ideal Board of directors. Bureaucrats still like to think that there must be, and that a quick addition to their boxes is job done. They then assume that their regulation will be risk free.

I should make here a brief note on 'risk'. Entrepreneurship – the creation of new products and services through the drama of business ventures – demands risk and reward. Risk encompasses failure. Without failure we cannot learn. It is not unlawful to fail in business, unless fraud or corruption is involved. It happens all the time. So, there is a contradiction in so many politicians and regulators promising 'growth' whilst trying to regulate without accepting that risk and failure are elements of it.

In making the move from managing to directing, the director induction process must ensure that a director commits to self-development: to become becoming better informed about these external complexities and risks, whilst keeping oversight of the operational trends. This is a strong personal and intellectual challenge that takes time and determination to learn. As a directing role is often given towards the end of a long managerial career, there is a reluctance to develop such new mindsets. Most peo ple do not like being exposed to the discomfort of continuing uncertainty, especially in later life. Yet I find that once a director has started such conscious learning, they find it a liberating, absorbing and personally satisfying process. On several occasions, I have had to accept the backhanded compliment that 'the directing role became so interesting that I have ruined my golf handicap'.

Many find this new learning process hard. Often their hope is that in board meetings they will be able to keep their head down long enough to not expose their ignorance of the other disciplines. They crave to be able to understand just sufficiently the other areas' 'buzzwords' that they can bluff their way in boardroom conversation and daily decision-making. This is unacceptable behaviour for a Level Four Professional Director. The open and continuous encouragement of 'naïve intelligence' is necessary.

Learning to rise through the four levels of directoral thinking is a life enhancing self-development process. In 1924 John Maynard Keynes set the bar high for developing such personal attributes:

> *. . . he must be a mathematician, historian, statesman, philosopher – in some degree. He must understand symbols and speak in words. He must understand the particular in terms of the general, and touch abstract and concrete in the same flight of thought . . . . . . No part of man's nature or his institutions lie entirely outside his regard. He must be purposeful and disinterested in a simultaneous mood: as aloof and incorruptible as an artist, yet sometimes as near the earth as a politician* [4].

Today we replace 'he' for 'they', but otherwise this quote passes the test of time comfortably. I find this is a useful definition of, and aspiration for, the attributes of a Level Four Professional Director. The irony is that Keynes wrote this originally as a definition of a perfect macro-economist. I think that his description fits much better a truly Professional Director.

But directors are not superheroes capable of massive insight and huge predictive abilities. They are humans with all their frailties. Keynes continued that: *economists* (and I would add directors) *'are at their best if they were humble, competent people on a level with dentists'.* This quotation can be too demanding for some existing directors. I do not expect omniscience in every director, but I do expect a continuous open-mindedness within an ever-changing PPESTT debating framework in which all directors participate and learn openly as a board.

There is another basic step needed to break away from the managerial/specialist mindset – to drop the assumption that there is always a final, single answer to every directoral question. Directors are faced with several parallel possibilities from which they need to resolve their problems based on their entrepreneurial instincts and values. And they may be wrong. If so, how nimbly can they access another possibility and apply it?

There is a famous quote from F Scott Fitzgerald that perfectly expresses this reality:

> *The test of a first-rate intelligence is the ability to hold two opposing ideas in mind at the same time and still retain the ability to function. One should, for example, be able to see that things are hopeless yet be determined to make them otherwise*[5].

This acknowledges the complexity, uncertainty and, therefore, the ambiguities of being a successful director. Risky decisions must be made by any Board to ensure sustainable growth. Risk-free decisions are not available. Directors comfortable only when reducing their thinking to a single 'either/or' solution do not make effective board members. Life is not binary or algorithmic. The new director role calls for the more subtle and integrated 'both/and' style of thinking needed to identify wider and better opportunities to reduce risk for better outcomes in a turbulent world.

Such thinking styles are learnable and measurable. I often use as a starter for boards to understand and assess the quality and range of their directoral thinking the *Thinking Intentions Profile* instrument from Effective Intelligence Ltd [6], as developed and tested over four decades by Jerry Rhodes and Sue Thame. This benchmarks both the board's personal and group thinking preferences when formulating and resolving Board problems. It maps their intellectual assets and deployment around a Board table. Sharing openly each director's thinking preferences gives the whole Board a usable map of their available cognitive diversity and their likely comfort zones (which they may overdo) and discomfort zones (which they may avoid) when they are designing their sustainable future.

In its basic form the Thinking Intentions Profile maps an individual's thinking *preferences* in relation to the weighting and priorities they put on their past, present, and future thinking. Each has a 'hard' and 'soft' side. So, 'hard past' shows their preference for logic and rationality. 'Soft past' concerns their preference for values and commitment. 'Hard present' highlights their preference for the tangible facts, whilst 'soft present' is the sensing of immediate possibilities and dangers – the micro-politics of the Board. 'Hard future' concerns the ingenuity needed to make the future happen. 'Soft future' is about long-term vision and aspiration. Each director has a unique blend of their thinking intentions. Understanding these is a key to effective Board participation.

The combined map of the Board can reveal some astonishing overlaps and black holes. As a crude statement, I see internationally that the majority of boards are locked into power battles between directors driven by strong 'soft present' (micropolitics around the board room table), backed up with strong 'hard past' (so they can rationalise by sounding highly logical, despite the hard facts). Decades ago, I had assumed that directors are always focused on making the future happen for their business. I find that this is rarely so. Soft future may exist in terms of vision. But the lowest preference I find for Boards internationally is for the 'hard future' (making the future happen). This alarms me greatly because I believe this is why directors are paid. This is why I focus so strongly on board learning and thinking.

In general, I find that to break their thinking out of the operational cycle directors need a strong sense of the absurd, blended with humility and a high tolerance of ambiguity. These are not taught at the business schools. But before we aspire to reach such heights of omniscience, most new directors just need a way out of their current muddled corporate thinking and jargon. They realise that, ultimately, they must build on those personal attributes that exist already in their head and heart.

The fundamental issue is that Boards are charged legally to take decisions using their independence of thought; carefully, skilfully, and diligently. Yet few new directors are truly 'independent'. Most still have the debilitating mindset that they are primarily dependent on those who appointed them. Additionally, directors are meant to pool their collective wisdom and, when they recognise that they do not have sufficient knowledge or skills needed to take wise decisions, they are charged with asking people who have appropriate knowledge and experience to advise them. They have a legal duty to test any proposition brought before them by asking critical questions, especially of the executives. This is rarely done.

The key board processes of problem-definition and problem-resolution demand high-level integration of all their specialist disciplines, plus the ability to 'horizon scan', to develop that full picture perspective for the future health of the company; to see beyond the obvious without becoming fortune-tellers. The ability to feel comfortable with such regular horizon-scanning, and to turn the often weak signals that are noticed into useful strategic thinking, is a developable skill for each director working from the PPESTT analysis. Only then can the Board examine much more clearly their strategic options for deciding future company health, development, and sustainability.

But many directors are still single-disciplined based, so outside their own discipline they have risen on a mixture of buzzword generation, and creative silences when faced with areas beyond their knowledge. Having cultivated an air of seeming to understand any Board topic, they have a real fear of being found ignorant when asked for an opinion or facts. This is unhealthy learning. It is where cultivating an ethos of encouraging intelligent naivety and critical questioning pays such big dividends.

For at least the first year of the induction of a new board member a wise chairman will *encourage* them to keep asking naïve questions without embarrassment. This is a powerful process to be developed beyond the Mutual Observation Period. The clarifying power of a seemingly simple, even naïve, question is a wonder to behold when all around are waffling. It helps inform not only the naïve questioner but often the other board members. It can spotlight the basics which have been forgotten or assumed but never recently tested. It also allows the others to catch up on questions they may not have dared ask when they first entered that Board.

As an example, I remember a case when three new directors were being inducted to the Board of a major, successful listed family brewer. At the end of a lively Board meeting, the first for the three new directors, the Chairman asked wisely if there were any deeper questions that they were hesitant to ask. After some embarrassing coughing, one new and very young director asked at what point the Chairman's son would become a director? The Chairman replied 'Never. He is a great young man, but I know that he does not have the capacity nor commitment to be a director who will ensure the future health of this old family business. He is well-provided for and has other interests in a different part of the world. The family wish him well.' Not only did this clarify the position for the new directors but the relief on the faces of the existing directors was visible. None had dared ask such a 'naïve' question. But once asked, the answer changed the tone of whole debate on board succession. It encouraged flexibility of thought and questioning by all board members and allowed much wider discussion and more informed decision-taking. Twenty years later that young director is now Chairman.

Not A Black and White Problem.

I use this board development process of encouraging naïve intelligence a lot. It is a very powerful start to any board induction process. The most memorable example I experienced was in South Africa with the Board of a massive state-owned enterprise which had run into deep and nationally well-publicised trouble at both Board and managerial levels. It was disrupting many stakeholders in the country's logistical systems and the national economy. The media accused it of blocking national growth. But then the politicians added complexity by introducing as mandatory their new national Black Empowerment policy backed by legislation. Now 40 percent of the new board must be black. Most of the old board were not.

The new Chairman began a delicate process of designing and selecting a new twelve-person board where key industry experience needed to be blended with the influx of five new black directors – all younger folk, the majority women. These had never been on such a Board before, nor knew the industry. He and the Chief Executive took a calculated risk and carefully selected a diverse group of younger, intelligent professionals as their new black directors. The existing white board members were highly sceptical, mildly bemused, and grumpy at being saddled with 'having to carry' such people when the business was already in such deep trouble and frequently under media attack.

What could these new politically inspired imports possibly add? And how quickly could they learn so they would not be a drag on the struggling board? The Chairman was careful to position the entry of these directors as an opportunity to input fresh thinking, diversity, and new energy into a floundering board, rather than blindly obeying a political imperative. These younger directors would have a long-term investment in their and their nation's future.

The newcomers recognised that they were being imposed from outside, and that they were inexperienced so open to both Board and public criticism. They were excited yet very nervous about this experiment. Tension was high on both sides at their first meeting. The Chairman was very aware of this, and we had discussed beforehand how he would play it. He decided to face the issue head-on and said to the Board: 'The company is in trouble and the only resource to resolve the issues is the combination of people around this table. I accept that some are grieving for those directors who have gone, but we must make maximum use of our new energies and ideas from those joining us. They have told me that they are very nervous and inexperienced both at being a director and at understanding our complex industry. So, we must now find a way to help each other to learn how to become a more effective Board. That will mean adopting humility on both sides. Our time is short. We must use the new members' intelligent naivety to help us resolve the deep issues we face.'

His advocating the acceptance of naïve intelligence from the start created a positive and reassuring atmosphere. The 'oldies' were on their best behaviour and very careful to ask the 'newies' frequently if they had any 'naively intelligent' questions to ask. There was a hint of facetiousness from them at the start. The 'newies' missed much of this as they were so enthusiastic to learn. They asked a lot of questions. They quickly showed that they were bright enough to learn from the older board members the nature of the company and the industry. But there was a bigger beneficial effect. The oldies began to ask intelligently naïve questions themselves. This was usually along the lines of 'just remind me what is meant by . . . .' and 'I have often wondered how that idea originated, please enlighten me'.

Within a year a mutually constructive atmosphere was created with noticeably more open learning. The energies of the whole board were successfully focused on the urgent, major issues. Small gains were made when older board members ran informal seminars for the newer directors outside the board meetings on, for example, the basics of finance. It surprised and horrified me that at school under the apartheid system young blacks had only been taught mathematics up to twelve years old, and then only as 'kitchen arithmetic'. Mathematics leading into science, technology and finance was banned. With the complete agreement of the oldies, we created training programmes to rectify this as part of the director development budget. The 'oldies' learned to face more openly the consequences of those wicked apartheid policies. The creation of a director development budget proved key to creating an effective board. Surprisingly, a few of the oldies asked later to join the programme so that they could 'update' their knowledge levels in areas in which they had previously hardly concerned themselves.

A touching scene occurred when the oldest 'greyback' admitted that he was intimidated by all the newies bringing their laptops to the board meeting and tapping into them frequently. One of the newies, a young woman, offered to update him on their use. Instead of exploding with anger he said that he would be grateful, so she fixed times when they could meet before the board. Later he admitted that he had learned so much, but that his real motivation at the start was not about his board effectiveness but 'to be able to look my grandchildren in the eyes by being keyboard literate'. Boards are made up of human beings.

The Chairman had started the board development process by asking three consultants – Sally, me and the lawyer Thina Siwendu – to conduct a deep review of the new Board's structure and processes. He needed to benchmark the necessary starting points for developing a Level Three Learning Board, and to persuade doubting politicians that the Board was progressing positively. We had developed a Board Assessment and Development tool. This comprised collecting individual scores of each director's understandings of the current position of the Board on the dimensions listed below, and then assessing the gap needed to resolve it. This gap analysis gave a map of the dimensions of each issue by each director, together with their priorities in bridging the gaps. This was then shared with all board members to create a map of the total Board's developmental needs for them to discuss and plan.

The detailed issues explored in depth through the Board Review were:
- The Dynamics of Board Working,
- Relationships between the Managers and the Board,
- Stakeholder Relationships,
- The Role of the Chairman,
- The Role of the Company Secretary,
- Things to be learned from good practice on other boards.

These gave the metrics needed to measure both each director's perception of where they were, and where they needed to be on each dimension, and the total picture needed to develop the Board's effectiveness. It created an agreed single script from which all Board members could plot over time the trends of their personal and board actions. It proved very powerful in creating a Learning Board.
I also encourage stakeholders and members of the public to use this six-section framework to ask naively intelligent, discerning questions of any Board.

The Learning Board Framework

The basic framework of *the Learning Board* model is:

The Learning Board process demands of the directors sufficient intellectual capacity to develop both their long-term and short-term thinking processes, and their external and internal perspectives simultaneously. It is personally demanding.

At its simplest, the model of the Learning Board is based on the Board's legal responsibilities. First, to create a sustainable future by designing and learning to constantly refine the path ahead – to give direction. Second, to ensure prudent control of daily operations, and deliver full accountability for the business – to ensure prudent control.

I encourage boards to see that there is an annual rhythm to a learning Board's year, starting with a review of their policy formulation performance, and ending with ensuring full accountability to their range of stakeholders. I ask them to see the Learning Board process as an integrated series of Board meetings. The policy review is followed by quarterly strategic thinking-focused Board meetings. Each month the Board spends only a minority of its time, usually 25 per cent, monitoring its Board Dashboard trend lines (see Chapter Five for details) to check the pattern of the business's operational performance; and around month nine in the financial year it is necessary to ensure that a major part of the Board meeting is devoted to ensure its accountability to the stakeholders by the year end, after discussions with the external auditors. In between there is much 'homework' to raise the level of Board intelligence. This becomes clearer if one divides the right-hand half of the diagram into a focus on giving direction; and the left-hand half to ensuring prudent control. It is a double loop of learning. This is where we move away from Managing towards deep and professional directorship.

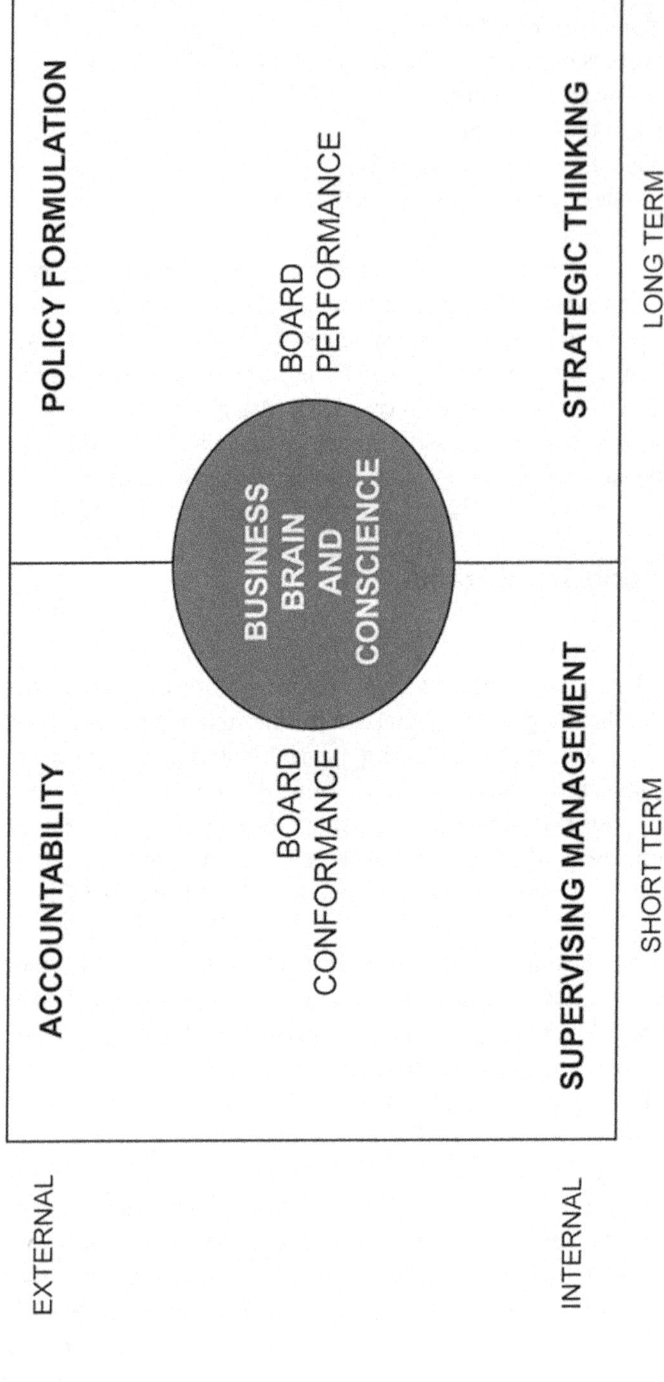

Figure 2: The Learning Board.

The two right-hand quarters of the Learning Board process focus on seeing the way ahead, designing the company's future:

Long-Term Thinking

Developing Policy – The focus is on long-term and foresight: externally orientated thinking needed to ensure the company's future health in an uncertain and dynamic world. It combines purpose, vision and values and hence the Board's conscience to keep its place in the wider ecosystem.
Strategic Thinking – This comprises long-term but more internally orientated thinking processes needed to convert Board horizon-scanning into tangible opportunities for growth using the finite resources of its people and the three capitals of Finance, Environmental impact and Social impact, to develop effective business strategies with risk assessments.

These two externally orientated quarters form the basis of the whole picture perspective. It may take over a year for a new director to develop such skills. Looking frequently upwards and outwards 24/7 for 365 days does take some learning.

Shorter-Term Thinking

Then the directors must integrate the Short-term Thinking elements focused on their overseeing management, and ensuring accountability roles:
Supervising Management – This focuses on the Board's oversight of short-term and internally focused thinking of the patterns of daily operations, without direct intervention from the boardroom table, and the creation of the information needed to be fed upwards by management to fuel the Board's dashboards and trend lines.
Ensuring Accountability – This focuses on delivering to the stakeholders and the external world the audited results including impact statements on financial, physical and social activities, and regulatory compliance, to ensure full governance reporting.

Ensuring accountability to the external world is the public-facing side of corporate governance. Here Board decisions on markets, resource allocation, people capital and social and environmental impacts are reported to the outside stakeholders at least annually through the accounts, audit and disclosure processes.

Supervising management is a common area of over-concentration for most Boards. It takes up too much Board time. Eighty percent of it is redundant if you have real-time dashboards. The Board's role is to seek *oversight* of operations, not to micromanage them from the boardroom table. They need to seek visual patterns in the operational data though their dashboards.

Early generative AI looks as though it may be a breakthrough in making more useful data and pattern analysis available. As so many directors have been managers or subject specialists, they usually feel they are proven experts and can do better than the new managers. But this is not their role. Two problems arise. First, they are not concentrating their scarce energies on their future-facing directors' role. Second, they are wasting time second-guessing the person appointed to fill their previous managerial role, taking up time and blocking their personal development. Hopefully, the emerging new global approaches to reporting, disclosure, and audit will help resolve this in the medium term. This issue will not go away.

All five elements of the *Learning Board* process are linked in a continuous cycle of changes and learning, scanning both the internal operational world and the external PPESTT world. They form a *lemniscate*, or double loop, of learning as seen on the cover of this book. The hub of this double loop of integrated corporate learning is the Board performing its prime role as the business brain *and* its conscience. It is the hub around which the Learning Board revolves. It is the Board's responsibility to scan these horizons frequently, learn from them, adapt nimbly, and so ensure that they sustain a healthy business relating to their stakeholders' needs. To do this well they need always to keep their company purpose, values, and conscience firmly in mind when taking strategic decisions.

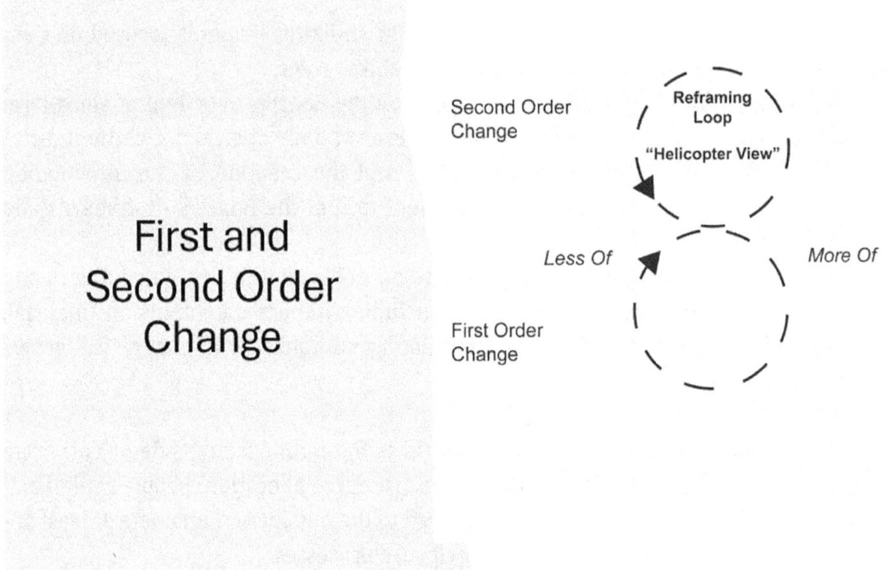

Figure 3: First and Second Order.

This is no longer an airy-fairy, soft, liberal, nice-if-you-can-get-it, set of wishes as so often portrayed, but the 'hard future' thinking demands that cope with existing and evolving financial, social, environmental, and legislative issues.

There is so much to absorb, plus crucial behavioural changes to learn, including how to stop taking instant managerial level decisions. And this is often at a time of life when many senior managers are happy to concentrate on their retirement rather than learn the new profession of directing. Therefore, designing a time and thinking space budget to allow them to practise becoming an effective director takes personal and Board commitment. New directors are expected to scan, read, digest, and develop ideas continuously to gain that higher level of insight into the topics under discussion. They are meant to do their 'homework' to develop foresight; then to use this information to contribute to critical internal debates with the Board, managers, and stakeholders about the future of their company.

Directors are not expected to deliver daily or monthly targets. To many managers making the transition from managing to directing, this statement just sounds weird and frightening. They stay silent. Setting such short-term targets is an abuse of their experience and energy, even unlawful. If they are registered, it is a dereliction of their directoral responsibility to not participate in the disciplines of the Learning Board.

A successful Learning Board process has two beneficial results. First, as the directors become comfortable with their broader and deeper strategic roles, they encourage the idea of the learning cycle to permeate all levels of the business. This leads to more transparency with the staff, suppliers, and customers, which in turn builds confidence with the stakeholders. Second, the stakeholders become more aware of the questions they need to ask about the Board's policy development and strategic thinking. Both need continual scrutiny. They are fundamental to ensuring the future health of any company.

However, these learning processes are often dismissed by dated directors as 'merely a nice to have' or 'irrelevant'. This is either through ignorance, or because Board members find them too hard to comprehend let alone deliver. They tell themselves that they just do not have the time to learn all this new stuff. Yet this is the basis of evolving international legal good practice for corporate governance.

Techniques for Developing the Learning Board

In Chapter Five I shall explore some of the well-tested processes for developing the *content* of Board policy-making and strategic thinking. Here I want to continue reviewing the thinking and learning *processes* and offer some proven techniques:

1. The Difference Between Puzzles and Problems

Step One is to learn to differentiate between puzzles and problems. Puzzles may look wickedly difficult and full of complexities. Many are. Yet the answer to their resolution is always contained within the boundaries of the statement of the issue, no matter how seemingly complicated. Their parameters contain the answer. This is the essence of the operational/managerial world and the essence of current AI.

Problems have no such resolution possible within their stated parameters. Problems are fuzzy and imprecise. They depend on the perceptions and values of the person stating them, and their acceptance by others. There is never a single or complete answer because the context is set by the questioner within a changing environment. They are not ultimately binary. This is the world of the professional director. It is full of ambiguity. One must often take decisions without being certain of the full facts, or the range or consequences of the outcomes. You place your bets and try to be nimble enough to respond to the dynamic external world as it changes around you. And you change your assumptions of 'the problem' as soon as is necessary. No wonder the title of F Scott Fitzgerald's novel was *The Crack Up.*

2. Learning One's 'Ps and Qs' Reg Revans [10], a key founder in the practice of action learning, helped me understand that 'action learning' concerns increased one's knowledge by the frequent questioning of accepted assumptions. He expressed this as:

$$\mathbf{L} = \mathbf{P} + \mathbf{Q}$$

Where **L** – is one's rate of learning. This is modified by the individual's ability to combine **P** – the existing Programmed Learning (what is already known and codified) – and **Q** – the ability to continuously ask discerning questions to test beyond the existing assumptions. This latter is best developed when an individual has the humility to ask those intelligently naïve questions without self-censoring the answers.

This is where an effective Chairman will push their Board to move beyond current business assumptions and standard, obvious, and fashionable answers to create new insights and entrepreneurial opportunities. In a world deluged in mere data it is crucial that a Board turns this into usable information to deliver their unique purpose and strategy. This is the new frontier at which the use and abuse of Artificial Intelligence is being tested.

Revans argued that the managerial world has a culture of asking questions focused only on deviations from existing plans – very much the **P** world. Managers can become very skilled at measuring and controlling such deviations – the cybernetic aspects of corporate governance. He argued that directors need to focus their attention primarily on the **Q** world, knowing that Boards must still commit to, and be held responsible for, their independent judgements and values. No algorithm will do this for them.

3. Good and Bad Organisational Learning

My colleague Keith Grint has helped me with two drawings to illustrate Good and Bad organizational learning. I find that directors recognise them instantly because they reflect the dreary, awful reality of so much organisational life. They have the added advantage of making people wince, recognize, and then laugh out loud at the too-human failings shown.

Bad Organisational Learning is found everywhere. In our daily lives we spend much of our time moaning about the lack of coordinated thinking across our departments, our organizations, and our governments. 'If only they had listened to me', 'Where is the joined up thinking?' and 'There is no systems approach used here', are heard throughout the world. If this lack of listening and adapting to others continues over time, then a corrosive culture of 'bad learning' is created. People become cynical and, ultimately, will seek to quietly disable their organization. It then becomes very hard to dislodge the bad learning culture. I must stress that this is not 'non-learning'. People learn all the time – good or bad. But a corrosive learning culture is focused on emphasizing the negatives, and how to personally avoid the consequences of the dire directoral and managerial decisions being taken. The organisational culture is rotting.

Grint's drawing for Bad Learning (Figure 4) (with agreed modifications by me) is:

Displaying this to a board, or indeed employees, usually causes both howls of pain, and much ironic laughter, followed by plenty of war stories. It is recognized instantly and internationally by so many as the frustrating position in which they often find themselves. When things get bad they feel that the only option is to be the first to blame others, then keep their head down. The big learning issue for me is that such a negative culture means that the issue is avoided, not resolved. It is left to fester and returns only to start yet another corrosive blame game. This creates a zero-sum, enervating, culture where there are only winners and losers. This is the breeding ground of intractable organizational issues. Sadly, the continuous blame game can continue as a malign form of organisational therapy – as long as you are not the one to be hurt.

Good organisational learning (Figure 5) leads to effective problem-solving and high positive satisfaction across the organisation. It is much more constructive in creating organisational learning to ensure long-term business health – the primary duty of a director and a Board.

The focus here is firmly on problem resolution, not on repeating previous mistakes. It relies on an early and honest reporting system, the rapid signalling of any deviations from plans or processes, no matter how small, followed by the guarantee of a process for immediate corrections. It is action learning as an organisational culture. It is systematic in its focus on demanding continuous learning and feedback at *all* levels, from the shopfloor to the Board. For example, such rapid feedback is already accepted as the basis of all effective organisational safety systems as seen in the nuclear, offshore oil and aviation industries. They actively encourage continuous improvements through the rapid sharing of open, anonymous, learning. It is the opposite of the 'blame culture'. It is the basis for creating a Board's prudent control mindset. It reinforces the positive managerial and operational learning culture of any effective business. But this can only be achieved if the Board is seen to be leading this culture by behaving in the same way. Too many Boards still believe in a 'do as I say, not as I do' approach. Any deviations between the Board's words and actions are

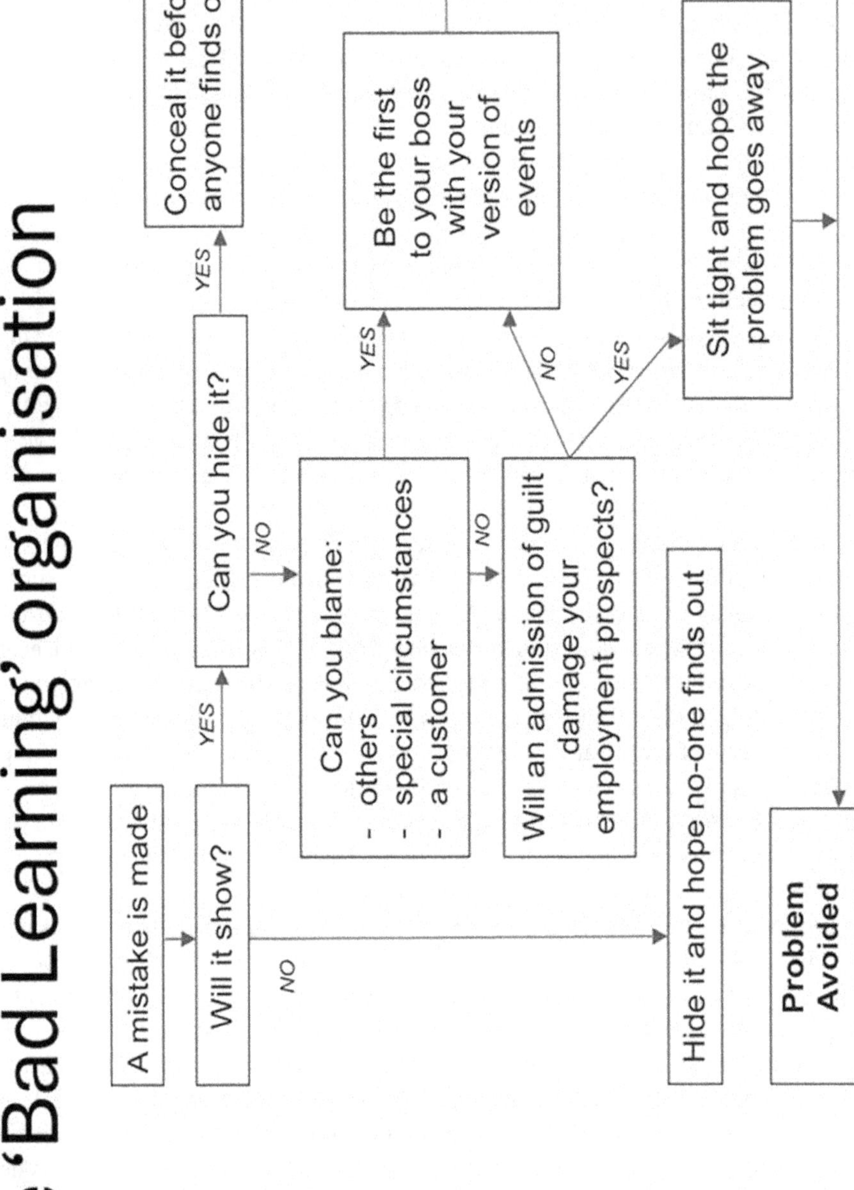

Figure 4: Bad Learning.

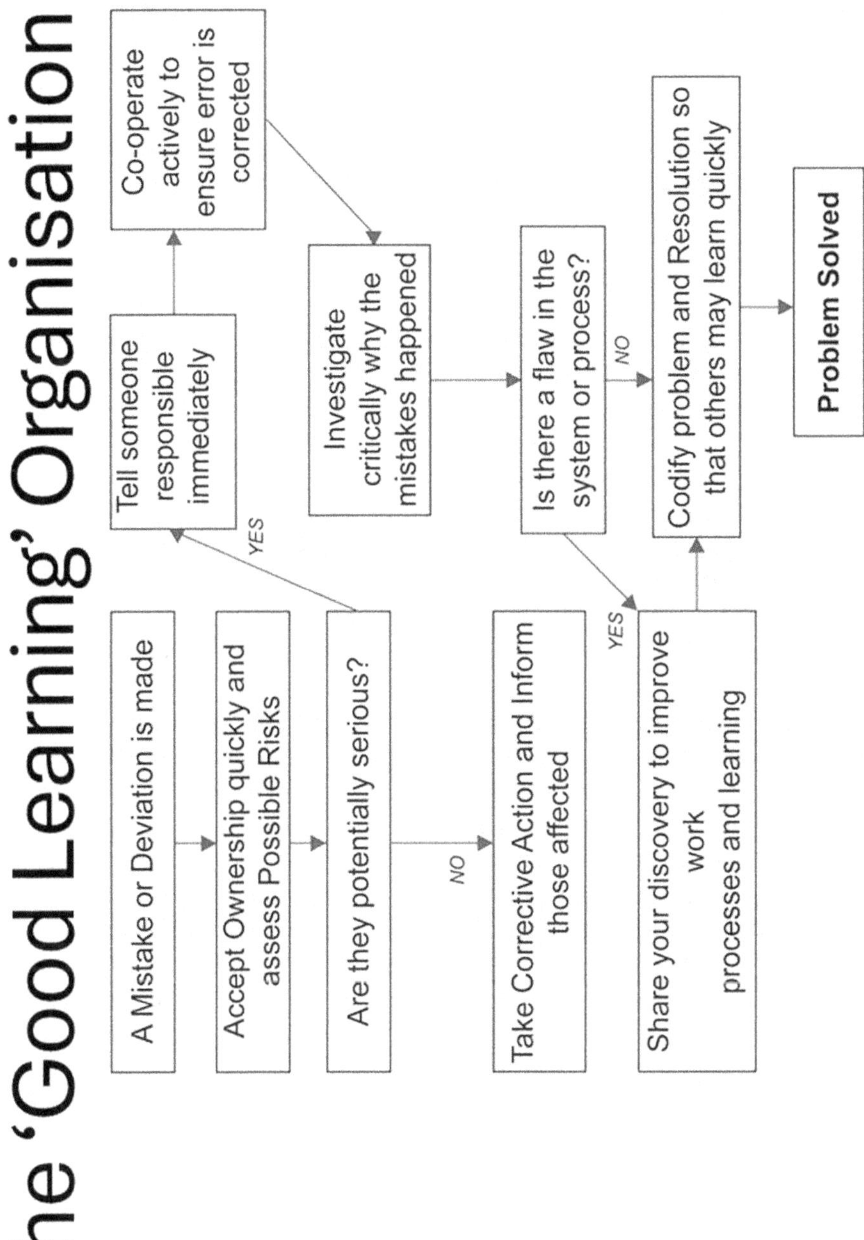

Figure 5: Good Learning.

quickly spotted across the business – and the staff will create a culture based on what they see is rewarded, regardless of the words used.

Once a board has learned its Ps and Qs and embedded a positive learning culture, the second breakthrough I work on is to get the Board comfortable with their responsibilities for first and second order changes. This is a further development based on integrating good and bad learning.

4. First and Second Order Change

Initially I used Prof Reg Revans' three levels of organisational learning and change (Systems Alpha, Beta, and Gamma) [9]. But I found that this confused my clients who wanted something easier to remember. I needed a model that balanced the interior, operational, busy, managerial world of 'puzzles' with the external policy and foresight world of complex and ultimately unresolvable directoral 'problems'.

When working briefly at the Stockholm Institute of Economics I came across the book *Change: Problem Formulation and Problem Resolution* [10] which fitted my needs. I have tested it over the decades with many Boards. The authors did not present their concepts in visual form, but I have. They argued that most organisational issues are unresolvable in the longer term if you restrict the problem-solving to single-discipline issues. For example, most 'finance' problems are not soluble by the finance function alone, they need a wider multi-disciplinary context to ensure lasting resolution.

The *First Order Change* learning cycle is where most people spend their working lives. They are bounded by a culture that argues that no individual can do much to change 'the system'. This is rationalised by prioritising actions shown in my diagram by the arrow cutting into this cycle labelled 'Deviations from Plans'. If the organisation is 'siloed' into separate disciplines, then framing the problem only within the boundaries of each single discipline limits effective multi-disciplinary problem-solving. Such thinking leads to binary decisions like 'let's do 'more of' or 'less of' what we are doing already'. This rarely generates creative solutions. And the problem will reappear months later because the business' leaders have deliberately avoided related, parallel issues. Such seemingly intractable problems that cross a chief executive's desk every few months typify the limitations of *First Order Change* thinking.

Second Order Change: I advocate that effective Board and strategic problems will always need resolving in wider, interrelated, perspectives for sustainable long-term solutions. This means opening Board thinking to the wider eco-system in which the business exists. This requires deeper and continuous study of the changing external contexts needed to reframe the problem to give it a much stronger chance of resolution. This is *Second Order Change* [12]. It acknowledges the uncertainties of interventions labelled 'Disruptions From the Environment' in the diagram. This is where directoral *judgement* is key in understanding the probabilities of such disruptions threatening the long-term health of the business.

This whole diagram demands the integration of both *First* and *Second Order Change* to achieve more robust, longer lasting, problem-resolution. This is the job of the directors.

The drawing of the operational first-order change is shown as an action-based cycle using managerial control systems to create daily levels of output – the key performance indicators. These feed in real time to the directors' dashboard.

In these drawings, and in the Learning Board model, I have assumed the acceptance of three levels of *simultaneous* directoral thought:

- Policy Formulation and Foresight,
- Strategic Thinking,
- Operational Thinking.

However, no world is ever stable and no matter how much systems engineering, Artificial Intelligence, quality and safety control, and cost-effectiveness are designed into the operational cycle, things will inevitably go wrong from time to time. I have shown this by the arrows piercing the operational cycle marked 'Deviations From Plans', and the policy cycle marked 'Disruptions from the Environment'. This is where the energy and intelligent learning of the people working in operations springs into life to bring deviant puzzle issues matters back into the planned processes. This is the daily drama of work in organisations.

As an aside, it is well known that too smooth a daily process can become simply mechanical. Humans do not like being treated as machines and if so treated, they get bored and frustrated. Then they often resort to gaming the system to see just how far they can break the rules without the whole system crashing. This is bad enough when done by accountants seeking cost efficiencies, but the consequences applied in safety critical industries are usually disastrous. Humans are naturally cussed and experimental. It is, therefore, always wise for directors to create a strong atmosphere of continuous learning and improvement in their businesses to avoid such self-induced crashes.

In the *Second Order Change* learning cycle we are looking as a Board at the directoral fields of policy formulation and gaining foresight – steering the way ahead into an unknown future, yet with our specific business purpose in mind. This requires constant monitoring of the external environment, then frequent adjustments to the board's direction-giving. This is the 'reframing cycle' and is often missed or considered only lightly by many Boards. Yet it is that intervening arrowhead of the 'Disruptions From The Environment' that creates business turbulence and focuses any board on the necessity to continually scan their horizon and adjust the tiller of their direction-giving.

The two learning cycles intersect in the area the *business brain and conscience*. This is the core of business intelligence. Here the debates between the Board and the executive decide where the business's scarce resources are broadly deployed to best achieve purpose and so deliver the varied wishes of the stakeholders. Combining and testing the entrepreneurial opportunities derived, and matching them with appropriate long-term funding sources, delivers purpose. I shall go into this in greater practical detail in Chapter Five.

I want to stress the importance of developing the *Learning Board* concept. The combined Board acting in its role as the *business brain and conscience* is legally charged with resolving simultaneously the problems found in both learning cycles. This highlights the eternal 'Directors' Dilemma' – how do we show the way ahead to a healthy future in a turbulent world, while also keeping our own scarce resources under prudent control? Linking this dilemma through adopting a whole picture perspective at the strategic thinking level seeks a balance between the two loops of learning. Indeed, the two loops are a continuous 'double loop of learning'– a lemniscate, or figure-of-eight, which cycles continuously and so defines the role of a director and a Board.

5. Directing As 'Seeing'

In this bridging chapter to the Level Four Professional Board, I finish with an idea and a set of seven line drawings that I have found help directors worldwide to discuss and understand their new directoral role. My long-time and esteemed colleague, Professor Henry Mintzberg, for decades associated with McGill University in Canada, has given me permission to use and adapt very slightly his concept of 'Thinking As Seeing' [9].

Board Thinking as Seeing

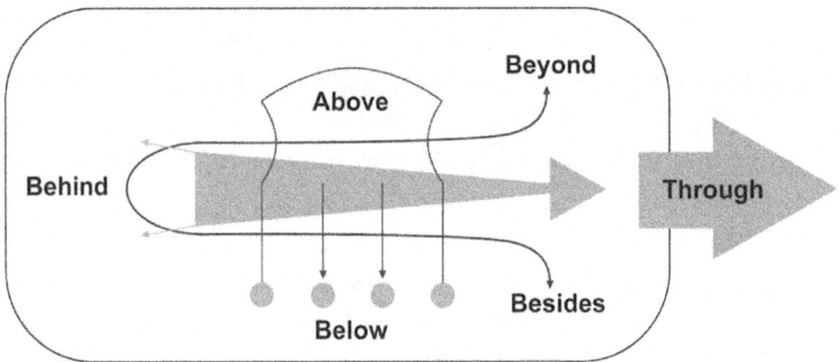

Figure 6: Thinking as Seeing.

Board Thinking As 'Seeing'

In 1995 I was increasingly disillusioned at what was being taught as strategy in the business schools and by many consultancies. They advocated what to me seemed to combine very mechanical, checklist style, over-quantified, unimaginative, and risk-avoiding processes with little entrepreneurial flair. I did not recognise this happening in highly effective boards. Sadly, much of this is still taught; but then few business schools consider themselves as learning organisations or even entrepreneurial. So, I decided to help my clients by bringing together the best people I could identify internationally and edited their essays into a book called *Developing Strategic Thought* [13].

Henry Mintzberg declined to contribute an essay but submitted six drawings:

Seeing Ahead

This thinking echoes the key message of this book – that directors must prioritise their limited time to focus on designing the future health of their business. Such entrepreneurship needs to be developed in the complex and changing financial, environmental, social, governance and ethical contexts, monitored by the Board. Directors must learn to spend the majority of their directoral time looking ahead.

Seeing Behind

This thinking argues that directors cannot see ahead without being anchored in their historical roots which have led to their present position, even if they are a new business. Mintzberg quotes Kierkegaard's wisdom that *life may be lived forward but is understood backwards.* It is impossible for a Board to have a completely blank sheet on which to design their future because even start-ups will bring their life experiences, values and prejudices with them. As these will form the basis of the future business culture they need to be shared, mapped, understood, and constructively criticised to stop them becoming a drag on organisational progress. Otherwise, myths develop about what staff can and cannot do, and especially what has been, and still is, rewarded and punished, in their organization. The folklore that 'culture' is 'what we do around here, when no-one is looking' is well worth exploring by the Board. You can only build on the strengths, and escape the weaknesses, of your past if you acknowledge them openly and are seen to learn from them.

Seeing Above

This is the world of the whole picture perspective. All Boards need to budget time and learning to embed this into the board's attitudes and behaviours. It needs to become their default position. It is how business issues are reframed and resolved effectively. But the Board learning process is more subtle than just looking upwards and outwards. It involves integrating other parallel inputs. It builds on that idea of holding two contradictory views simultaneously and still being able to operate. Mintzberg argues that the key here is to search for *noticeable difference* – what he calls 'Seeking The Diamond In The Rough'. This means seeking rigorously the facts rather than the current 'fake it till you make it' culture as shown in the Theranos case (see below).

Mintzberg encourages us to seek the entrepreneurial gem of an idea that will change the business.

Seeing Below

This is where boards can encourage creativity and opportunity emerging from your own workforce. Toyota have a principle of accessing 'the gold in workers' heads'. Here is where the Board's ability to use the cybernetics of prudent control, regular reporting, and auditing comes into play. Oversight is a legal requirement for any board. The data collection is delegated by the Board to management. But the Board is ultimately responsible. During my early drafting of this book the astonishing crash of the FTX crypto exchange was all over the media. The investigating auditors were amazed by the lack of even the most basic of controls, or naively intelligent questioning. At Theranos, none of the directors seemed interested in checking out the actual experience of the people at the customer-facing sharp end. These were making it clear that they were not achieving what the company was claiming. This is part of the syndrome of 'the investor fairy story' mattering more than the facts or the truth. In November 2022 the founder of Theranos was sentenced to 11 years in jail for defrauding investors (Ref). To me this proved the toxic mix of the current ignorance of effective governance, plus unbridled greed of investors, executives, and directors, plus not listening to your own people, so often overcomes prudent controls with disastrous consequences. This is especially true in the unethical Silicon Valley Bro atmosphere of 'move fast and break things'. This is why it is so important that directors check frequently on the fundamental purpose and truth of their business model.

Seeing Besides

This is about thinking more subtly to gain competitive advantage. It takes Board thinking beyond the obvious 'industry formula and norms'. Mintzberg is more nuanced and says:

> I believe that you can see ahead by seeing behind, and see above by seeing below, and still not be a strategic thinker. It takes more. It requires creativity. Strategic thinkers think differently from other people; they pick out the precious gems that others miss. They are innovative entrepreneurs . . . . . . challenging the traditional world that wears blinkers . . . . . . and thereby differentiate their organisations.' But truthfully. It is their ability to see both the big picture and the small, but identify the key differences that makes the big differences for customers and clients. This is what any Board needs to distil and pursue.

Seeing Beyond

I encourage all Board members to take personal responsibility for monitoring changes in the Political, Physical, Environmental, Economic, Social, Technological, and Trade Flows (PPESTT) spheres to develop foresight. It is their homework. In Chapter Five I go deeper into this. Here I will just say that I have helped Boards learn how to cover all six areas within a period of 18 months. This need to broaden a Board's perspectives is increasing in response to legislation.

Seeing Beyond involves the constant search for those 'weak signals' others miss, then tracking the changes beyond the industry's accepted boundaries to detect those future changes that may affect the business's existence and its opportunities. Immediate action may not be needed. But awareness and being sensitized is necessary if a Board is to respond quickly.

Seeing It Through

Which brings us to the blindingly obvious – it is not worth a Board investing in any of these interactive thinking processes without them being able to see it through – to implement the results. They must help deliver the long-term health of the business. Entrepreneurial thought must lead to stakeholder-rewarding outputs and consequent surpluses or profits. Mintzberg makes the pragmatic point that none of the seven processes mentioned above is worth investing in unless the Board has the *intellectual* capacity and moral commitment to take their strategy through to completion. This demands rapid feedback, the ability to adapt, and to value the consequent continuous learning.

Onwards to Crafting the Level Four Professional Board

Having started to develop the processes of the board's thinking, constructive criticism, and integrated intelligence we can make the final move to Level Five Board Maturity – creating a truly Professional Board.

This is where both the content and processes of Board thinking, and conscience, combine to ensure comprehensive problem formulation and problem resolution.

We are now a long way from the Accidental Director, and Grudgingly Compliant Boards. Developing The Learning Board approach is the essential launch point for true directoral professionalism.

References

[1] How employers can prevent AI work slop, Financial Times 22 October 2025
[2] Bob Garratt, The Fish Rots From The Head: Developing Effective Directors, Profile Books, London, 1996, 2003, 2010
[3] Bob Garratt (ibid)
[4] Bob Garratt (ibid)
[5] J. M. Keynes, "Alfred Marshall 1842 – 1924" The Economic Journal, 34 (135) (1924); 311–372
[6] F. Scott Fitzgerald, The Crack-up, Alma Classics 2018

[7] Jerry Rhodes and Sue Thame, Effective Intelligence – The Thinking Intentions Profile, jdr@thunks.com
[8] Reg Revans, The ABC of Action Learning, Gower, London, 2011
[9] Keith Grint, Fish Rots from The Head, ibid, pp 57
[10] Reg Revans (ibid)
[11] Paul Watzlawick, John H. Weakland, Richard Fisch, Principles of Problem Formulation and Problem Resolution, New York, 1974
[12] Elizabeth Holmes sentenced to 11 years in jail over Theranos fraud case, The Times 18 November 2022
[13] Henry Mintzberg, Strategic Thinking As 'Seeing', Chapter 5, Bob Garratt (ed), Developing Strategic Thought, Profile Books, London 2012

Chapter 5
Level Four Board Maturity: The Board as a Professional Team

Level Four Board Maturity – the Professional Director – features directors who can not only learn continuously and responsively but do so as a team. The idea of the Board as an effective working team is rarely discussed around the boardroom table, yet they are bound together legally: always jointly and severally liable. They are legally a collective identity that is more than the sum of its parts. To achieve this, they need to contract jointly and consciously to broaden their directoral maturity and 'give back' to their stakeholders by giving them their prime attention. They do this by rising above the operational world and directing their thinking, debating, risk-taking and implementation, by focusing strongly on the policy, learning formulation, and the implementation of strategy. These are competences that are under-appreciated.

The Level Four maturity mindset is to always put the stakeholders first, even when it hurts the Board in the short term. They do this by optimising their entrepreneurial skills to deliver simultaneous benefits for their business, their environment, and their community. Level Four directors accept naturally that the company is their primary client. It takes determination and time to learn.

Directing is still not widely considered as a serious, discrete profession. The power players in many societies still view it as merely an optional and exclusive luxury. Many do not know, or care, of its societal and legal underpinnings let alone accept the key competences and assessment processes necessary to deliver its craft. This has always puzzled me because we are talking here of the top people entrusted by our society to give direction and ensure sustainability to our human institutions. Often the only selection criteria used for directors are the volume of shares owned, or personal patronage. Sometimes short-term managerial success through the artificially boosting of the share price is thought sufficient to join a Board. This leads frequently to directoral conflict when reality bites.

Indeed, the fear of missing out by Boards and share buyers is a common phenomenon that leads to the herd mentality seen since, for example, The South Sea Bubble of 1720. The excited chasing of the 'fairy story of the New Thing' as my colleague Gunnar Walstam calls it, usually relies much more on the fairy story than the reality. I have referred to the shameful example of the Theranos scam (see Chapter Four). 'Fake it until you can make it' seems the ethic of the day. In US business it now seems acceptable to make exaggerated claims, lie openly, and hope that there are sufficient investors who are stupid and greedy enough, backed by social media campaigns, to believe it. This combines currently with the brutal ethos of both 'move fast and break things', and 'get in early, talk up future profits, load up with cheap debt, and get out

 | https://doi.org/10.1515/9783112231340-005

before the fools move in'. Ironically, Theranos was in the reputedly ethical medical analysis industry. This is the antithesis of the professionalism I advocate.

The vast amounts of cheap money available since 2008 and the subsequent policy of quantitative easing, especially in the US, encouraged uncritical investors to pile into companies encouraged by fund managers and day traders expecting quick riches with few questions asked, and no deep testing of reality or ethics. Thorough due diligence was not demanded. Risk appetite was absurdly high. There was negligible stress testing of the business model, and business judgment, and the conditions under which were they likely to fail. This is now being asked by the US courts. Such thinking as seen in Section 172 of the UK's Companies Act on the Purpose of a company was not recognised. There seems little thought of seeking positive long-term investment impact on financial, environmental, and social capital returns. This is the antithesis of being a professional. It is not unlawful for a business to fail, provided it is not shown to be fraudulent or corrupt. But I do wonder if some are designed to fail after the initial investment rush. These are often called Ponzi schemes.

So, what Is 'professional' about The Professional Director? The Oxford English Dictionary defines a professional as *'one who exercises great competence and skill, and who is able to instruct others to follow'.* It assumes levels of proven expertise and that a professional will always put their client needs before their own. This definition predates by some 200 years the demand for more effective and professional governing of our organisations, private and public. Professionals are careful, skilful, diligent, and ethical, with a primary focus on the prioritization of their *client's* needs. Many are already bound to be by their specialist professional codes. So, why does this thinking not stretch upwards to include directors? I argue that a major mindset change is needed by directors so that they see themselves as professionals leading the total learning and health of their company.

Although stated in many Companies Acts or Ordinances internationally, the concepts of the need for directoral 'care, skill and diligence" and the key idea of 'independence of thought' by each director, are often sidelined by Board teams at the expense of the stakeholders. Shareholders are wrongly given priority. Most are more comfortable focusing only on shareholder needs, on the misguided assumption that shareholders own the business. The idea of fulfilling wider stakeholder needs is seen as 'a nice idea' but 'not yet the time' and 'too hard to enforce'. This is self-serving nonsense, but will continue if politicians, regulators, and the directors themselves, do not know, let alone enforce, their own laws. It is still convenient in too many companies, families, governments, and charities to reward each other with directorships without demanding the reciprocal duty of learning their professional craft. This is especially true if the directorship is seen as a reward in return for external status, or existing personal relationships. None of these ensure competence.

A key argument throughout this book is that developing directoral competence is fundamental to the effectiveness of all our human institutions – private, public, and not-for-profit. In turn, our institutions create and stabilise our society and reflect its deep values. To reach such governance competence a professional mindset, values and consequent behaviours must be learned and committed to by all Board team members. Understanding starts with the Mutual Observation Period. Commitment comes at the swearing of the oath before other Board members. This is the induction ceremony to the Board team. As a society we do not encourage such bonding behaviours and attitudes sufficiently.

In addition, among those Boards that are not reckless in their risk-taking, one can observe the opposite tendency: heightened risk-aversion among many directors and politicians. Too few accept that entrepreneurship is *the* driver of future business growth, and under-estimate its potential beneficial impacts on environmental and societal health. Too many politicians are still comforted by the implausible concept of the state-funded state and the magic money tree. And too many companies still launch on markets untested or dysfunctional products and services in the hope that they might just work. They then adopt a tin ear to the anger shown on 'customer satisfaction' returns. The Silicon Valley ethos of 'fake it until you make it' echoes Antonio's worries in *The Merchant of Venice* as his ships sail out of sight that 'my fortune is now in the hands of others'. He did not have the advantage of cybernetics, but with modern telecoms and GPS systems allowing instant feedback, there is ample data and feedback. Yet many Boards act as though Antonio is still right and that such rapid feedback and learning cannot exist. They avoid the fact that their Board's role is not to just say 'yes' or 'no' to over-ambitious and ill-tested propositions by the chief executive. It is to design and direct their company's future.

Building the Board Team

Because directors are both jointly and severally liable there must be some agreed form of emotional and intellectual bonding. A team must be more than the sum of its individual parts. Yet few Boards see themselves as 'a team' with collective responsibility for their group decisions. Their default position is too often that they are a group of individuals brought together quarterly merely to discuss and agree the CEO's propositions. This is unlawful. Only as a team can the Board achieve optimal performance using independence of thought and care, skill and diligence. In my terms there are currently few Boards working at this level.

Level 4 Boards demand continuous maintenance, and often last for a maximum of five years, even when a talented and motivated group of direction-givers commit to use creatively their diversity to achieve their mutual purpose. Even then its competence will change because of changes in the mixture of the Board and external dynamics. These will force them back towards Level Three or lower. Then they need to relearn quickly. The change of just a single Board member demands a temporary return to a less mature stage before their induction brings the Board back to Level

Four. Few Chairmen accept this need for new learning and renewal. Even fewer make it happen.

The common perception of 'a team' is of a small group of people who regularly work or play together and are bound by a common objective. They are physically and psychologically together for the majority of their time. Executive teams and sports teams are like this. In my terms they are a 'team together'. However, a Board of directors is rarely a 'team together'. They are part-time, often 'outsiders', and initially rarely know each other well. Curiously, this is accepted in society. Given the rise of social media, they are lucky to meet physically once a month, and often only once a quarter. Even then they are not together for long. A total of six hours of work and a little socialising is often seen as a lavish investment of their time per quarter. Too many Boards that I meet remind me initially of the definition of many universities – a group of super-egos whose only common bonds are the central heating pipes. What can hold them together?

Level 4 Boards are, by definition, a *team apart*: a collective identity with a distinctive, high-performing characteristics. I first came across such an idea in the book *Superteams: A Blueprint For Organisational Success.*[1] Creating a team apart needs very skilful handling and bonding by the Chairman, many of whom are only vaguely aware of this. I am always keen to ensure that a potential new Board member has that Mutual Observation Period of six months for both parties to decide if they want to mutually commit long-term. If they do, then a personalised individual director development process is designed over a period of at least a year, with agreed assessment criteria. The aim is to blend their new unique mix of ideas and experiences with those of the other Board members to optimise their abilities to ensure lasting organisational health. To do this they must recognise that each team apart has unique specialized developmental needs.

The problem I encounter frequently is that most Board meetings are driven by formulaic, fixed agendas and an acute shortage of time. Their mission often then becomes to work rapidly through the Chairman-derived agenda, and to get out as soon as possible so that they will not miss their flights home. Many have told me privately that their wish is always to return to some 'proper' (usually managerial) work. They hope no one saw them furtively using their mobile phones under the Board table to deal with 'more important' matters elsewhere. For such folk directing is often rated as a burden, rather than their primary role. They are Level Two directors. The idea that their time should be 'wasted' on careful thought and debate of intractable problems, then taking risk-balanced decisions, seems mad to them.

A key to the creation of an effective Board team, and the cement that holds them together, is the realisation that each director has a legal right to decide what is on

1 Hastings Colin, Bixby P, Chaudry-Lawton R, Collins, *Superteams: A Blueprint For Organisational Success* Fontana, London 1986

their Board agenda. The agenda is not the Chairman's prerogative. This shocks many directors because it means that they have a duty to create time to debate each agenda item thoughtfully, skilfully, and especially diligently. In law the Chairman cannot decide alone what is and is not on the Board's agenda. A CEO has no right to determine the Board agenda. If any director tells the Company Secretary or Legal Counsel their wish is to have an item placed on the next Board agenda, then it must be put on it. No one has the right to censor this.

The decisions from the resulting debate, and any dissent, must be recorded accurately and circulated in the minutes rapidly. AI may be of some use here. Minutes must be written immediately after the meeting. It is good practice to circulate draft minutes within 24 hours whilst memories are fresh, and corrections can be easily made. Queries should be sent to the Chairman within 48 hours of the draft. Then the Chairman circulates these agreed minutes within a week. I have seen this simple process have a highly transformative effect on Boards. It frees a lot of time. It prevents the start of the next Board meeting being blocked by unnecessary disputes over the last minutes. I remember a very wise Chairman telling me what he thought the worst sound in a Board was. I did not know, so he replied 'The sound of minutes being opened at the start of a meeting, physically or online'.

Building a team apart takes patience. It must led by the Chairman. It must include some face-to-face team meetings, despite the wonders of modern digital technologies. The 'feel', 'touch', and 'emotional temperature' of a Board and its personalities is as important in creating a positive culture as the words heard and seen on screen. I was amazed by the speed with which so many Boards were able to switch to Zoom or Team-based meetings during Covid. This held many businesses together during trying times. However, since the end of Covid I have been more moved by the surprisingly emotional restart of face-to-face meetings. The energies released at being in mutual physical contact have been a joy to see. The personal tales of work, families, friends, scandals, professional bodies, national politics, and the international dynamics of trade, plus stories of how Covid had impacts on the physical and social environments, have been a delight to witness. Directing is a very human activity.

Each Board needs to become more skilled at learning as a team. When directors are not meeting face-to-face, they must remember that their joint legal liabilities for their decisions still demand the careful building of trust in each other's competences and ethics. They need to develop simultaneously their thinking and their implementation craft. This is a fundamental step in building Level Four Board professionalism.

It is a paradox that to focus intensely on delivering its Purpose the Board must constantly seek to widen its horizons and try to understand the consequent uncertainties. We are back to that original meaning of 'governance' as balancing both the organisation's clear direction when steering it through turbulent and highly uncertain waters, while simultaneously ensuring the prudent control of its daily operations. The Board's care, skill and diligence duties demand that it tests its purpose by launching specific products and services without damaging its physical environment, its local community, or the company's existence. Many Level One and Two directors see these as near impossible to conceive, let alone implement. It is only when a director starts on the path to Level Three Learning Board maturity and then aims for Level Four professional maturity that the directing and Board roles are realised.

Such mutual realisation comes through the creation of Board Vison and Values and the consequent organisational culture that flows from them. 'Culture' is a fashionable governance phrase and much abused, so I shall investigate its meaning and use below. To have verifiable meaning the company's stated Vision must reflect the Purpose and Objects in its constitution. This is both a legal and moral requirement that reflects publicly and transparently the moral values that create the Conscience of the Board. But in developing a Level 4 Board one must create an effective 'culture' – the emotional temperature and rewarded behaviour of the organisation.

Many Boards find it difficult to discuss such 'emotional' issues and shy away from anything labelled 'cultural'. It is easy for a Board to make specious statements about their espoused values and consequent culture. It is done frequently and usually leads to customer and public cynicism. There are often too easy ways to disprove such public statements simply by Boards checking their espoused values against reported behaviours, especially with customers. Social media is full of this. The public are then right to cry 'hypocrisy' and to attack statements as 'values-washing'.

Culture

But cries of hypocrisy can be made of all sides. The current push by many pressure groups, backed by some regulators, to advance the current vogue for, say, 'equality, diversity, and inclusion' (EDI), seem at first sight a noble cause. But unrelated to any entrepreneurial meaning it is prone to immediate charges of 'wokery' and later bureaucratisation as it becomes part of an ever-increasing tick list. Even worse is when such fads are written into criminal law. Ironically, negative feelings about coping with 'culture' can become a culture in itself. Culture is always present in organisations the question for me is how to develop it positively? We need a better acceptable definition.

Before I go deeper into 'culture', let me clarify first what I mean by 'values'. Values are those deep beliefs driving the Board team on the relationships between the company, the stakeholders and the wider public. Values determine the priorities of the Board regarding its opinions, attitudes, and behaviours towards its stakeholders. These determine the 'emotional tone' of the messages from the business. These are experienced both internally by the staff and externally by the customers and public. 'Living The Values' makes good PR-speak, but the harsh experiences of customers and staff rarely reflect positively the company's rhetoric. A classic example is the inconsistency of the customer service message that declares 'you are important to us so please wait whilst we connect you quickly' while leaving you with endless music of horrible sound quality, interrupted by repetition of the opening statement on how important you are. You are given no idea of your position in the queue, the likely waiting time, or offered a 'call you back' facility.

When I have a new or potential client, I phone their main switchboard and measure the time it takes to get a reply, and assess how helpful the operators are to get me to my deliberately vague desired destination. This information, plus the physical design of their entrance hall (from vainglorious grandeur to grotty make-do), tells me much of the values, priorities and emotional culture of that business. I then encourage all the directors to try and make contact by their website and to telephone their organisation as if a member of the general public with a complaint, to test the 'tone' of the responses. My simple test for any business is: Do their words and behaviours match those fundamental human organisational values of accountability, probity and transparency?

Like values, 'culture' is a highly fashionable word, dreadfully abused by companies and pressure groups. It is over-used and backed by ill-thought out and untested legislation. Hastily applied laws in the area of human values rarely achieve their purpose and often lead to debilitating infighting. Yet the careful and timely development of an organisation's culture is critical to its long-term survival. The link from espoused values to perceived culture is direct.

The simplest practical definition of 'culture' is 'the way we do things around here'. My colleague Coralie Palmer has much experience in social enterprises and uses the phrase 'accepted habits of thinking and doing.'. More cynical but common is 'what we do when no one is looking'. The most complete definition of culture that I have found and use frequently is that of Clifford Geertz:

> *An historically transmitted pattern of meaning embodied in symbols; a system of inherited conceptions expressed in symbolic forms by which men communicate, perpetuate, and develop their knowledge about, and attitudes towards life . . . . . . Man is an animal suspended in webs of signification he himself has spun. I take culture to be those webs, and the analysis of it, to be not an experimental science in search of law, but an interpretive one in search of meaning.* [3].

Some directors object to such high-flown language, so I take them through the definition phrase by phrase and then get them to tell war stories about how they and others talked themselves into the belief system that created their present mess – those webs of signification by which they have come to feel trapped. Understanding their current culture, its strengths and weaknesses, usually becomes explicable.

A current problem I have with 'culture' is that it is advocated most vociferously by politicians and regulators who use the word in public as a silver bullet to solve intractable organisational problems instantly. They are not experienced anthropologists and are content merely with hectoring sound bites that demand action by others but no accountability for their advocacy. It takes time and patience to change an organisational culture, years or even decades. Politicians rarely have this time as they are trapped in their own dysfunctional culture of offering maximum four-year solutions to long-term problems.

It is easy for a Board and an executive team to make grand statements of the 'Vision and Values' of an organisation and the need to build a supportive culture. Indeed, it is done all the time through Annual Reports and encouraged even by most corporate governance codes, for example:

> *The governance of individual companies depends crucially on culture. Unfortunately, we see examples of governance failings. Boards have a responsibility for shaping the culture, both within the boardroom and across the organization as a whole and that requires constant vigilance. This is not an easy task. Our recent guidance on risk management highlighted the need for Boards to think hard about assessing whether the culture practised within the company is in line with what they espouse. Boards should consider what assurance they have around culture. Are performance drivers and values consistent? How can culture be maintained under pressure and through change? Is the culture consistent throughout the business?* UK 2014 Corporate Governance Code [4].

Fine sentiments, but without any definition of 'culture'. So, how do you assess regularly the consistency between performance drivers, rewards, and the company's espoused values? When the going gets tough, who is really rewarded in the business and on which criteria? I am not aware of any anthropologists being involved in designing such systems. So, I commend following, for example, Gillian Tett of *The Financial Times* and now of Kings College, Cambridge, as both a trenchant critic and a trained anthropologist. She is well worth reading by Boards seeking help in the murky area of culture.

I have found the frequent use of opinion polls or social surveys are of little use unless they can test rigorously the businesses' espoused values against reality. Even then, I have not seen a poll that reports regularly on the differences between the espoused values and the values in practice. Such measurement would at least give a dimension to the size and range of the problems to be tackled, and the variations across the different groups within the business.

Yet we are all sensitized to an organisation's culture as soon as we meet it. For example, the gap between the practical reality of group behaviours – the true culture – and the ideal was brought dramatically alive for me when I read Alan Greenspan's *The Map and The Territory* [5]. Here one of the so-called 'Masters of the Universe', previously the Chairman of the US Federal Reserve, reflects on the Western Financial Crisis of 2008 following the scandal of the sub-prime loans debacle and the consequent implosion of Western financial markets as trust in its integrity was lost internationally. Here the differences between the values of probity and stability espoused by many bankers and their greed-based behaviours were so far out of line that it nearly brought down the world's financial systems.

When interviewed, in his answer as to why the crash occurred, and why was it that they did not see the crisis coming, he avoided the obvious cultural and ethical dissonance and just said that 'our models did not work' (sic). He had 250 PhDs working on them, but the models were tuned only to the neo-classical economic concept that, despite any shocks, markets would always return to equilibrium given time. When they did not self-correct, causing a major crisis, no one knew what to do. The UK's Gordon Brown finally managed to convince other national finance ministers to intervene immediately with massive 'quantitative easing'. This new printed money released the immediate pressures and fears of a global economic crash, but has created many still existing international debt-related long-term problems.

Greenspan admits that they had not factored in two very human forces that were spooking the markets. First, 'the nature and speed of market dynamics' (sic) and, second, 'people' (even siccer). I am mind-boggled that the human, emotional aspects of wealth generation and destruction at the global level were not considered important enough to even be a minor factor in 'The Model'. Peoples' greed and fear are always powerful human motivators as the reaction time to either is instantaneous. Fear Of Missing Out is always present in financial markets. This determines the astonishing speed of market reactions beyond the control of all governments. With modern instant news links and social media criticism it was predictable in 2008 that world markets would be destabilized instantly and then panic would lead to chaos. This was not considered seriously in the Fed's risk analysis. When the tidal wave hit the Fed, they were unprepared for the consequences. We are still suffering from such outdated and inward-looking modelling.

In retirement Alan Greenspan is only a little contrite. He admitted that he went to study a new discipline of which he had underestimated its importance – anthropology – 'because I now realise that people are important'. He wanted to begin to understand much more about people and their values so that he could reassess their importance in macro-economics. Little has changed so far.

Policy Formulation, Foresight and Strategic Thinking

Building an effective Board team is an essential step for Level Four Board maturity. It is a foundation stone of professionalism and good corporate governance. Here I return to the process and practice of the four elements of the Learning Board I described in earlier chapters (see Figure 1). This helps each Board identify its unique balances between the four elements.

- Policy Formulation and Foresight,
- Strategic Thinking,
- Overseeing Management,
- Ensuring Accountability.

Below I show four examples of how to develop mature Board team thinking, implementation, and so learn the craft of directing.

Taking that ancient Greek meaning of governance as being 'the steersman', my focus is on giving effective direction and control. A Board needs to know constantly where it is, externally and internally, to reach its purpose. I have the Board draw agreed 'Future Maps' to discuss their start and end points, and the [outline?] of their likely uncertain territory in between. I have found these the least developed areas in so many Boards' thinking. Some Boards have never considered deeply their short-term, medium-term, and long-term perspectives. As this can sound intimidating, I often start the Board in pairs to draw cartoon-style one page of where they think the Board is, and another to show their aspired endpoint. Sharing these causes a lot of laughs and eases any initial tensions. But it has the serious intention of leading a Board into the two areas to which they pay least attention, and where they are most uncomfortable.

'Policy Formulation And Foresight' and 'Strategy Thinking' are key. These are never delivered by a quick 'away day' at a pleasant hotel. They are a continuous and core part of any Board's agenda.

I have mentioned adopting the 'Whole Picture' perspective as the necessary default position for all directors. However, I do want to stress here the importance of Boards debating, challenging, and critically reviewing to be able to design their future; then committing, implementing, and learning rapidly from these Board team processes. A disconnected and directionless Board, or an all-powerful management team, spell long-term disaster for any business. Developing confidence to debate openly and without recrimination, builds trust within the Board and between the Board and Operational Management. It is, therefore, an essential for any professional Board.

I am often brought into a Board to help resolve the power battles within it, especially between the Chairman and the CEO. I have learned the fundamental need for each Board to understand, agree, publish, and implement those legal powers that it exercises uniquely *as a Board,* regardless of what the executives, or shareholders, feel or think. These 'Reserved Powers of the Board' are rarely published, reviewed regularly, or debated. Yet they are the basis of Board power. They are sometimes mentioned at an early Board meeting and then filed away by the Company Secretary. They are rarely seen as a key working tool. So they are often discounted in the action-orientated power games between the Board and executives. Too often such unnecessary power plays lead later to a dangerous waste of top-level time and resources. So, these vital Reserved Powers of the Board must be recorded and publicised to every director as part of their induction pack. Once agreed, these Reserved Powers form the basis of the Board's Strategy Responsibility Grid, of which more later.

Figure 7 shows the total Learning Board process. Note that the arrowheads show that each quarter flows naturally into the next as a rhythm of continuous learning. These are the quarters in which Artificial Intelligence claim it may make rapid strides. Currently I feel this is most likely in the internally focussed Supervising Management and Ensuring Accountability areas and least helpful in Policy Formulation and Strate-

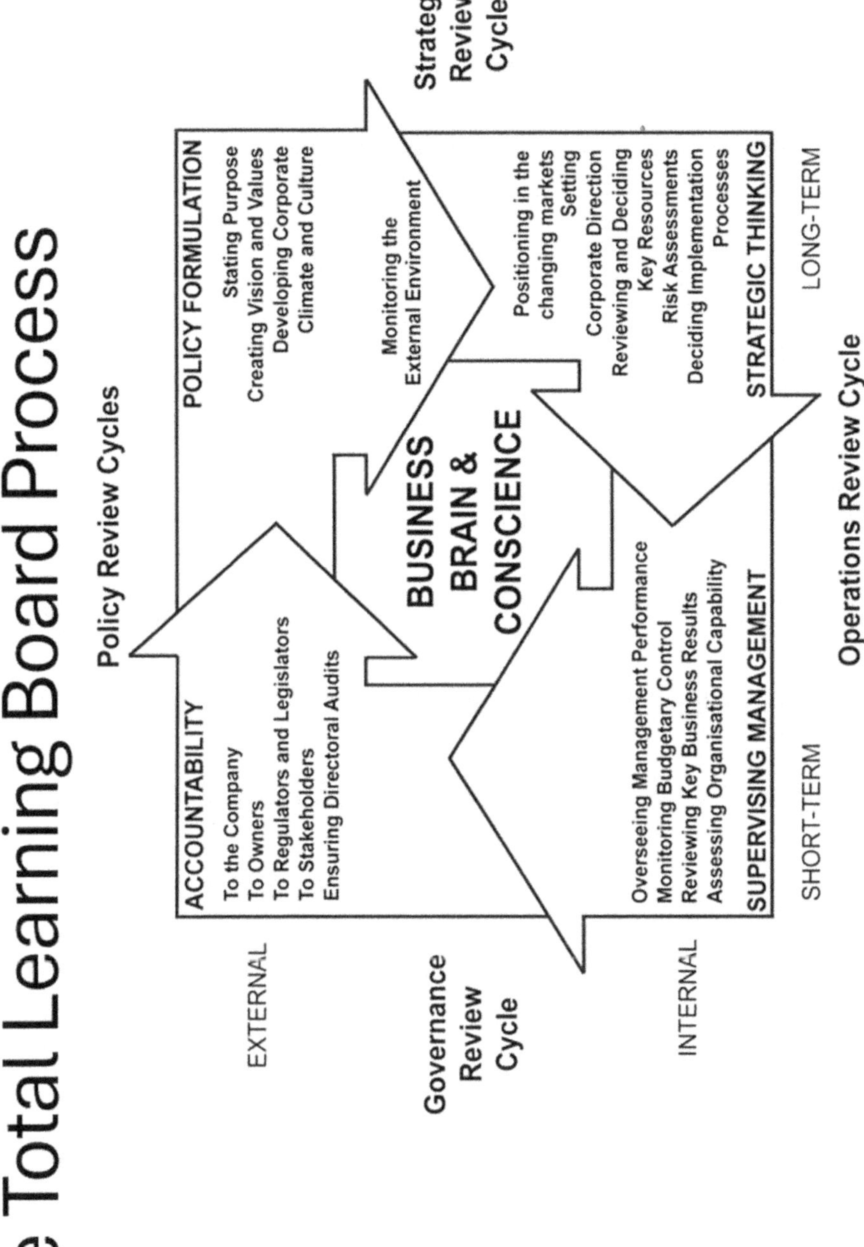

Figure 7: Total Learning.

gic Thinking. Below I have added the necessary thinking styles needed for team development.

Policy Formulation and Foresight	(combining long-term *and* externally orientated thinking)
Strategic Thinking	(combining long-term *and* internally orientated thinking)
Supervising Management	(combining short-term *and* internally orientated oversight thinking)
Ensuring Accountability	(combining short-term *and* externally orientated thinking)

Committing personally to this continuous total learning process is the acid test of a Level Four Professional Director. The alternative is to continue being a 'director' in name only.

Before we move to the practical thinking and techniques for crafting professional directorship, I have noticed two basic questions that effective directors always keep in their heads before getting into the complexities of Policy Formulation and Strategic Thinking:

- How do we make a profit or surplus currently?
- Is this sustainable for the future?

Without such foci companies die.

Developing Board Policy As A Team

Policy Formulation and Foresight are those aspects that create the boundaries for Board members' thinking about their vision, values, and purpose. These give the reason for their very existence as a team, and a steer as to where they are going, and why.

Understanding 'why we are here' is the cornerstone of Policy Formulation: the Purpose of the company stated in its constitution. The Memorandum and Articles of Association, or the Company Ordinances. I am frequently surprised how many directors, managers, employees, and stakeholders do not know this, or read it once and then forget it. They treat the company as an anonymous corporate blob with unlimited life and resources, and with the ability to do anything it wants. It is not and cannot be. It always has limited resources. Its Purpose should be seriously reconsidered by the Board at least annually and the result published as the context for the annual report to the stakeholders.

On the other hand, so much rhetoric and virtue signalling has been written about company Purpose over many years that I shall not list examples of the fatuous boilerplate 'corporate speak' and woke gibberish currently in circulation. In practice I check three key questions when dealing with a client team on the issue of their Purpose:

- Are the Board emotionally and financially fit to pursue their stated purpose?
- How will the Board continue to create wealth by the way they deploy their capitals – financial, environmental, and social? Although their ultimate existence is determined by their cashflow, do they understand the business eco-system by which that profit or surplus is sustained, for how long into the future, and how does this relate to their stated Purpose?
- How do the Board regularly review and assess their learning of these triple wealth creation processes? Is the speed and regularity of their learning sufficient to guarantee them a healthy future?

Business trends have often encouraged a company's lawyers to write the Purpose clause in such broad terms that it seems to be able to do anything it likes. This weakens considerably the Board's clarity of focus. In the Companies Acts the 'Objects' clause is that part of the company's written constitution that states the purpose and range of its activities. It sets limits on the power and capacity of a company to act. But in recent times 'Objects' clauses have been deemed unfashionable, often unnecessary. Many companies have dropped them quietly or absorbed them into the Articles of Association. Ironically, they were seen as too 'catch all'. This is being reconsidered by Next Generation directors as their existing catch-all Articles have little real meaning or focus for future direction-givers.

There is a growing case for asking companies to restate in their annual reports more limited and specific Objects so that stakeholders can understand and critique a company's performance and proposed activities. What appears to many directors as a minor and legally redundant clause is beginning to be of growing importance as, for example, the ESG movement and Net Zero demands change the focus in many companies. Reframing the Objects clause seems a good start.

This is the area which most Boards tend to avoid. The mantra that 'business has nothing to do with politics' is heard often. But internationally politics is increasingly interested in having more say over the power and wealth of business. I find globally that most directors do not want to be involved in 'politics', especially party politics. This is usually wise. Yet most mistakenly conflate 'policy' with 'politics'. This is a fundamental misunderstanding. Many actively try to avoid both because they tell me that trying to cope with these issues 'makes their brain hurt'. I have sympathy for them. Yet formulating their future policy is the primary task of any Board of Directors. It sets their ultimate boundaries in a very messy world. Corporate policy concerns the directors' *vision* of their future in that wider 'political' world, and is underpinned by their agreed values and behaviours developed to help achieve their goals.

Directors do live in an increasingly party-political world. This does not mean they must get involved in party politics. They need to take decisions relating to the deployment of their scarce resources in this political context. Such decisions are seen as 'political', both within the company and externally. They will be interpreted by the wider public as evidence of a Board's 'political' stance. Their decisions will have knock-on effects in the wider stakeholder community which, in turn, many outsiders will consider 'political'. These decisions are taken by the Board, and the team needs to commit to them, unless the wider dynamics change significantly. They will be judged by stakeholders as a clear indication of the company's espoused values and conscience.

This statement may seem blindly obvious, but it does make many directors very uncomfortable. It is made worse when they realize that developing the company's Next Generation Purpose and Policies will now be set in the new global ecological and community contexts. They just do not feel competent, or willing, to broaden their thinking to take on an increasingly political world. It can feel like having to eat an elephant in one go. But I remind them that the answer to the question of 'how do you eat an elephant?' is to take it slowly and in small portions.

This is where getting the Board aligned to face the challenges, and then attuned to take it slowly and methodically by dividing it into clear and achievable stages, becomes a crucial test. It is a test of the Chairman's competence, their understanding of the Reserved Powers Of The Board, and the stakeholders' tolerance. It is here that a Board's skills at Policy Formulation and creating Foresight are developed.

I have found much early resistance in getting a Board to move towards serious consideration of their Policy Formulation and Foresight duties. So, rather than attempting to eat the whole elephant at one go, I often start by getting them to agree to experiment by returning to the PPESTT (see list below) framework as the basis for more digestible learning. Again, I do this by getting the Board to agree to form 'buddy pairs'. Each pair agrees to support each other in crafting their professional learning across the total PPESTT spectrum over the following 18 months.

Ideally, I seek the maximum difference in each buddy pair so that naïve, critical, yet supportive, questioning is necessary between them from the start. I ask each pair to select and scan the changes in their external environment in just one of the PPESST areas:

- Political Change
- Physical Environmental Change
- Economic Change
- Social Change
- Technological Change
- Trade Flow Change

I then ask each pair to contract with the other Board team buddy pairs to give a 10-minute review (maximum two pages) every quarter of their findings and thoughts on their selected PPESTT area, focusing on the two or three key points they feel the company must be tracking in its horizon scanning. Time is budgeted for a quarterly Policy Review session either at or before a Board meeting. It usually takes a lively hour to debate. This is to encourage, supplement, and reinforce their 24/7 scanning duty to sensitise themselves to ensure a more informed watch on external changes. Initially this can lead to levels of scepticism, or even downright cynicism. So, I encourage each director to select a few media sources that will help them and their buddy pair to track their issues for just three months, and to discuss this with each other informally at least monthly. It is a formal part of their homework.

Despite the initial scepticism I find that at the first Board Policy Review session the extent to which each pair wants to inform and discuss with the others is usually much more than either side had expected. Suddenly the Board's role in external horizon-scanning makes more sense. And it is not as difficult as first thought, provided they scan their newspapers, newscasts, technical papers and social feeds for a few minutes a day. This budgeting of time to scan and think about the future implications of the changes that they see happening starts building a firm foundation as a Level Four Professional Director. Many have found it intellectually liberating to finally break out of the claustrophobia of their inwardly focused managerial and specialist mindsets. Some have found it a useful way to engage with their children when discussing many current issues.

Next, I encourage each pair to drop the specific area they have been studying for the last three months and swap to another element of the PPESTT framework, with the promise that they will report back to the Board on this area in the next three months. The process is then repeated on three-monthly cycles for all six PPESTT areas. By the end of 18 months all directors will have studied and discussed all the areas, including those about which they knew little. This builds up confidence and momentum for more thoughtful horizon-scanning to design the company's future.

Often to their surprise, they find that they now have much more discerning questions to ask of managerial and specialist areas which they have previously avoided. From this point the importance of policy review and the development of more informed foresight is given much higher priority by the Board. Their horizon-scanning 'homework' becomes an automatic part of their professional directoral duty and life.

I have been pleasantly surprised by how personally liberating this seemingly simple, mechanical process has proved for so many directors. It takes them into areas about which they know little, or were intimidated by, supported by an intelligently naïve colleague. It broadens their intellectual curiosity and deepens the range of questions that they feel more confident to ask.

Social Housing Association

The clearest example of this effect that I experienced was with the Board of a social housing association. A newly appointed director was proving 'difficult' for the other Board members to accept. He was appointed as a tenant-director and saw his role purely as supporting all tenant demands regardless of the business needs of the whole organization. He would not participate in any Board developmental activity. In a long personal conversation with him I found that he felt intimidated by the other directors, all of whom had degrees. He had little formal education and proudly declared that he was there to support the working class. He admitted privately that he was running his own form of class warfare on the Board and felt justified if he gained a few tangible benefits for those tenants who had voted for him. He admitted that he was frequently frustrated as he had not been very successful at convincing other Board members.

He was frightened to join a buddy pair for the PPESTT reviews as it would show clearly his lack of formal education. He felt that he knew nothing about any of the six areas. I suggested that he might be surprised at how many of the other directors felt the same. Reluctantly he agreed to try, chose a buddy to pair, and was surprised both by what he did know and what the other did not. The quarterly Board Policy Review developed into a constructive mutual questioning and learning process for him and across the whole Board. At the end of the first year, he took me aside and said that the Policy Review process had given him the best 'university education' he could have had – and it had not cost him a penny! He now felt confident in asking intelligently naïve questions and could evaluate the quality of the replies from the executives much more easily. And he could explain to his constituents his wins and why the Board sometimes disagreed with him in favour of the interests of the wider association.

I also advocate a Board reading programme. This can raise looks of anguish around the boardroom table. It is to make two points. First, that key need to widen directors' perspectives. Second, to create time to think and so break the managerial impulsion to action. We agree a few books, or papers, that the Board will all promise to read and discuss at their Strategic Thinking sessions. The choice is theirs. For example, I have found that internationally a book like *Prisoners of Geography: Ten Maps That Explain Everything* by Tim Marshall [1] is a mind-opening paperback book for many directors. It allows them a very different and unusual world view. It covers the consequences of geography and demography in unique ways outside the usual bounds of business and politics. It helps them kill many of their preconceptions and too-easily accepted social media non-facts. It helps reframe the Board's debate and their world view. The regular reading and debating of such short books and papers helps Boards build higher levels of confidence in facing their seemingly intractable polycrisis problems. Board reading development can be broken into chapters for buddy-pairs to read and debate. In my experience it provides lively and enlightening policy and strategy reframing sessions when, for example, considering the likely consequences of trade flows, foreign markets, technological advances, and social movements.

Developing Team Board Strategy

The acid test of a Level Four Board team is whether they can move from high-flown policy and foresight into creating and implementing practical strategy. Many directors tell me that getting to grips with so many clashing, indecipherable, and contradictory dynamics happening simultaneously is impossible in today's world. It all seems outside of their control. I feel like that sometimes. Yet it is our directoral job to do our best to resolve this by learning from our strategic actions. We are back to F Scott Fitzgerald's *Crack up*, with its need to reconcile contradictory forces, by making the seemingly impossible work. Which is a good definition of strategic thinking and implementation.

They ask how they can be expected to predict accurately the future. They cannot. And it is unwise to try too hard to do so. But Boards can train their personal and corporate brains to both loosen up and broaden their thinking range, to develop their strategic thinking skills, and then respond nimbly and thoughtfully to the evolving trends as we saw in Chapter Four. To do this well they need to learn how to develop those intellectual perspectives, to tolerate the uncertainty and yet make tough decisions and learn quickly from them.

To this end the arrowheads shown linking each quarter of the Learning Board model are a carefully chosen symbol. They are a key part of the Board's learning dynamic, ensuring the links to the messy external world and allowing better learning for the deployment of their limited resources, using those three capitals of finance, environmental resources, and human resources. Every Board must blend these to deliver effective strategic thinking. Because many Boards do not do this in a regular and systematic way, their puzzlement and frustration continue.

How does one start strategic thinking to open their minds to better horizon-scanning and using the whole picture perspective to reduce, but not eliminate, their uncertainty? A discipline I have found helpful concerns learning to enjoy broadening the corporate mind. A third concerns ensuring a clear definition and agreement of the duties of directors and managers before they set off on the great Board strategy developmental process, turning their strategic thinking into overseeing the management's operational deliverables.

In Chapter Four I talked of the importance of opening each director's mind by accepting the challenge of using the PPESTT analyses as a normal part of their 24/7 responsibilities – their 'homework'. How then does a Board take this further in a time-effective way? I like to start by talking with each director about their view of their very personal career timeline to create their perspective, and then to get them to focus wider on their Board's timeline.

There are many proprietary brands offering such help. They usually use expensive 'away day' types of workshops to try to broaden Board thinking. Some have limited use in starting the breakaway from the tyranny of managerial figure fixation. But few have any systematic learning follow-through. My preference is to start from each individual director's position of comfort, derived from their personal histories, and, once they are comfortable, for them to share these later as part of the Board's group learning process. As an example, I give each of them a copy of Sally's and my personal timeline (referring to my late wife and business partner Sally Garratt). This describes the influences that shaped us until 2001. Then I leave them with a blank sheet to complete personally in any way they wish to describe their last decades.

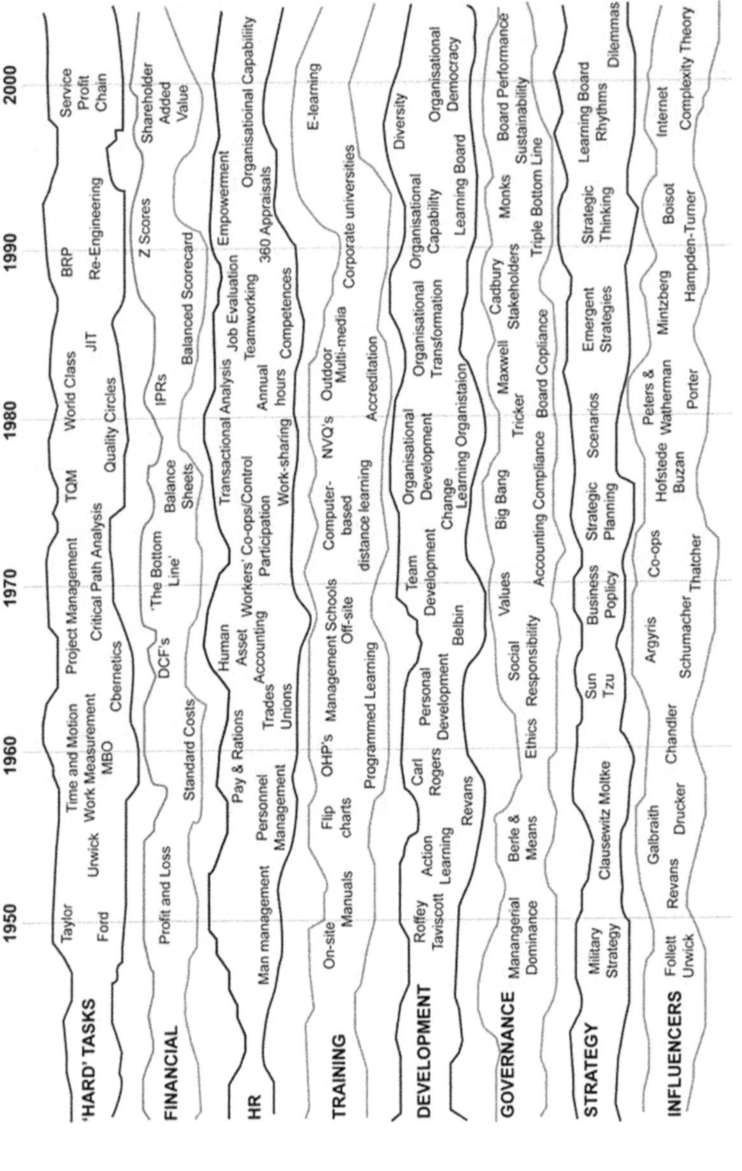

Figure 8: Personal Timelines.

I encourage them to fill in notable events in their own discipline and then in any others that had a knock-on effect on them, positively or negatively. This is a confidential exercise which usually takes around an hour. Some find this sudden challenge intimidating and are only comfortable sticking to describing the history of their own discipline. These will rarely make it as Professional Director. Most are intrigued and set off apace, first in their areas of professional interest, and then try to link these to the other Board disciplines and wider external issues. Many privately refine the exercise over the following months.

Then I bring the whole Board together to share results and encourage them to consolidate these historic trends and dynamics into a Board map agreed with all the other directors.

Often, they are surprised at how wide the gaps in perceptions of each other's disciplines are, and how little they know about those gaps. This Board team gap analysis is often a half-day exercise. This helps build their confidence in starting to ask each other better quality 'naïvely intelligent' questions of the other disciplines and so develop openness, trust, and curiosity in their fellow directors. Most importantly, it also highlights their personal and Board development gaps for which more knowledge and skills may still be needed from external experts for the directors to become capable of designing and delivering their future.

Later I ask them to begin to plan with the other Board members, and the senior executives, how these gaps can be narrowed, and their knowledge extended to create their corporate future. This usually leads to much information-swapping and to a lively debate about what the other disciplines have been up to over the previous 20 years, how effective they have been, how this has formed their world view, and how this has impacted on their business. My objective is twofold. First, for everyone to begin to appreciate the dynamics of all the other disciplines involved and how these may help or hinder the business's future. Second, to reinforce their approach to open questioning around the boardroom table and with the executives before they converge on a resolution.

At the end of this initial development process the Board agrees a corporate timeline that forms the basis for creating the 'Future Map' for developing the business. This widening and broadening of the Board's problem-solving processes reinforces the legal reality that they are jointly and severally responsible for the giving direction to their business.

The quarterly-reporting PPESTT/buddy pair process is a powerful start to broadening and deepening a director's confidence in Policy Formulation and Strategic Thinking. Henry Mintzberg's 'Thinking As Seeing' (Chapter Four) is then a useful 'mind map' of the thinking processes needed by any professional Board to build the bridge between scanning the future external environment and turning this into their unique data, and the insights needed to refine the Board's strategy for the *Future Map*.

But the Board's thinking processes must have hard content to be effective. How can a world full of seemingly random data be turned into tested, useful information? Such information is vital to turn data into usable P + Q (Programmed learning + Questioning ability, see Chapter Four)-style questioning that answer those two questions on current and future viability. With the current rush towards god-like veneration of Artificial Intelligence, these remain vital questions for direction-givers to answer. How can the Board test and agree the basic facts from which they are developing their future?

I remind Boards of the security services' basic process to start validating any data used to turn their data collection into 'hard' information. In an age awash with dubious and contradictory 'facts', massive 'data scraping', and fashionable stampedes because of fear of missing out, it is essential to ask the following questions of any data that the Board wishes to turn into usable information:

- What is the source of this data?
- How reliable is that source?
- Can it be cross-checked?
- Does it help in resolving the problem?
- How can the consequences of its use be monitored to ensure its continuing validity?

I challenge Boards to then design and develop their *Future Maps* based on these answers. Most tell me that it is impossible to spend time thinking about their companies in periods as long as 50 years. Yet they are usually uncomfortably aware of the looming public global demand for answers to such issues as Net Zero to satisfy their stakeholders. They often reject my request as absurd because they say that they cannot even predict what they will be doing next year. This is true, if you focus only on short-term returns. The financial tyranny of quarterly and annual performances, set in the context of most investors' short-term expectations of ever-growing returns, is still deeply ingrained in most directors' mindsets and blocks truly strategic thinking.

Yet with the weakening of the acceptance of shareholder supremacy model, plus the growing pressures of having to create a future that balances those three demands on scarce resources, major reframing is needed to create a Board's future perspective. As mentioned, a major societal problem is that politicians are locked into that same short-term thinking cycle, often driven by a political voting cycle of around two to three years, regardless of their rhetoric about the longer term. It is ironic that although politicians are frequently criticising business folk for their over-use of short-term thinking it is those very politicians seeking immediate political advantage who are most trapped in blocked learning cycles.

There is growing interest on all sides in developing an alternative approach based on more creative 'long finance' strategic thinking. Good examples can be found in family offices, sovereign wealth funds, or in the financing of major successful infrastructure projects like the Kings Cross Redevelopment in London. The focus is on the creation of an asset that lasts for many generations with the same owners. Immediate, short-term returns are not fundamental to this model. The fund-raising is not via a three- or four-year, get-rich-quick, private equity style scheme, with much share 'flipping'. The focus is often on long-term performance bonds with investors contracted to an initially slow return that will speed up to give superior performance over, say, 20 years. This is becoming known as 'sustainability investing' and looks promising.

Broadening the Board's mind by exploring such patient finance options points a significant way ahead for any Professional Board's strategic thinking, if they are seriously to deliver their legal duty 'to ensure the long-term health of the business'. Family offices and sovereign wealth funds are prime examples of the need to think in timespans of *generations*. For them it is a necessity to protect the very long-term family or national interests. Many are now operating more as classic merchant banks, working on developing mutual long-term projects based on trust between their clients and themselves. Their values and actions towards accountability, probity and transparency show a more co-operative, 'open book accounting' basis of the business relationship. It is the antithesis of day-trading and FOMO (fear of missing out).

It is here that I see great hope for a strong 'sustainability' approach to future business. This is because the Next Generation, noticeably in many family offices, are beginning to reach positions where they can influence strongly the development of our future world. They can do this through their more equitable reallocation of their, often substantial, resources of finance, environmental, and social capital. Their corporate values are expressed by seeking actions to balance returns on those three capitals. It is interesting to note that such patient projects often take more risks in the very early stages of their development because they have time to learn what will work best without the pressure of immediate returns. The longer-term returns seem much more reliable and sustainable. This stands in stark contrast to the frantic current 'fake it until you make it' approach of many Californian chancers.

If the patient capital approach is not possible for your organisation, then all is not lost. There are other ways of broadening the Board's mind. I have worked with Boards with truly scarce resources creating Future Maps with longer-term timespans by examining their aspirations, gut feelings and fears amongst the sea of messy future possibilities.

For example, I often ask a Board to study the single page drawing of the Path To Net Zero published in 2022 by the International Energy Agency [6]. This is not to endorse the concept of Net Zero, but as an exercise in thinking long-term. I find the drawing a good example of a big, bold, and concise Our Future thinking map. Its design allows a Board to visualise, debate and agree its specific policies and strategies to achieve its Purpose within a single A4 sheet.

I ask them to produce their own version to explore what, keeping to the 2050 Net Zero objective, this means for their unique business? The IEA map shows both a time-

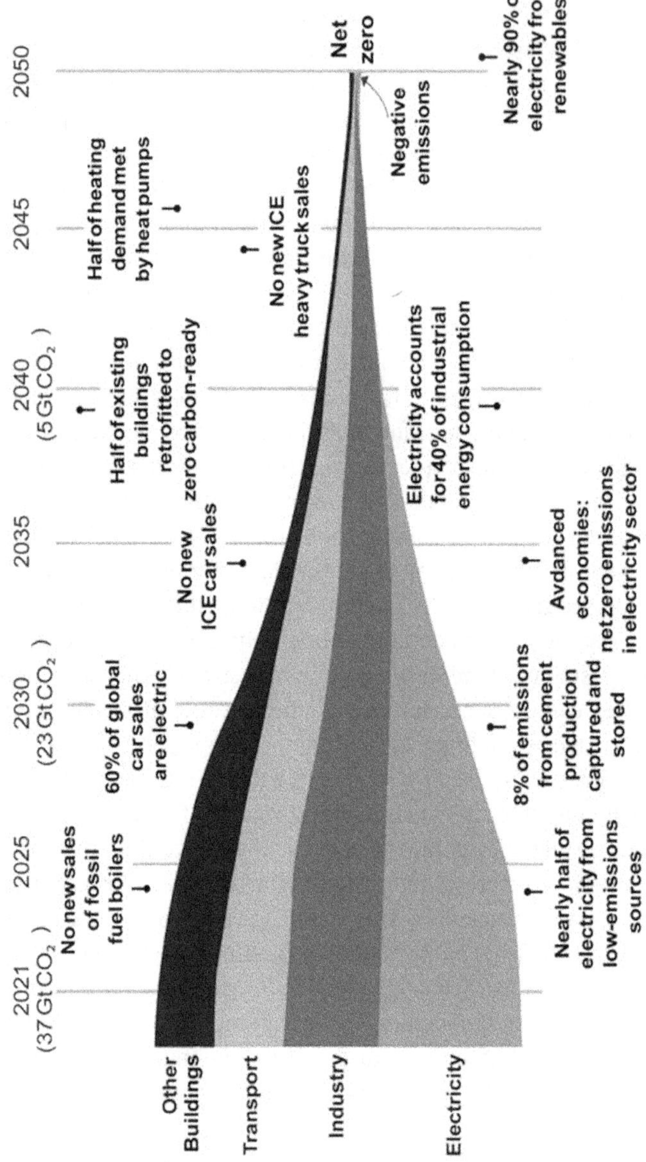

Figure 9: Path to Net-Zero.

line on the horizontal axis and an industry analysis on the vertical axis. To ensure intellectual rigour I ask them to keep strictly to the timeline and its key milestones.

But then I ask them to decide the specific trends from their sector that they wish to use as their inputs and comparators. The Board often needs a couple of attempts to gain their agreed *Future Map* for the business in 2050. This then becomes their regular comparator against, for example, their quarterly strategic update on the Board agenda – with sufficient time budgeted for rigorous debate, amendment, and decision-making. This is a key function of Level Four Professional Boards. It is a professional job and needs to be treated as such. It is a long way from micro-managing the executives from the boardroom table.

However, it is not only the content and processes of Board decisions that need clarification. One of the biggest blocks to effective decision taking is the unresolved power struggles both within the Board and between the Board and the executives. Egos can easily overpower rationality.

Many business strategies crash and burn because of the lack of clarity and ensuing conflict between the Board and the executives during the strategic thinking processes. This is rarely discussed openly and rigorously around the boardroom table, so many assumptions over responsibilities are made. This leads to many unresolved issues that surface later, usually at inconvenient times. Mini-social silences then exist, especially between Board members and executives, with few wishing to vocalise the issues for fear of retribution. What is *not* said can be more powerful than what is. This sounds easy to resolve, but human nature intervenes, and the mixture of inflated egos and wrong assumptions about roles leads frequently to unnecessary, and energy-sapping, boardroom battles. This seems particularly true in the US where the cult of the superhero CEO is still in strong play battling both Boards and shareholders.

To resolve this potential lingering sore quickly I use a battle-tested single A4 sheet figure – The Strategic Responsibilities Grid. This clarifies the roles of the Board and the executive. I encourage the Chairman to hold a special, single-issue Board meeting to ensure that all concerned understand and commit to this grid. It is the framework against which strategic progress is measured.

The vertical side of the grid outlines of the four stages of strategy development:

- Developing The Strategy,
- Ratifying The Strategy,
- Monitoring The Implementation Process,
- Developing Necessary Support Partnerships and Alliances.

Remembering that the Board has sovereignty over the total process.

The horizontal parts of the grid take each of the four stages of strategy development and focuses them on the formal agreements needed by all parties involved to create, implement, and monitor the strategy:

The Strategic Responsibilities Grid

Stage of Strategy Development	Board Authorities	Managerial Authorities	Clarifying joint or unclearly assigned authorities
Developing Strategy	- Understand the external environment/changes - Main forum for debate and discussion of vision, values, goals and key issues - Develop and agree vision, values and culture - Provide advice and support to executives during the development of the plan - Comment on executives'drafts - Check compliance accountabilities - Agree final structure of strategy	- Undertake research to provide information for the development of the strategy - Embed the 'learning organisation' culture through the organisation - Provide feedback on environmental and social scanning rapidly to the	- Who will write drafts of strategy and implementation plans? - Who will authorise the use and payment of consultants and advisors? - Who will control the budget for strategy development?
Ratifying the strategy	- Approve strategy implementation and feedback process - Delegate to senior management/executives	- Present implementation plan to board - Develop implementation plan - Allocate resources to implementation	- Who will disseminate the strategy? - Who will complete the details of the strategy
Monitoring implementation	- Monitor overall progress of strategy implementation - Help executives in problem solving and trouble shooting - Communicating with shareholders/stakeholders	- Manage implementation process - Manage progress - Manage resource committed - Sign off completed tasks - Report frequently to the board	- Who is reponsible for speed and frequency of the feedback?
Developing partnerships and alliances	- Identify and approach potential partners - Use board networks - Communicate with existing partners - Approve formal partnerships and alliances	- Help identify potential partners - Help approach potential partners - Negotiate detailed agreements - Manage partnerships and alliances	- Who will finalise partnership agreements?

Figure 10: Strategic Responsibilities.

- The Board Responsibilities (as stated in the Reserved Powers of the Board document),
- The managerial responsibilities (usually a mixture of the main devolved research inputs needed plus the executive plan for implementation and rapid feedback to the Board),
- Clarifying the joint or unclear assigned responsibilities (reducing the chances of conflict over the ownership and development of the strategy by openly laying them on the table and reaching agreement).

This grid is key for clarity as the increasing use of many subcontractors and supply chains has made such assigning responsibilities more complex. The Chairman must lead this process and the Chief Executive be seen by the Board to commit to it positively and openly. In my experience agreeing this grid at the start of the strategic thinking process has reduced weeks, even months, of unnecessary argument around the boardroom table and many false starts. In the UK an example is the continuing mess over the installation of the HS2 high-speed train system. This has had so many political interventions that it is now a shadow of its original plan, having been scaled back owing to vastly increasing costs. If the grid is done well and applied, the energies released enhance designing, implementing, monitoring and learning to create an effective strategy.

Remember that the word 'strategy' is derived from the ancient Greek *strategia*. It concerns the functions of a military general. It is about the *broad* deployment of an organisation's scarce resources to achieve its objective. It is not about planning. Planning belongs in the world of management puzzle solving.

When I start with a Board team, I offer a reminder of what has proved successful in designing an effective strategy over the past 3,500 years. Throughout history, for any strategy to be effective, it must be capable of being described in one paragraph. This allows it to be memorable and, crucially, easily communicable to others throughout the organisation. It is even more effective if it is contained in one easily remembered sentence. Remember that strategy concerns the Board's *broad* deployment of the business's scarce resources. An effective strategy needs to integrate five decisions:

- Holding and protecting what you value – your core assets,
- Advancing into new territories,
- Retreating from ineffective resource use,
- Combining forces to reinforce your resources,
- Withdrawing totally from failing activities.

I argue that all business strategies must have clear answers to all five categories simultaneously. These elements are as applicable to not-for-profits and legislators as for a business. If it does provide such answers, then the strategy must be well-publicised and phrased in simple language so that every member of the organization knows the current strategy and the reason behind it. This may seem a simplistic statement but so many organisations let strategies get blurred by adding detailed plans to them. As the number of pages increases so the chances of a reader understanding the strategy decreases proportionally. I am reminded of General Montgomery's strategy for defeating Rommel's army in the North African desert: 'We shall push at speed across Libya from Egypt to meet our comrades pushing East from Algeria. We shall then bottle up the enemy in Tunisia and biff them hard!' This is easy to remember, applies to everyone in the organisation – and it worked.

I am often surprised when sitting with a Board just how unclear members can be about the thinking *processes* needed to design and deliver an effective strategy. The right words are usually there, but not necessarily in the right order. Often there is little evidence of a coherent flow of thought, backed by analytical content, the actions needed for commitment. There is often even less thought on the necessary implementation, rapid feedback and learning processes. Random, ultra-fashionable, but energy sapping ideas often predominate. This is where the Board's Strategic Decision Grid gives a powerful, single page, discipline to bring the Board's strategy process back on track.

So, I advocate starting with the Board agreeing the axiom that Entrepreneurship + Environmental Impact + Social Impact + Accountability + Board Maturity = Effective Corporate Governance (**Ent** + **EnvI** + **SocI** + **Acc** + **BM** = **ECG**) to give the context to their process.

Because Boards have a legal duty to monitor constantly their changing environments to ensure the long-term health of their business, this demands an agreed time and money budget for the Board. But there are other 'free' resources which are rarely considered. This is where the stakeholders, especially staff, customers, suppliers and communities, can play a powerful co-operative, strategic role.

What questions need to be asked frequently to ensure such co-operation? Here we return to a more complex version of Mintzberg's six ways of seeing. This demands a Board team agreeing their integrated strategic view. This combines their horizon-scanning information – their internally generated information from staff, customers, suppliers and stakeholders. The Board team is the central processor of such data. This can be handled successfully provided that the directors learn to tolerate higher levels of uncertainty and ensure more rapid learning when placing their strategic bets. Successful directing is the acid test of their emotional resilience in times of uncertainty.

I then encourage the Board to work through this three-level process to learn by refining and critically testing their strategy. But how can they then take their problem formulation deeper in a systematic manner to explore the likely competitive business eco-system that the organisation needs to be able to sustain itself? I insist that the Board commits first to the discipline of reviewing rigorously their strategic homework on at least a quarterly basis.

I worry that often much of this future-thinking process is subcontracted to external consultants or the executive team. This allows a Board to both feel free of its statutory obligations and gives someone external to blame when things go wrong. Neither approach is valid. But such behaviour often leads to a Board reducing decisions on strategy to a binary 'yes' or 'no' with little true discussion or critical review.

However, I do note those ideas and models that stick in directors' minds as useful over the years, These are easy to remember and discuss, are easy to use, and seem cross-cultural. Amongst them one name stands out: Michael Porter's approaches continue to influence much strategic thinking and analysis. Other brands are available, but I have noticed that his work has remained continually in use in framing Board's analysis of their changing competitive environment. I believe that this is because his approach is decidedly entrepreneurial. It appeals to folk wanting to understand the leading edge of developing the future health of their organisation.

I have found two of Michael Porter's seminal ideas used frequently by Boards to crystalize key aspects of the 'hard', analytical content of their strategic analysis. He has kindly let me refer to these in my previous work. They encourage learning through thoughtful implementation processes. I reprise them here. [6] The simplicity and utility of his Competitive Advantage models are noteworthy, especially The Five Forces model, as a framework for a Boards' focused introduction to competitive analysis. When combined with The Value Chain model, they allow a Board team a good launch pad to monitor the integration of its external world and internal daily operations. I commend Porter's continuing work in this vital field.

The Five Forces model describes five dynamic external forces working continually to reframe the competitive eco-system in which any company must learn to survive.

Porter's Five Forces

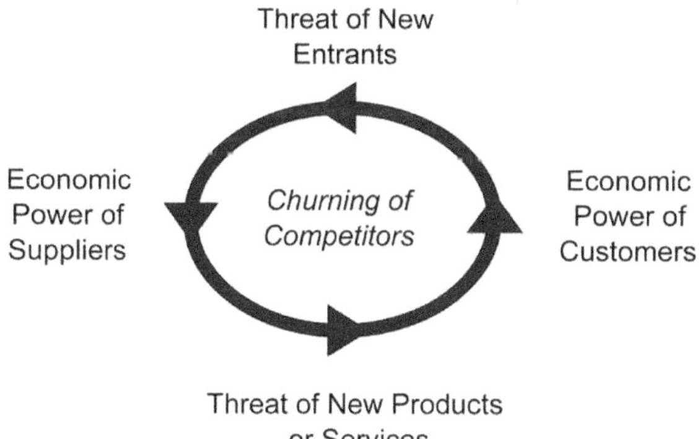

Figure 11: Five Forces.

The beauty of this model is that directors find it easy to *visualise* and remember the five dynamic forces, whilst allowing discussions with the executives and specialist staff of its content and the implications for their business. The model illustrates four opposing and dynamic competitive forces:

- The Threat of New Entrants,
- The Threat of New Products or Services,

And
- The Economic Power of Suppliers,
- The Economic Power of Customers.

At the centre of the model sits the business, coping as best it can with the fifth force the 'churning' manoeuvres of the existing competitors – their frequent reframing, refunding, and repositioning in the current markets. All staff have opinions on this, and talking with customer-facing staff helps the Board better understand what is happening in the business. I refer you to Michael Porter's excellent books for the more detailed explanations of the models.

Here I will comment only on some of the regular learning I have observed from Boards using such models. Below the macro-environmental dynamics of such global PPESTT analyses there exists a second level, the *competitive* world in which the Board fulfils its primary role of broadly deploying its scarce resources to sustain and develop the business's future. But what dimensions, metrics, and consequent learning should they use to do this effectively?

A business is always watching who might enter their market and what new products or services might disrupt both their immediate plans and their longer-term strategy. This is a constant concern of Board teams and all the executives. The turbulence is reinforced by technology, which develops at a seemingly unstoppable rate – unless one can find a way of cutting off the electricity supply to allow a Board sufficient time to think.

As I write the media world is fixated on the rise and seemingly unstoppable rise of 'Artificial Intelligence'. Some see human beings becoming redundant in the foreseeable future. At the other extreme some see massive opportunities to shape what we have known as the working and social world, if they move fast and have rich backers keen on the creation of vast data monopolies that will ransack the world's intellectual property assets before trying to sell them back to their legitimate owners. It is easy for a Board to panic, or feel disabled, in such circumstances.

So, a Board needs to think deeply and critically rather than just surrender to new technological advances. Yet despite the Silicon Valley credo of giantism it must be remembered that it is not always possible to enter markets easily. The barriers to entry need careful and constant monitoring for this part of the strategy to be developed effectively.

Two key questions need to be asked. First, what is the price of entry? An easy assumption is that in an age of global trade and easy credit it is possible to fund in the short-term any semi-decent idea, including many that are implausible. In the new cyber age, it looks to be as simple as a having a good brain, a laptop, some homegrown algorithms, and a fast-growing social network with plenty of followers. Life is rarely that simple even if the start is spectacular. It may still need years of careful investment in building a robust physical or electronic infrastructure, and overcoming much local politics, before any return is possible.

Barriers to entry include the developmental time needed to even enter a market. What are the legal, national and international trade barriers to be overcome? What are the registration procedures needed? How strict are accreditation procedures? What regulatory barriers are there? It may be easy to launch and copyright a new app, but to get certification for a new drug from the US Food and Drug Administration may take a minimum of 10 years. Do not assume that a competitor's PR rhetoric means that something that might happen will happen. What is the probability of any novel product or service occurring and in what time frame? Will that new product deliver the wonders it promises? How will our Board know? What are its intelligence sources and how reliable are they? New products and services are popping up everywhere all the time, from graphene to those currently much-hyped, frightening, and media-fixated, aspects of Artificial Intelligence.

Example: London Taxi Wars

As an example, I have watched, with a vested interest as a frequent user and grandson of a London 'cabbie', the continuing competitive clash between new and old strategies, technologies, and cultures of London's competitive taxi companies, highlighted initially by Uber's attempts to dominate the London market. I stress that this is my personal experience. It is not an academic case-study. However, I have found it an interesting saga of the real-time evolution of differing business strategies.

Just a few years back Uber announced it had been licensed to enter the London 'mini cab' market i.e., that part of the market that can be accessed by the public only by booking by telephone or online, as distinct from the much more strictly licensed 'black cabs' which historically, over two centuries, ply for hire directly on the streets. Black cab drivers need to pass an onerous test following around three years of part-time training, known as 'The Knowledge', which is set by Transport for London officials. During this time 'cabbies' must fund themselves through other work whilst they learn *by heart* and are later tested regularly and frequently on the location of every street and major building in a six-mile radius of London's Charing Cross. Over nearly two centuries they have built Londoners' trust as reliable, honest, and highly knowledgeable, if a little pricey. Psychologists have proven that such Knowledge-based cabbies' brains have physically changed as their hippocampus is larger than the average person's to cope with the extra knowledge they carry. London 'black cabbies' are a special breed.

Determined to move fast and break things, Uber entered the London market by offering much lower fares, the use of GPS location rather than the bothering with The Knowledge, fast responses, and a 'cool' image that contrasted with the nearly 200 years history of traditional black cabs. Uber's ultimate business objective seemed to be to break the semi-monopoly of the black cabs so that they could create a new monopoly through which they would control the trade by prices. The initial offer of low fares had great public appeal, especially to younger people who needed taxis after, say, clubbing late at night – a time when black taxis were often less available. Initially it went well, and the 'black cab' trade suffered.

But then issues arose that challenged the Uber business model's credibility. The real cost of entry was multiplying. These included a growing number of public complaints that their drivers relied totally on GPS and had no idea of where they were going, so they took longer than the black cabs, which had the rights to use bus lanes, of which there are many in London. Some Uber drivers started gaming the system if there was a large demand for taxis in a specific area. Uber had initiated a system of 'surge charging' to cope with growing demand. Fares would suddenly go up if there was an increased demand in a specific area. Some drivers seeing the increase in demand on their screens would wait outside the area until surge charging was triggered before responding to calls, thereby ensuring higher fares. Much more serious were some recorded instances of assaults on women passengers, especially at night. These began to create bad publicity for Uber through the findings of the criminal courts [*need a reference*]. The public began to lose some of their initial confidence in Uber and lowered their expectations of its drivers. But it was still relatively cheap.

However, then the barriers to entry became more noticeable. The issue of Uber's chosen form of employment contract became public when local and national politicians started to intervene. A major legal case was lost by Uber when the courts deemed that Uber drivers were not self-employed, as they had insisted from the start, but had a contract of employment with a named employer who controlled their source of employment. This meant for Uber as a company that they had to start paying employment taxes, insurances and the usual staff benefits including holidays. This had a noticeable dampening effect on its bottom line and, therefore, its business model. Its costs and prices rose, and the customers noticed. But it also had a major effect on its supply of drivers. Many had liked being self-employed and able to control their time and to some extent the employment taxes they paid. It did not help that the maximum number of passengers such taxis could carry was usually four. The black cabs technological response was to buy electric cabs that were distinctly more comfortable and could seat six.

Many Uber drivers refused to pay such taxes and left. The Covid-19 virus intervened, and many drivers found more amenable jobs driving 'white vans' to deliver goods during the pandemic. They found life was better when they did not have grumpy passengers moaning at them. This created problems for Uber as with fewer drivers they could not always satisfy demand; yet they could not then automatically use surge pricing as their fares would often rise above the fixed fares of the now resurgent black cabs. During Covid the black cabs renewed much of their stock to those new larger, six seater, electric cabs, and had good digital communications. Young people began to find that, especially at night, it was becoming cheaper and much more comfortable for them as a group of up to six to use a black cabs again.

I wait with interest to see how this will eventually play out. But it looks currently that Uber's ability to flood a market in the short term, using cheap debt to cover initial negative cashflows, may prove expensive in the long run. It seems that insufficient weight was given to evaluating 'old' black cabbies' resilience, and Londoners' initial cultural tolerance of an incomer whilst they learned, churned and repositioned themselves to a changing market.

But then the Knowledge cabbies struck back again. Others from the European Union had entered the black cab market such as Gett and FreeNow. They used all the new technology but were becoming increasingly expensive as they started adding on a range of 'extras' depending on time of day, booking process, and type of cab used. This caused increasing confusion and annoyance as passengers found it increasingly difficult in assessing their final fare – it was no longer what was shown on the taxi's clock and the effects of the promised driverless cars.

With the aid of a credit card company that gave them access to their technology the black taxis created Jump. This allowed customers to pay exactly what was on the clock, much to customer's relief. Most of the incomer taxis became greedy and had increased the percentage fee that black cab drivers paid them to as high as 20% per trip. This hurt their earnings. Jump charged nothing extra to passengers and charged only a small percentage to drivers through the credit charge transactions. In the first six months this looks like being a popular success. I await the longer-term 'churning' consequences with interest.

The continuing battle of supply-and-demand between customers and suppliers is the stuff of business, especially at the operational level. I do not intend to write yet another economic treatise on it here. Rather, I will comment that directors and managers see it played out every day. Sometimes it is seen in rational responses, as in the repositioning of the supply of energy and grain to Western Europe that followed the invasion of Ukraine by Russia in 2022. The horrendous rise in energy prices, shipping costs and consequently food costs caught everyone by surprise. Yet the fast-learning responses in finding alternative international suppliers, the rebuilding of gas storage facilities, and the increased move to wind, water and solar energy sources is a pleasure to see. Boards were forced to work flat out to stabilise their markets but then had to think about the strategic implications on their longer-term energy and food supplies. Net Zero-style thinking suddenly began to have more meaning.

Yet people can be quite irrational. Fear-of-missing-out is still a major human driver often exaggerated by social media. One whiff of a shortage and panic can easily spread, for example, causing a run on food shops as we saw in the early days of Covid. At the extreme end of human cupidity, I remember the world shortage of Cabbage Patch dolls one Christmas and the massive rise in prices that followed this nonsensical trend.

For Boards the question is always 'what is the balance we need to strike between our suppliers and our customers to ensure the return we need to sustain their needs and our business?' There is never one easy answer in a dynamic world. This is why the Board's 'brain and conscience' role is critical in combining the external and internal worlds of Board team thinking.

A constant puzzle for directors is how they are meant to keep in their heads the complexities of daily operational outputs sufficiently for them to be able to question credibly monthly managerial performance to ensure Board oversight. With so many diverse specialist inputs, what questions can the Board reasonably be expected to ask and be able to process? Here I have adapted Michael Porter's work on Value Chains, which has proved helpful to many Boards in framing such questions. This is my version of a Board dashboard to monitor monthly operations.

The initial Porter design looked on the horizontal axis at the flow of work through a business: from inputs through processes to outputs. On the vertical axis was the organisational superstructure needed to ensure the prudent control of the organisation. Through rigorous questioning within this framework Boards, using their monthly Board dashboards and trendlines, are encouraged to better interrogate the answers from their executives and specialists. This allows constant refinement of both the current workflow and its superstructure. Most importantly, by not actively intervening, Boards are able to track the pattern of the performance trends of each aspect of the business without having to lose their directoral oversight perspective. They use their value chain as a Board dashboard.

My adaptation is based pragmatically, first on the infrastructural issues that have become more prominent since the original model – that is, Corporate Governance, Organisational Capabilities, Human Asset Investment and Development. Second, it expanded the range of questions to be asked during the daily flow of work through the business –on the detailed Pre-Work Logistics needed before work starts, the changing methods of Delivery to Market, and the precise demands of After-Sales Service in different market segments. Such questioning is not only the basis of focused discussions

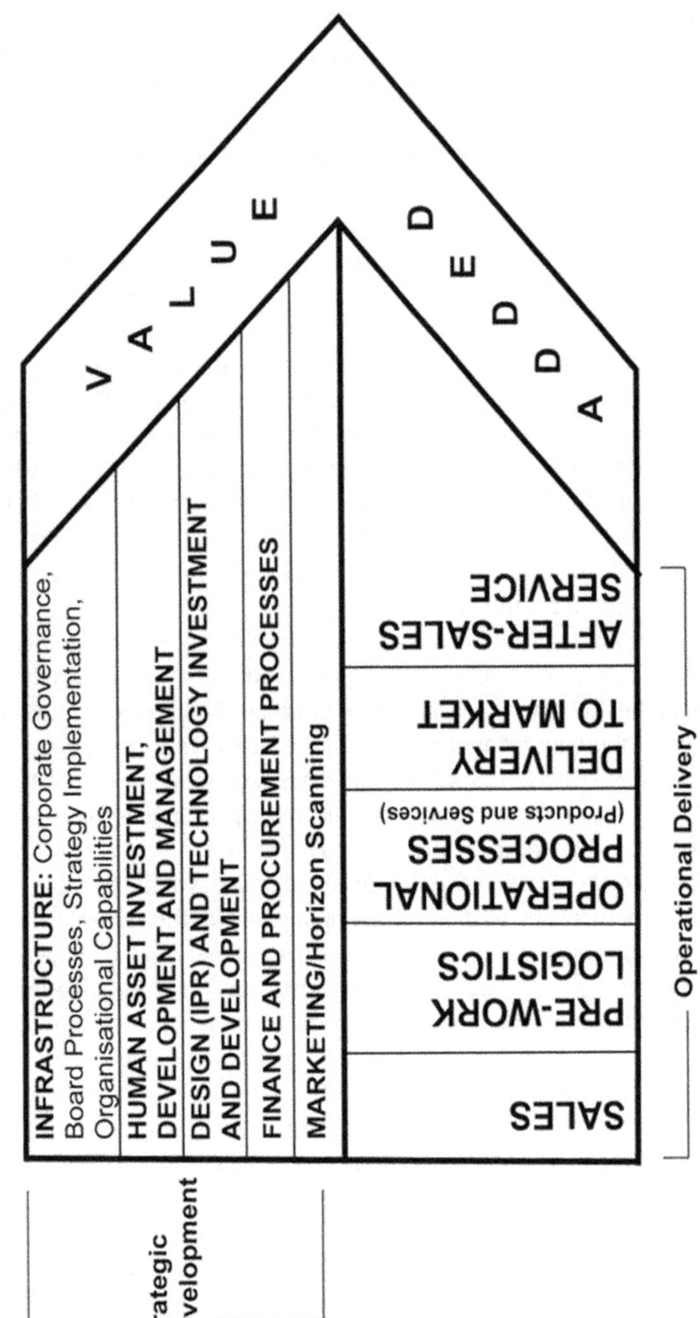

Figure 12: Value Chain.

between executives and directors, but it allows more transparency for all stakeholders. Some will also have shareholder rights to allow them to probe deeper into the decision-making processes.

Used well, all the staff, not just the executives, need to be involved in such an organisational learning process. This is their working life, and they release their learning willingly, if not always optimally. They will have positive ideas as to how to improve processes. If they are not heard, then negative behaviours can be employed that block the delivery of the offered product or service. Negative recognition is seen as better than no recognition. There is a perverse form of human satisfaction to be gained by doing the wrong things and being shouted at, if the right things are not rewarded. The delivery driver, phone or online complaints operator, can be invaluable in rapid feedback as to how customers are responding to the delivered product or service. Or they can ruin your reputation. Suitable reward systems for such real-time feedback are rarely in place or seen as cost effective, so this valuable information is rarely fed upwards.

The use of such tools as the Five Forces model and the Value Chain brings the Board up close to everyday reality in the company they direct. The Board's role is then to balance the trends from their Operational world with the wider trends from the macro-world (PPESTT) analyses. The combination of this double loop of learning is a truly professional job. It needs to be rewarded as such. Sadly, it is usually the executives who reap the big financial rewards with the directors running a poor second, often having to accept just job satisfaction plus ultimate responsibility without appropriate compensation.

This is where the power of the SWOT analysis (the perceptions of a business's Strengths and Weaknesses, Opportunities and Strengths) can be brought back into continuous organisation-wide learning. SW represents the internal company world, OT represents the dynamic external world. Everyone in an organisation is aware, consciously or unconsciously, of having a personal SWOT analysis relating to their organisation and themselves. Few are encouraged by Boards or the executives to turn this into constructive learning. Yet such personal insights are the main source of real-time data-gathering and information sifting processes.

A commonly used tool like the Value Chain, deployed as an analytical language and thinking frame for all, can help ensure better internal operational debate, insight and learning discipline. When added to the Five Forces model, it gives the Board more confidence in their decision-making in what can appear an increasingly irrational world. Sadly, much of this data can be actively suppressed if they contradict organisational politics, silos, and culture. We see this highlighted with such continuing UK inquiries as the Grenfell Tower disaster, and the Post Office Sub-postmasters scandal.

This is where Boards are wise in being seen to encourage a positive emotional temperature in their business of 'no blame' – a move to the 'good learning' culture. This is developed through an anonymous, no-blame. fault reporting system. For example, the airline and nuclear engineering industries have become skilled at ensuring rapid anonymous accident reporting coupled with the fast public publication of their investigations to reassure the public. These are growing examples of Keith Grint's 'Good learning' (Chapter Four ibid). The UK Army has developed Rapid Wash-Up sessions at the end of each daily mission with all ranks encouraged to comment, non-hierarchically and without rancour. This is seen to work well despite initial misgivings. Sadly, The UK's NHS has failed miserably to do so, despite the huge amounts of long-term national data from which they can access and learn. Many others, and especially financial services and insurance businesses, are still lagging.

Moreover, it is often forgotten by Boards that their staff members and customers are also members of their wider communities. Listening to community-based staff allow Boards to take a much wider view of their business's total performance as seen within their community eco-system. Such perspectives are rarely used regularly to investigate environmental and social impacts of the Boards' decisions.

Although there are many proprietary products on the market for each Board to choose, I stress here that every Board needs to develop and agree three basic elements to their unique strategy development process:

1) The Strategy Development Grid (as shown in this chapter),
2) The External Environment Scanning Process (as shown in chapters Four and Five),
3) The Operational Performance Monitoring Process (as seen through the Value Chain).

So, I finish this chapter by encouraging professional directors to develop and use regularly their Board's strategy development processes. They show the range of skills needed by a Level Four Maturity Board to deliver continuing organisational health.

At the centre of the 'Learning Board' process is the area of the previously mentioned 'business brain and conscience'; the area where the Board team assembles the often contradictory internal and external data and refines this into information for the strategic debates on which it makes its long-term decisions; and then creates its rapid learning systems to deal with the consequences.

Many Boards still use simplistic either/or thinking processes to strategy on the assumption that there must ultimately still be a single answer. There never is. So, their process needs to be that 'both/and' approach as advocated throughout this book. The validity of such Board debates needs constant testing by using scenarios. These are pictures of *possible* futures. Scenarios are *not* predictions. I am careful here not to use the term 'scenario planning' because this is not the world of predicting the future, nor of detailed resource allocation. That is for the executives later. Here I am looking at stretching the intellectual abilities of the Board by them creating and assessing the range of their *possible* futures.

I start by getting them to take each of the PPESTT elements and ask them in small groups to think about the many external issues that continue to worry them. What may happen in the Physical Environment in a ten-year time span; what might happen in the Political Environment in the same time and so on? Then I ask them to create on one side of paper a one-line description for each of the six PPESTT elements. The combined result is a scenario – not a prediction. They can develop as many scenarios as they like. Bringing the Board together to debate a few of the other Board member's scenarios frees up a lot of Board thinking without it being quickly blocked by demands for an immediate planning process.

If this exercise is conducted before or during, say, a quarterly Board meeting the Board becomes more sensitized to impending external environmental changes, and existing internal blockages. It is then better prepared, and toughened, for the necessary planning debates with the executives. Scenario Thinking is the core of the Level 4 Maturity Professional Board.

References

[1] Tim Marshall, Prisoners of Geography: Ten Maps That Tell You Everything You Need to Know About Global Politics, London 2016
[2] Clifford Geertz, The Interpretation of Cultures, Basic Books US, 1973
[3] UK CG Code 2014.
[4] Alan Greenspan, The Map and the Territory, 2013.
[5] IEA Path To Net Zero
[6] Michael Porter, Competitive Advantage, 1985.

Chapter 6
Issues Blocking an Integrated Learning System for Effective Corporate Governance

I know of no country that has an integrated system for defining, developing, and assessing effective corporate governance. Politicians and the public frequently talk about the urgent need for developing such competence. Little happens. This chapter describes the thinking emerging in some countries about restructuring the relationships – legal, practical, and ethical – between the key players. I define the five key players as:

- Directors,
- Legislators,
- Stakeholders,
- Regulators,
- Public Oversight.

Currently there is no agreed way of linking these into a coherent learning system. And because of the general indifference there seems little interest in doing so. However, because of the growing dissatisfaction with corporate governance incompetence there are a number of publicly aired questions about how we might design our future organisational governance. The status quo is now unsustainable because of that rumbling public disquiet. My musings here are very personal reflections on creating such a learning system. They lead to the final chapter – the Challenge for Next Generation Directors.

I know from conversations that many of the next generation directors are keen to face the challenge. This enthusiasm sits in stark contrast to the dated directors who admit to running out of steam, ideas, and motivation. They have let the early, heady, start of 1992 erode into niggling bureaucratic wrangling with only marginal gains. This is why effective corporate governance now has such low esteem in the publics' mind.

I start with the acceptance that our ineffective institutions are a continuing burden on all citizens. So, how can future directors be held accountable for seeking to resolve those global, economic, environmental, and civic, poly-crises, crucial to sustaining human existence? This is a crucial role for every director and Board to pursue in their communities, however small their individual contribution may be.

As politicians and legislators have failed to create an integrated system of corporate governance it is now up to the directors themselves to complete the task by asking tough questions publicly of all five major players. Will you commit to moving the concept of corporate governance away from finance fixation towards an integrated

 | https://doi.org/10.1515/9783112231340-006

mutual learning system including environmental and social impacts? I am optimistic but still mildly sceptical.

The Five Key Players

All five key corporate governance players should be contained within a *system* of continuous learning: But currently these five players remain unconnected. Often, they are sniping at each other. They are not a mutual learning system. They are disconnected islands in a turbulent stream and so incapable of mutual real-time development.

I am frustrated with the low quality of corporate governance at all levels of society. For example, when I started drafting this book the UK government had failed to launch its long-promised ARGA agency, has scrapped their promise of a radical overhauling of the existing corporate governance rules including proposed new audit committee reporting responsibilities on environmental, social, and governance issues, and has published instead a very middling new Code, not a structural reform. When I questioned politicians about this lack of progress, I was told that improving corporate governance could never be a party political priority. So, from being a world leader in 1992 the UK is becoming an also-ran. Sadly, no other country or institution has yet taken up a leadership role. Indeed, the recent implosion in minority shareholder protection in the leading US state of Delaware gives a dreadful example of regression.

I reprise the opening theme of this book, that most of our current leaders are not trained for their governance roles, are often ignorant of them, are not assessed as to their competence, and are too concerned with protecting their immediate personal and political role advantages to be able to give effective direction for the long-term benefit of all. They are increasingly risk-averse and do not understand, or are frightened to execute, their 'business judgement' and accept the consequent personal risk-taking involved. I argue that this is due to their lack of commitment to professionalism in directing and corporate governance. This leads to their eroding moral leadership in this key area of societal cohesion.

There is, however, growing hope, especially from the younger generations of potential directors – the Next Generation – who are much more aware of these issues. Hopefully, they will be able to rebalance the three capitals, supported by those often unreported 'iceberg' organisations whose directoral thinking and investments must be necessarily beyond short, mere political, timespans. I refer to the Family Offices, the Sovereign Wealth Funds, the bond traders, and those private investors who must always invest across generations. These are usually outside media scrutiny and public awareness and are, therefore, under-researched. Yet they have massive funds, bigger than many stock exchanges, possibly totalling hundreds of trillions of dollars. Given the more inclusive and community-based values of many of these next generation directors I see them having an increasingly positive and integrative influence on the direction of future national and international investment and corporate governance.

A More Systems-based Approach to Corporate Governance

I have no magic solution to creating a brave new world of effective corporate governance, except that resolution must start with the public and politicians breaking the social silence by admitting that there is not yet a system; and one needs to be built. This will build on open, regular, and communal discussion, and learning of the importance that effective governance is to social cohesion and the development of our human society.

Recognising the Unresolved Questions for the Five Stakeholder Groups

I have been developing some ideas as I travel the continents. I am convinced of two things. First, that the solid legal foundations laid down 50 years ago in the Company law of the UK and Commonwealth are still unique, robust, necessary, and transferable internationally. They are the foundation stones of my learning system. But they require much better implementation, testing and mutual development, especially through case law.

Second, that any proposed structural solutions (the easy bit for bureaucrats) must include the creation of new networks of continuous learning (the difficult bit). Corporate governance needs to return to its roots to create a much more cybernetic approach to its growth. Currently the five main players are so fragmented that they rarely speak regularly even with just one other party, let alone all of them. And then rarely as part of the public discourse. Nowhere is there a co-ordinated systems-based, focused debating forum to allow such regular learning. This lack of connection and continuity means that it is not possible to create an ecology of learning for mutual benefit. I do detect a growing demand for such linkages internationally but so far without leaders.

So, in this chapter I suggest some starter questions for all five groups to stimulate such debates. The energy needed for such a wider reframing must come from many more diverse folk, well beyond the current establishment players and especially beyond the worlds of finance and accountancy.

Many of these new perspectives and energies will come from the insights of younger directors. They will design their future and learn to reject the current laxity and restricted perspectives of dated politicians and corporate governance practitioners. This gives me hope. There are growing signs of innovation far beyond the 'Western' mindset. Some small states are seeking to develop effective corporate governance to cope with their existential issues. They seek to use the risks and rewards of national scale entrepreneurship to effect economic growth while ensuring social and environmental sustainability. These emerging Small Smart States – like Qatar, Botswana, Estonia, Trinidad, Armenia, Jamaica and Jordan – aspire to become more like Switzerland and Singapore. Westerners will need to face the humility of having to learn co-operatively with such innovators from other geographies.

However, I have not entirely given up on the present generation of directors internationally. Indeed, it would be churlish of me to do so both because there are some outstanding current advocates, male and female, creating their organisations' futures through developing the good practice I mention in the context for this book. Indeed, I acknowledge that those who do seek to improve have provided four decades of income for me.

The final part of this chapter contains my experiences in facing the unresolved questions needed to restructure corporate governance. I seek answers to seemingly intractable governance questions that appear in all nations.

For a sustainable future we must pose these questions openly, and demand that all five players answer them honestly and co-operatively. Then we can learn more systematically how to create a professional, and ethical system of corporate governance. However, it will need also a parallel, more informed and energised public to keep asking these questions; and asking and asking, until they get reasonable answers from the other four existing players and ensure accountability.

Seven Unresolved Questions for Legislators

1 Why are the legislated Duties of a Director, and the Purpose Of A Board, not treated as the backbone of the Commonwealth's case-law approach to Effective Corporate Governance?

At the risk of over-repetition, I demand acceptance of the Seven Duties of a Director are under Section 171 of the UK Companies Act 2006 and the six aspects of the Purpose of a Board under Section 172 be built into every director's induction oath.

Such a mandatory 'declaration' or oath at registration would position corporate governance competence and assessment as a key stabilising force in our society. This is of increasing importance as we enter the complex polycrises looming in geopolitical environments.

There is an obvious lack of political commitment in many countries to encourage prosecution in the civil and criminal courts to test the legislators' intentions on corporate governance. More, and faster, case-law decisions would bring many directors quickly to adopt a more professional line, or get them to drop out of their directoral roles altogether.

2 Why do legislators have no regular monitoring of the effects of their legislation?

It takes much time and political infighting to pass a law, so why do legislators have no regular reporting system to monitor the effects of their legislation? The passing of a law seems to be seen as the end of the political process; not the start of continuous learning to test the validity of that law. For example, the UK's 2006 Companies Act took some eight years to go through both Houses of Parliament and yet little has been heard of its implementation since, despite the 2008 global financial crash which featured institutional failure in major banks. There are plenty of business scandals and a few court cases to study and test the validity of this law. Who in parliament is responsible for monitoring its implementation and refinement? Why is there no independent public body to do so?

3 Why is there no nationally agreed all-party declaration on the fundamental importance of effective corporate governance being the foundation of our national institutions – public, private, and not-for-profit?

I argue for political parties to agree a Compact on the primary importance of effective corporate governance in all the organisations working within their national boundaries.

4 Why do legislators confuse themselves and the public by allowing unlawful and lax use of the word 'director?'

For example, do we really want the current use of the word 'director' to cover everyone from a person setting up a £50 company to the leaders of a multinational? Why do we obscure the clarity of the statutory basic law by allowing the random, non-legally defined, use of such phrases as 'Executive Director', 'Non-executive Director', 'Executive Chairman', and 'Senior Independent Director'? And this is before the fashionable yet legally meaningless importation of such US titles as 'Vice President' or 'President'. All of these have become used and abused lazily in secondary legislation, especially in the financial sector, without ever being tested in primary law. Many of the words and titles used have no statutory base but are treated as though they were Gospel.

5 Why has no government faced the issue of clarifying company Ownership?

Why has no-one attempted to resolve the puzzle left by the 1890 Salomons' Judgement as to who owns a company? If we continue to have our economic system based on a 'legal fiction' (an increasingly doubtful proposition), then can we at least clarify the daily operational consequences?

6 Why do governments encourage the growth of money laundering, modern slavery, and corrupt payments by creating legal entities to protect them?

Why is it considered legitimate to allow the deliberate obscuring of the ultimate, beneficial ownership of a company by, for example, creating Limited Liability Partnerships? These are proven to be used as fronts for money laundering, corrupt payments, and modern slavery. It seems impossible to find out who the legal owners are behind such entities, with consequential issues of the real sources of funding. Yet there is little public knowledge of, or outcry against, such usage. There are no current serious attempts by legislators to stop them.

7 Will you advocate strongly for a globally accepted comprehensive corporate reporting system?

The estimable Mervyn King of South Africa is rightly campaigning for a global system of accounting and corporate governance reporting. He wants a global level playing field. This is a long fight against massive odds. The need is obvious both for developing effective corporate governance and for allowing more rational investment decisions, nationally and internationally. Why is there so little interest in so doing? Surely the transparency being advocated will benefit all.

These are just some of the questions that need answering by our legislators. Sadly, the legislators continue to dabble in adjusting the minutia of corporate governance codes, and rules, and then commission yet more inquiries, rather than return to the basic law and face the structural weaknesses of the lack of implementation of their own legislation.

Five Unresolved Questions for Future Directors

The essence of this book contains five fundamental questions for existing and future directors.

1 On registration will you commit by oath to your fellow directors and the public to live by the legislated Duties of a Director and the Purpose of a Board?

2 As a registered director will you accept the need to, and budget sufficient personal time to, develop your necessary competences?

3 Does your Board have the systems in place for effective director selection, induction, development, competence, accreditation, and deselection?

Given the emergence of the polycrises, will you have the humility to use an 'intelligent naivety' approach to widen your future perspective to learn better to cope with the uncertain future? I keep in mind the Peter Drucker quote that *trying to predict the future is like driving backwards down an unlit country road at night using only the rearview mirror.*

4 Will you strive to build your business model and business judgment on more integrative sustainable lines – linking your deployment of the three capitals of finance, environment, and community with more systematic learning between your Board, the legislators, stakeholders, regulators, and public oversight?

5 Do you recognise that you are held publicly accountable for the four issues stated above?

If a director and their Board can answer these five fundamental questions positively, then they are on the way to creating a future Professional Board.

Two Unresolved Questions for Stakeholders

1 Who is now a 'stakeholder'? The long-held notion in the West that only shareholders 'owned' a company has been eroded both by the legal facts under Common Law, and the fast-growing pressures from community and environmental groups to ensure that their 'emotional ownership' of corporations is raised to equal importance as the shareholder 'owners' when making a board's future business judgements. The younger generation directors are more aware of these stakeholder pressures and the consequent need to rebalance the Three Capitals. The rebalancing of future ownership power is central to this.

2 How will stakeholders resolve this ownership issue? I still find this messy and intractable. It involves facing increasing controversy in those areas of society, environment, ethics and accountability, previously considered well beyond the normal remit of 'business'. It is an area where cool rationality hits strong emotions mixed with deep personal and political values.

The question of ownership creates strong reactions. The economic and social history of the world, especially the Western world, is played out by the Board in a three-dimensional game of corporate governance chess. On one dimension the current political debates between 'free markets' and 'communism' continue their dialogue of the deaf. On another very different dimension more inclusive and co-operative values are being prioritised by many of the next generation and increasingly the Small Smart

States. And on the third dimension, time and circumstances create changing risk and opportunity.

To allow me to stay sane, I currently categorise the confusing issue of defining stakeholders into three broad categories:

- Financial Stakeholders
- Internal Operational Players
- External Environmental and Community Players

And then I add the dimensions of:

- Legal Ownership
- Emotional Ownership

The legal ownership issues are clearly shown in the Introduction and Demystifying sections of this book. However, the emotional issues are less explicit. They are a deep aspect of suppressed social mistrust and power wants and needs. Think of the emotional ownership of a sports team, a city or region, a political party, or a religion. There is usually little immediate connection with legal ownership, but massive emotional ownership. A decision that a dispassionate legal shareholder might consider as following logical business judgement can create huge opposition in a socially dynamic, media-influenced community. This is often reflected in 'knee jerk' local opposition to business proposals. All stakeholders have their roles to play in creating a healthy business. Yet few talk with each other in a positive and regular way.

My experience in this area applies as much to not-for-profits, state-owned enterprises, and community businesses as to private sector companies. Indeed, the former's strong emotional ownership roots are often the drivers of their successes but also of their many failures.

Four Unresolved Questions for Financial Stakeholders

A prelude to the questions: Throughout my non-career I have experienced the deep tensions between financial 'investors' and 'traders'. The capitalist concept of long-term investment to ensure a steady, growing return over many years is still fundamental to my meaning of 'finance'. The importance of the survival of pension schemes, insurance companies, Family Offices, and Sovereign Wealth Funds is key to my understanding. The sums involved are so large that, when combined, they, rather than mega-corporations, are the foundations of much current Western wealth. They provide most of the finance of governmental and social services and, hopefully, the public's discretionary spending.

But things became distorted, noticeably in the US and UK, when the opening up of the financial markets encouraged short-term gamblers and agents for new funds to become greedy. Indeed, greed was considered 'good' by many. The quest for immediate profits was upgraded to become the apex of the new international financial system.

And traders, including many CEOs, were greatly over-rewarded for such immediacy. Many became fixated on having to make rapidly rising short-term profits, the antithesis of long-term investing. Matters became worse as many agents were set short-term performance targets, often quarterly, which led to the inevitable 'market churning' to create specious returns. A cancerous sub-industry was developed with little public outcry, except on a rare, big-impact event such as the short-termist, risky trades that resulted in the financial crash of 2008 (discussed later in this chapter).

Little value was added to these 'investments' but the traders had learned how to manipulate the system to create seemingly continuous positive returns. The rise and rise of such fund managers and traders combined with the arrival of 'venture capitalists'. Their business model was too often to take an underperforming company, load it with debt, 'improve' its performance by immediate heavy cost cutting, pay hefty dividends to the shareholders and themselves, and ensure that they left the business within four years before the obvious grim long-term consequences of their short-term actions became manifest. The same model was used in many countries for the 'privatisations' of national utilities.

I see these political and ethical battles played out daily on social media with increasing public anger, disgust and intolerance. I understand that in such emotional battles players are liable to take sides, and then to restrict their information flows to reinforce their values at the expenses of the opposition. Their choice of self-reinforcing social media algorithms will then drive them to more extreme views without consideration of any opposing views. But this is not the stance that a professional Board takes. Their social media 'likes' need always to be treated with great care.

Watching the widening mix of stakeholders, I am increasingly worried by such bi-polar thinking and decision-making, especially the much higher risk-taking involved. To balance my thinking, I review the Purpose of my clients' organisations and work with them on creating an agreed grid based on how they wish to position themselves; prioritised on their judgement of their basic business dilemmas:

- Short-term focus versus Long-term focus,
- Individualistic focus vs Community focus,
- Immediate gratification vs Patient integrative gain,
- Over-reliance on Debt vs Avoidance of Debt.

Drawing such a weighted grid with a board can be a revelation. It usually creates much debate as to what are the scarce resources and values the company will deploy to create their future.

This is such a contentious area that I stick closely to the Common Law findings that shareholders do not own companies. They can influence strategy through their votes but should not intervene in the daily operations of a business.

So, my **Five Questions for Financial Stakeholders** are:

1 How clearly and publicly stated is your business model?

Do your investors, especially the pensions funds and insurers representing the savings of millions of citizens, understand your model, and the short, medium, and long-term business judgements within that model? And do the Boards in which you are investing agree with you? In other words, does it work?

2 How have you balanced your tactics for short-term gains with your long-term value-added strategy?

Many businesses still only exist for the short-term perspective, especially since the global pandemic. They survive mainly on the easy availability of low interest rates and the unwillingness of governments to force closures. This began changing in 2023 as interest rates rose closer towards historic norms. Given the growing popularity of market-tracking investors, I wonder about the continuing viability of such 'impatient', shareholder/traders, fund managers, Private Equity, and many forms of venture capital. The days of a debt laden 'investment' coupled with a quick exit seem in retreat.

This may be good news for 'patient' investors as they can then adopt a more Warren Buffet-style approach of seeking out undervalued businesses, or exciting new ventures with long-term potential, in which to invest and develop their value over the decades.

3 How long can the concept of your company continue as merely a financial entity when the demands of the other two capitals of Community and the Environment are backed by rising legislation and popular discontent?

The next generation questions the singular focus on finance and values of much current business 'success', For example, the majority acceptance by the next gens of the need to strive for NetZero or its equivalent by 2050 means the conscious phasing out of fossil fuels and their substitution by new technologies, as part of the urgent need to counter climate change and biodiversity reduction. How will your Board widen their investment perspective to cope?

4 Can your investment strategy help the company ensure that its espoused ethical values and behaviours exclude instant personal gratification, and consequent greed, and encourage more thoughtful, integrative, and longer-term business judgements?

My concerns here are two-fold. First, that simple greed is both an addiction and morally indefensible, and that addiction is a foundation of the current 'free market' religion that is now deeply embedded in much Western business. For example, note the rise and rise of 'day traders' especially in the US, as a relatively easy, yet obsessive, money-making life-style choice. This leads to the massively increased daily churn of stocks and shares without adding any real value to them. The middlemen in such a system always take their cut which guarantees their cashflow, but to what societal end?

Second, successful unrestricted greed leads to monopolies which consequently hurt communities, cultures, and the environment. For example, we see the meteoric rises in the share prices of Google. Meta, X, and now Artificial Intelligence, from mere start-ups to globally dominating their fields in a handful of years. And the long-term benefits and problems of cryptocurrencies are yet to be tested. They had little time to consider their environmental, community, and cultural impacts. That slogan 'move fast and break things' is based more on the rush to create a monopoly than the excitement of pure innovation. Easy money and that impulsion to load acquired companies with heavy debt has created a culture of short-term trader non-investors expecting unreasonably large immediate returns to shareholders. This is without consideration of the longer-term consequences for the company, the environment, or the community. FTX and Theranos, companies that ended in scandal, exhibited these traits.

5 Have you helped the board truly consider the consequences of their proposed Debt/Equity ratio on their future trading?

Four Unresolved Questions for Operational 'Internal' Stakeholders

When financiers could simply assume that the Board in which they had invested could tell the managers and workforce what to do and this would be done without question, business life was easy. Compliance and unquestioning submission reigned. However, in the West, Japan, and to a lesser extent China and Russia, we see the combined effects of rapidly declining populations, rising education levels, changing social values, digitisation, social media, an over-reliance on globalisation, and growing mass migration all creating a polycrisis at the operational levels of businesses.

The global Covid pandemic illustrated strongly that an adherence to 'just-in-time' deliveries, long supply lines, workforce disruption, and customer uncertainty has forced a rapid rethink on the validity of these assumptions. This has caused a major rethink of value chains and their relation to the internal stakeholders – the staff, the suppliers, and to a growing extent the customers, as demonstrated in Chapter Five. Although the pandemic is over, elevated levels of uncertainty have persisted, so the switch from 'just-in-time' cost efficiency to resilience has continued. This development reinforces the need for the Board of Directors to fulfil its second corporate governance role of 'ensuring prudent control' of the business.

So, I ask four questions of the internal control system, especially the managers, regarding these newly evolving 'stakeholders':

1 Have you created a robust and continuous Board Dashboard through which the Board, management, and operational suppliers can monitor instantly disruptions, and learn quickly to improve their performances on behalf of the wider stakeholders?

Within that framework how will you track continuously such issues as:

2 People – especially the employment conditions, educational improvement, social contracts, and increasingly the imposed external legal aspects on your people on such issues as modern slavery, diversity, corruption, anti-money laundering etc.

3 Suppliers – how will you monitor the future robustness of your supply chains that ensure your business and services continuity?

   The Covid-19 crisis and the later wartime disruptions to shipping channels have resulted in rapidly diminished use of just-in-time delivery processes, and increased the need for ensuring both alternative suppliers and buffer stocks to maintain quality and quantity standards. This has had a knock-on effect on costs that is unlikely to go away. How will you keep your suppliers on board? For example, will you contract with them better cashflow payments to guarantee mutual continuity of supplies in difficult times?

4 Customers – will the Board Dashboard allow it and the management to stay in constant touch with customer trends, both in terms of developing appropriate goods and services, and monitoring the social trends that affect the public perception of your business?

This can be a sensitive area; trust in a company can be affected when it declares one set of values and follows another. How will the Board ensure that the company is not accused frequently of 'washing', green or otherwise?

Three Unresolved Questions for Environmental and Community Stakeholders

This is where emotionality, personal values and deep beliefs meet the cold logic of legality and precedent. It is where a Board needs to be able to keep its parallel contradictions in play long enough to devise a both/and solution.

I have little doubt that the 'stakeholders' of an organisation – private, public, or not-for-profit – will have a bigger voice around the boardroom table in future. How much of a voice and what power they have in operational and strategic thinking, (but not decision making as this remains the Board's prerogative), depends on the specific circumstances and the complex interplay of their unique powers of finance, community and environmental resources. Sadly, most of these powers are currently seen as being in opposition to each other. There are good historic reasons for this. Yet the polycrises are now forcing all five players to reconsider their positions to demand co-operation to reach, for example, Net Zero by 2050.

So, my three questions are:

1 Do you accept that you are facing a polycrisis which threatens your organisation's existence?

Since the Covid-19 pandemic we have seen a noticeable drop in outright resistance to such a question as wars, wildfires, floods and mass migrations are creating a new public perception of reality.

2 Are you seeking to form a compact with the other four governance players to be able to reach your aspirational target?

I am hoping to bring together for debate and development all five players at national and international levels. The environmental and community lobbies will inevitably have a more powerful future say in the debate. The 2024 Lord Mayor of London Mike Mainelli's concept and practice of recreating the informal London 'coffee shops' as havens for democratic off-line testing and debating of often contradictory ideas seems to fit this well and is to be encouraged greatly. Who will set up the coffee shops?

3 Are you willing to accept that if co-operation is a better path to mutual salvation, then the old conflict models need to be dropped?

Some NGOs now use social media opposition as a way of life, even as a source of funds. This can be a block to co-operation. I have come across too many examples in my travels. Typically, it occurs when the vocal opponents of a proposed new project suddenly win their case and have to assume leadership. Some find it very hard to accept and prefer to maintain their oppositional lifestyle rather than accept their new responsibilities.

The worst case of this I saw concerned the development of a massive oil pipeline crossing three countries which would affect the lives of hundreds of indigenous tribes. Several international NGOs were outraged by the project and led a long and ultimately successful campaign that gave the local people (who were not opposed in principle) the rights to determine the precise path of the pipeline and many of its environmental, and social, consequences. I was wrong-footed when the NGO's then questioned the locals' carefully fought-for decisions. The NGOs thought that they should now lead the project and take the final decisions as they 'knew better' than the locals. They were deeply offended when they were, in turn, accused by the locals of 'imperialism' and seen by them as no better than the oil company executives they had so recently opposed. The NGO assumed that the power of corporate governance was too important to be left to the tribes.

Four Unresolved Questions for Regulators

1 Will you agree to work towards an integrated national learning system with directors, legislators, and stakeholders to allow more open public oversight, debate and fast sharing of future corporate governance learning and development?

2 Will you agree to pause on the creation of new codes and regulations until a time when there is an agreed integrated national learning system in place?

A sub-theme of this book has been my concern that regulators, often administrators inexperienced in this specialist field, are charged by politicians to oversee the corporate governance sector, unaided. Too many see their success in the number of additional regulations and codes they can generate and impose. They cling to 'the metrics' as if for their own dear life. Too few are willing to take the hard road of advocating creating case-law to clarify existing issues. My view is that this just adds more bandages to an already suffering body. At some point the patient dies of asphyxiation. Let us release the bandages until we are back to the basic legislation and then learn mutually from all five players how to create a healthily regulated national system. Let sunshine be the best disinfectant.

3 Can Corporate Governance Regulation Act More like Rugby Referees?

I have asked this question earlier but feel it worth another airing. I see and discuss the issue with many regulators. They are often confused by their roles and scared that their lack of knowledge and skills in the corporate governance area will be exposed in public. They are therefore likely to be in thrall to vocal but ignorant politicians. I have mentioned that such dated regulators act more like soccer referees – even with video-assisted referee (VAR), issuing immediate penalties only after an infringement and without immediate detailed explanation. I notice that by contrast, in rugby the role of the referee has developed in a very different way. There the referee is running with the game in real-time and issuing warnings *before* offences are committed. Penalties are given for infringements but there is little dissent by the players as the warnings had been given. How can this model be adapted for corporate governance?

One way I notice is in the emergence, particularly in non-Western countries, of early experiments in strengthening the role of the registered Company Secretary – an officer of the Board – to become something akin to the rugby referee; running with the strategic and day-to-day operational packs and able to offer instant warnings of infringements of the law before they are committed. Such instant warnings and internal consultations with the Company Secretary and Legal Counsel can resolve matters rapidly and cost effectively. They are more likely to be accepted and recorded. This strikes me as a useful way forward which, when combined with strengthened whistleblower legal rights for staff members, can encourage better Board and managerial decisions.

4 Quis custodiet ipsos custodes?

But my lasting concern is who will guard the guards themselves? For two millennia the question 'Quis custodiet ipsos custodes?' has been of prime historical importance for governance issues.

Currently with the lack of legislative responsibility and learning following the passing of an Act or Ordinance, I argue that no one is accountable for guarding the guards. That is where my proposed national corporate governance oversight system is needed.

Unresolved Issues if the Public is to Oversee Effective Corporate Governance

I see the public as the future stewards of effective corporate governance. Most are unaware of their potential role. Currently they experience the consequences of the existing fragmented system but have no part in it. My emphasis here is on building sufficient public confidence to hold the other four players to account by asking discerning questions, especially of the current under-performing Boards and legislators. Building public interest and knowledge will encourage the next generation to develop a more structured, systems-learning approach to integrate all five concerned parties.

What is needed is a more pragmatic, grass roots approach which diffuses learning rapidly through the next generation of directors sharing newly learned good practice, underpinned by the ancient community values of accountability, probity and transparency. We need to build more inclusive, caring, corporate governance communities.

Integrating The Five Main Players

Proposed inter-connectedness of the five major players

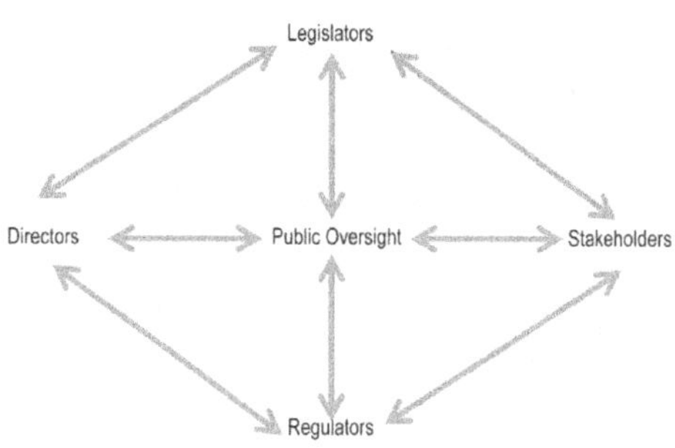

Chapter Four: Figure One: *The need for future inter-connectedness of the 5 major players*

Figure 13: Five Major Players.

The current 'players' – stakeholders, directors, legislators, regulators, the public – are too fragmented and isolated. Because the public are unaware of the Duties of Directors, and the Purpose of a Board, there is little pressure from them for directors, stakeholders, legislators, and regulators to speak constructively with each other or the public. There are no regular public debating fora for them to exchange ideas and information. There are no 'corporate governance coffee shops' to debate ideas and practice. And there is no regular public oversight of the total process. Each may have an increasingly urgent need to speak with another, but the idea of learning openly from each other on a regular basis is only considered in a national emergency.

I am increasingly optimistic that the great majority of the current 'blockers' of effective corporate governance – legislators, regulators. 'owners', fund managers, sham 'directors', plus public ignorance and apathy – can be re-educated at little cost to become active advocates of sustainable, effective corporate governance. It is in all of their interests. The existential context is only too obvious to allow the prevailing stand off to continue.

Improving Our Rate of Public Learning

I have highlighted the growing number of unanswered questions that all five parties must resolve to ensure a viable future for them, their successor organisations, and their communities. Throughout my working life I have used the concept that:

> *In an increasingly turbulent world, our rate of learning must be equal to, or greater than, the rate of environmental change (L ≥ C)*

to quote Professor Reg Revans [1]. Developing such elevated consciousness by applying action learning – open learning and feedback in real time – to our daily directoral activities is the key to future governance sustainability.

How can we increase this rate of learning? Few will now argue that our economies, communities, and environments will return automatically to the old normal. Turbulent geopolitics, climate change, demographic destabilisation, mass migration, continuing economic, social, and geographic instability, bio-diversity collapse, and political polarisation, amongst many other international issues, will generate growing risks and uncertainties that will test all directors' and legislators' resolve and intellect. This is why I advocate all five parties learning how to use and debate, for example, PPESTT analyses, buddy pairs, and dashboards to get the ball rolling.

How Can Companies and the Public Combine to Integrate a Learning Approach Nationally and Internationally?

My argument is that in a dysfunctional world, where national and international power groupings are failing to provide good national and corporate governance, the primary burden for creating a sustainable human future will rest firmly on directors – private, public, and not-for-profit. Politicians cannot do this. Directors must take those key decisions to reallocate their scarce resources and ensure prudent control of their often-modest companies. Each company's learning may be partial and only marginally significant but combined with the learning of many others it has a multiplier effect. I know that a bottom-up approach of mass learning within and between companies, shared regionally, nationally, and internationally, can be highly effective.

At first hearing this may sound impossible. But we know that the diffusion of continuous and co-operative learning from these many organisations an international dialogue, knowledge base, and intellectually tested framework, can be created that will affect the long-term effectiveness of future corporate governance and improve community health.

It is significant that autocrats in many countries have learned to pass conspiracy laws that start by indicting just two energised persons. They have learned such small combinations can challenge the status quo. Larger scale bottom-up approaches can be very effective in creating change, when combined with informal internet-based groupings that bloom into wider public movements.

The fundamental question that such national and international co-operative learning must answer is clear – how do we ensure effective direction in a turbulent world whilst keeping our organisations under prudent control, and within the key values of accountability, probity, and transparency? Equally clear is that state controlled, 'big bang' solutions of even more legislation and more sanctions cannot resolve the complexity of the human condition within our organisations. Humans need discretionary power and will always use their creativity to game the system. In a time of great public disillusion with our organisations these top-down solutions are being rejected rightly as bureaucratic, expensive, and doomed to failure through lack of commitment by any of the participants.

To Design a Constructive Future You Must Understand the Past: 1776 and all that

But then Boards ask, 'How can I do this?' Having read this far you will not be surprised that my response starts not with an instant, simplistic, answer but by exploring with a Board a longer-term historical perspective to help them reset their conceptual frameworks, raise their strategic foresight, and broaden their business opportunities. I seek to refocus their entrepreneurial energies towards higher levels of optimistic aspiration for their and humankind's benefit. I ask the reader's indulgence for the next five pages as I conduct my own international historical review as an example of the type of conversations from which we learn.

The Age of Enlightenment Spawned the Age of Unenlightened 'Hard' Business.

Readers of my earlier books will know that I am intrigued by the year 1776, and the positive and negative step changes towards human development brought about during this Age of Enlightenment. Here commerce, science, arts, technology, and moral philosophy converged seeming initially to herald a more liberal, challenging, richer, and evolutionary Western world. The idea of *doux commerce,* or soft capitalism, was advocated strongly by such thinkers as Montesquieu, Voltaire, and Adam Smith to counter examples of the growing rapacity of the new business and self-serving political greed personified by such as the British, Dutch, and Danish East India Companies.

The year 1776 saw the near simultaneous publication of Adam's Smith's *The Wealth Of Nations* (which has shaped much of Western moral and political thinking through the concepts of the importance of Moral Philosophy and Business Economics); the publication of Jean Jacques Rousseau's *The Social Contract* (which advocated human liberty and the development of more democratic institutions); and the Declaration Of Independence in the nascent United States (whose political and economic consequences are still under critical assessment because they combined slavery with a concept of democracy). These three texts helped create the optimistically beneficial base for the modern Western world.

This convergence was hailed by many intellectuals as the start of a brave new world. As in every revolution it over-promised and under-delivered. But it went horribly wrong when the destructive aspects of 'hard' commerce overtook the notion of 'soft commerce'. This led to industrial capitalism, empire building, and increasingly rampant greed by business titans seeking monopolies and forced labour. In turn this disregarded the interests of the physical environment and local communities. It still does. Yet I find that most of the next generation of directors are increasingly aware of these contradictions and the consequent deterioration of the organisational world they will inherit. They want to do something to correct this for their organisation. They seem ready to accept the *Ent + EnvI + SocI + Acc + BM = ECG (Effective Corporate Governance)* axiom. Indeed, some have welcomed it as an antidote to the last throes of the current increasingly corrupted Western business world order.

Voltaire's notion of 'gentle mercantilism' was quickly lost and the business model grew away from the medieval merchant adventurers and their personal risk-taking and, backed by the much-improved technologies in shipbuilding, navigation, new sources of finance, and limited liability, moved towards the mass exploitation of others by corporations. The colonialist flag followed trade, enthusiastically backed by emergent big business.

For example, although trade combined with slavery has existed throughout recorded history, as seen in Assyria, Phoenicia, Greece, Rome, The Vikings, Portugal, Spain, the African, Chinese, South American and Arab worlds, it later helped create a supercharged European business model. This grew rapidly from the granting of Royal Charters in England, Denmark, Sweden, Holland, and later the creation of similar business models in France, Belgium, Italy, and Germany. 'Hard business' models were created more intent on monopolistic domination than peaceful trade. For example, in 1601 in the UK The Honourable the Irish Company was allowed by the English government the 'settlement' of what is now Northern Ireland, 'planting' large numbers of Scottish settlers, as a political and religious initiative, backed strongly by finance from the Livery Companies of the City of London.

A different model was to lease 'uninhabited' Caribbean countries like Barbados to indentured white English farmers (originally with their six black slaves). A similar Charter was granted in 1606 to develop The Virginia Company at which time there were four times as many white settlers in the Caribbean than in the East Coast of the nascent United States of America. The trades in tobacco, sugar, and then slaves became highly profitable and many 'adventurers' exploited these opportunities. The Age of Unenlightened Hard Business began to run uneasily in parallel to the aspiration of the Age of Enlightenment. In 1600 the East India Company was formed. It grew to have its own army and civil service and rejoiced in its piratical and privateering origins in South Asia. Its increasingly outrageous behaviour was only brought to heel by the UK government in 1858.

The 'Royal Adventurers of England Trading With Africa Company' was established in 1672 based on a more mechanised and rationalised business model. This was fundamental to the industrial growth of the slave trade. It created a profitable triangle of trade taking manufactured goods from Europe to Africa, slaves from Africa to the Caribbean and nascent US, and sugar and tobacco back to Europe. The money was good and the morals low – often explained away by the adventurers and clergy as 'bringing civilisation to the natives'.

This corrupting and popular business model was the antithesis of what Voltaire, Adam Smith, and Rousseau were advocating with their 'soft' capitalism ideas. However, companies in France, Spain, Portugal, the Netherlands, and the growing United States joined in greedily. This was despite the latter's paradoxical support for the French Revolution and the idea of Freedom, Egality and Fraternity. African leaders and Arab traders expanded their historical business interests by capturing slaves and driving them to the profitable West African coast. There were notable ironies. For example, in Barbados many of the original indentured English and Scottish agricultural workers could not repay their bonds, let alone buy their promised land, and so became effectively white slaves, often inter-marrying with the later flood of black West African slaves. And the very ships that had carried slaves later became part of the growing UK anti-slave trade naval patrols from the mid-1770s until the UK's abolition of the slave trade in 1807, and the banning of slave ownership in 1833. I note also that African Corsair pirates were still on slaving raids for white women on the south coast of England in the late eighteenth century. These contradictions were noted by a growing politicised public and helped create the anti-slavery movements, the growth of trades unions and an increasingly literate and enfranchised working class following the UK's Reform Act of 1832.

The Modern Context

Although many Western nations and businesses became wealthy through this expansion of world trade, the consequences back home were not a boon for all. The newly emerging working class benefited little as they moved in large numbers from the countryside to the rapidly expanding and unhealthy towns and cities. They responded by organising into trades unions to protect their interests, and fight slavery. There was growing public awareness that 'big business' and its strong financial links to governments were not good for them. I find this perception is still a very strong and widely held view internationally. It simmers just below the surface in so many countries and companies. The 'Them and Us' perception is well-established. The age of unenlightened government and governance persists.

For example, during my travels I am frequently reminded of an event that has stuck in the public mind globally despite it occurring in 2005. It is a turning point in the world's perception of the US. I, and millions of people around the world, was shocked by the US Government's slow response to its own citizens' plight following the devastation of Hurricane Katrina. Ordinary folk in Africa and Asia watched their TV screens and were astounded that the US government did not seriously help their own citizens for nearly two weeks. The devastation of one of the worst storms for over 100 years, plus the slow response times, shocked and disillusioned these overseas observers about the priorities and benefits of reputedly top Western 'governance". Until then most had accepted a rosy picture of the US being the most advanced and socially integrated country in the world which would automatically help any of its citizens in distress immediately. The image of the US's streets being lined with gold – 'the gold mountain' – was then still prevalent. When this became visibly untrue it fed general distrust of both US government and the governance of their institutions.

Many people began to ask two basic questions: First, is the US really a nation that comprehensively cares for all its citizens? They realised slowly that the answer might be 'no'. Second, they then began to question the quality and quantity of effective US government and corporate governance. I was shocked at how shocked and naïve the global public were. It is to counter such growing public doubt and incredulity that rising next generation directors must respond by breaking the silence on corporate governance.

The 2007 – 2010 Western Financial Crisis

Matters were then made much worse in the public's mind by examples of excessive business greed, particularly in the US. The Western Financial Crisis of 2007–2010 and its continuing consequences was the trigger that undermined much public confidence in government and organisational governance globally. This confidence has not been restored. Consequentially, trust in our leaders continues to fester. This financial crisis was triggered by the sub-prime mortgages scandal in the US. At first it seemed impossible to imagine that it happened in an assumed sane world built on the values of business equity, justice, customer satisfaction, and moral sentiment.

But it was horribly true, and at its most blatant in the US, where rampant financial greed was suddenly highlighted as being consciously against the longer-term interests of customers, bankers, shareholders, the financial system, and the nation itself. The essence of the sub-prime mortgage scandal was to assume that a few traders can make short-term gains at the expense of the nation by selling long-term mortgages to people who they knew would not be able to repay. This was unethical, unlawful, and almost certainly criminal. It was against the longer-term community good. It grew out of a response to 'monetising' the depressed US housing market and the search for 'creative', financially engineered, short-term, ways of stimulating profits regardless of the long-term consequences.

Many bankers, insurers, fund managers, and credit ratings agencies focused enthusiastically on creating these instruments for immediate gain. A new financial field was developed rapidly and without probity. New financial instruments such as 'mortgage-backed securities' and 'collateralised debt obligations' were launched on to a greedy market. I argue that at the heart of these new instruments was a morally rotten concept – that of bundling many bad mortgages into a tradeable instrument because it was topped by a highly doubtful triple A credit rating. This latter then made it possible to trade these bundles on open exchanges to the detriment of the public. It was a corrupt game of pass-the-parcel which initially made very attractive paper profits provided no-one dropped the parcel, or opened it.

In the short-term such bundles created large profits for the traders. But as soon as the mortgagees failed to pay their mortgages such bundles stank like rotting fish. The resulting foreclosures panic by the banks and fund managers who were financing the game led to the financial crisis and, because of their real-time links, the potential global meltdown of national financial centres. Short-term disaster was avoided by central banks hurriedly combining to declare massive zero-rate lending facilities especially through the creation of 'quantitative easing'. The debilitating long-term consequences of this to national economies are still being felt as interest rates rise towards 'normal'. Public disillusionment with their governmental leadership and corporate governance rose noticeably. It continues.

Such scandals as Theranos and FTX have had global publicity and reinforced the public's perception of the many inadequacies of current corporate governance – especially the inability of boards and shareholders to ask such basic questions as 'does the product really do what you claim?', or 'how does this service make profits in the longer-term?'. The rush to acquire Artificial Intelligence monopolies on cheap money is a clear example of this continuing trend.

In the UK one can see the tolerance of, and subservience to, prioritising financial rather than moral priorities, at Public Inquiries such as the governmental service provision levels in the continuing scandals in the Blood Transfusion Service, featuring the infection of hospital patients with infected blood [3], and the appalling treatment of the Post Office sub-postmasters (see Chapter 2), and the inability of governments to apply their own laws to railway or water companies. These do little to re-establish public confidence in the basic laws already passed but not implemented.

Are there Alternatives?

I repeat and amplify Alan Greenspan's words that 'we know that the current models do not work' [2]. So, what might be the alternatives? Having seen the results of Communism and extreme socialism I resist these as essentially authoritarian and inhumane. Current noble attempts to recreate better future companies, for example the 'Benefits Corporations', are well-intentioned, but insufficient in their scope and connectivity. They seem too social-values motivated without sufficient understanding of the necessary legal and governance foundations. Being 'good people' trying to do 'good things' is worthy but no longer sufficient. This alone will not lead to organisational sustainability, and beyond. We need to combine human values with a harder, entrepreneurial edge to cut through the current impasse. I am not denigrating well-intentioned folk, but as I showed with the international NGO example above, they can do harm by pursuing their specific social vision without empathy for their stakeholders and organisational nous.

The current alternative organisational structures I see proposed are wide open to the charges of both 'values washing' and 'greenwashing'. In turn, they have generated strong 'anti-woke' opposition, being denounced vociferously as 'ultra-liberal', 'socialist' or even 'communist', often without good reason. Paradoxically, in a polarising and anti-rational world these same opponents strongly pursue such highly discredited notions of prioritising 'shareholder value' and ill-defined notions of the supremacy of 'free markets'. Such cases sound as if they must be for the benefit of the many yet, for example, with so many minority shareholders marginalised in practice, they tend to benefit already over-rewarded CEOs and a few major shareholders. This then concentrates existing executive power and wealth.

I know that effective governance in times of uncertainty can be reframed rapidly for the benefit of the organisation. This is why I want to see people experimenting, learning consciously, and sharing openly at their work level; then feeding this learning upwards to help create better models for the organisation, the nation and government to understand and copy. But we need be ruthlessly systematic in our thinking about preserving democracy and its implementation to achieve this.

We must face this question if we are ever to have all five corporate governance players learning simultaneously. In Ed Straw's thought-provoking book *Stand And Deliver: A Design For Successful Government* [4] he says:

> *A key issue for democratic politics, in the UK and many other nations, is what to do about voter disengagement. The faith that the electorates have in government – of whatever party – to make their lives better is dramatically decreasing, while the incompetence of our political structure and those elected to office becomes increasingly apparent. The problem is now so acute that many believe that we are in danger of losing an entire generation from the political process . . . Governments are 'organisations' – bigger, more complex, and more important than most, but organisations nonetheless'.*

We have never developed the idea of having a stakeholder electorate in and around the corporate governance of our companies that demands the release the innate learning within. This is why we need to reframe our concepts of legal and emotional 'ownership', and 'stakeholders'.

A Proposal for National Standing Commissions on the Effectiveness of Corporate Governance

To this end I propose for any nation a Standing Commission on Improving the Quality and Practice of Corporate Governance. Will you support this?

This would be created by a national parliament yet be independent of it. Its role would be to collate, integrate, and disseminate the continuous learning of all five players – legislators, directors, stakeholders, regulators, and public oversight – so that the silence on corporate governance is broken and its benefits enjoyed forever.

References

[1] Reg Revans, The ABC of Action Learning, Gower, London, 2011

[2] Alan Greenspan, The Map and the Territory, 2013

[3] Infected Blood Inquiry, website of the public inquiry https://www.infectedbloodinquiry.org.uk/

[4] Ed Straw, Stand and Deliver: A Design For Successful Government, Layerthorpe UK, York Publishing Services, 2014

Chapter 7
The Challenge to Next Generation Directors to Create an Ecosystem for Developing Effective Corporate Governance

The Challenge for Next Generation Directors

I finish this book on an optimistic note. I restate my challenge to the next generation of directors; to be truly radical, to return to roots and start designing corporate governance anew so that it becomes a profession and a craft. It is the cement of our future institutions. Our existence depends on it. In addition I argue for bringing together the five main players in corporate governance – directors, legislators, stakeholders, regulators, and the pubic, to form a national learning system for the continuous development of the profession.

From my hundreds of conversations with next generation directors in many countries I know that many are eager to grasp the opportunity. They want to rise above the stagnation of current corporate governance to create a better world. So, I reprise for the final time that those roots were well planted more than 30 years ago in the UK's Companies Act 1992 but that many of the branches and fruits have been allowed to wither. Non-financial aspects were rarely encouraged. So, financial cankers were allowed to grow.

I have listed below the major challenges that I see need addressing initially by the next generation directors.

The Board of Directors

First, to commit to and deliver the legally espoused role of the Board of directors to promote the success of the company. 'A director of a company must act in a way that he/she considers, in good faith, would be most likely to promote the success of the company for the benefit of its members as a whole; and in doing so have regard (amongst other matters) to:

- The likely consequences of any decision in the long term,
- The interests of the company's employees,
- The need to foster the company's business relationships with suppliers, customers and others,
- The impact of the company's operations on the community and the environment,
- The desirability of the company maintaining a reputation for high standards of business conduct, and,
- The need to act fairly between members of the company.

 | https://doi.org/10.1515/9783112231340-007

For The Individual Director

Second, to live the seven general duties of a director on their Board:
- To act within their powers (their constitution),
- To promote the success of their company,
- To exercise independent judgement,
- To exercise reasonable care, skill, and judgement,
- To avoid conflicts of interest,
- Not to accept benefits from third parties,
- To declare interests in proposed transactions.

The director's role is to ensure the future sustainability of their organisation by having the intellectual, practical and ethical capacity – the nous – to implement and learn from their directoral decisions. Then to be held accountable for the consequences of their simultaneously showing the way ahead in turbulent times whilst ensuring prudent control of their current operations.

I argue that future effective directors now need to deliver the axiom:

Entrepreneurship + Environmental Impact + Social Impact + Accountability + Board Maturity = Effective Corporate Governance.

And all of this must be achieved by being seen to live out in public those basic human values needed to overcome the poly-crisis – accountability, probity, and transparency.

This is my challenge to next generation directors!

Signs of Spring

Why am I optimistic? Hopefully, failing approaches to government and corporate governance are reaching their nadir – provided the next generation then work on building a more integrated future for the economic, environmental, and social deployment of their capital. But will the next generation have the intellectual capacity, craft, raw energy, and moral sentiment to rectify these matters?

I believe that the answer is 'yes'. Two current examples are making breakthroughs. The launch of ISO 37000 sounds like yet another bureaucratic 'do-gooder' initiative. But it is the first international benchmark designed for comprehensive good governance. It 'promotes the tools and practices necessary to enhance boards' performance and efficiency whilst behaving ethically'. It is not overly prescriptive or too full of boxes to tick. It is backed by helpful advice including anti-bribery processes, and IT governance. It was written by a team of Next Gens. I note the enthusiasm of the younger generation to use it as a much more interactive, networked system of continuous learning. This gives me hope. It is worth studying.

Similarly, I note the growing corporate interest in 'sustainability'. This has its strengths, and its opponents. I see the enthusiasm of many of the younger directors to develop these ideas by sharing their action learning through focused practice and rapid feedback. They are not narrowcasting them on social media as a moral cause which can be solved by a mixture of protesting and shouting 'washing', green or otherwise. The recent establishment of the Cambridge Institute for Sustainability and Leadership is a nascent good example of seeking to rigorously develop such systematic learning.

The Silence is Breaking

We now see in many countries the desire for more open and informed debate and decision-making by people keen to have a greater say over their daily and lifetime work. The breaking of the public silence is starting. But the forces being unleashed are clearly not of the Panglossian 'best for all possible worlds' type. At one extreme we see 'wokeism' and the desire to legislate on all aspects of an individual's right to speak, behave, and think, unless it is in line with vaguely defined 'woke' fashion. It demands 'rights', but no social duties, around fashionable 'isms' which then are demanded to be made law. In this world all is for the best – provided you do exactly what I say. There is no freedom for learning or critical debate. It is the opposite of good governance. The good news is that its media prominence is beginning to allow critical public debate to erode the social silence.

At the other extreme are the advocates for free markets, small government, and the authoritarian enforcement of their perceived 'the will of the majority'. Come to think of it, both extremes seem to have remarkably similar ethics and an underlying desire for absolute power to force individuals and groups to do things in the way only they can they specify. Such advocates have never heard of The Law of Human Cussedness. This states that whatever the rules, humans will immediately seek to game them, play the system for their own ends, and subvert them, satirising, and demeaning them. My challenge to the Next Gens is to counter both extreme positions to create more humane organisations through developing professionalism through open and continuous learning.

Voltaire died in 1778, still a believer in 'merchant capitalism' and the idea of freedom of exchange of ideas and trade. He was increasingly worried by the seemingly unstoppable rise of industrial and colonial capitalism. Indeed, he warned of the inbuilt contradictions of global expansion and its powerful advocates – 'those who can make you believe absurdities can make you commit atrocities'. It is such modern intellectual atrocities as 'move fast and break things', 'greed is good', 'monopoly is the aim of every business', and the glorification of 'shareholder value' that many of the Next Generation directors are rightly questioning. As these directors are elected or selected to take up their new powers I hope that they will take more balanced and longer-term beneficial strategic decisions. I applaud them for trying.

Reasons to be Cheerful but Aware

I am not a supporter of the naïve Dr Pangloss, but I remain optimistic. My travels have shown me wars, plagues, famines, poverty, oppression, genocide, and gross injustices. Yet I am constantly amazed at the resilience of humans and their desire for meaningful, innovative, productive, and environmentally balanced family and community lives. The current social silence renders many of them frustrated and inarticulate. Yet, despite everything awful I see in click-bait social media, with their motto of 'if it bleeds it leads', I notice growing improvements over the past 40 years in the human condition, and communications.

My optimism is natural, but I was encouraged hugely following the publication of Hans Rosling's *Factfulness,*[1] and the many optimistic publications that have followed.

Rosling attempts to demystify many of the currently widely accepted depressing, and baseless, 'facts' through careful statistical analysis. He stresses as provable positives that:

- In the past 25years the proportion of the world living in extreme poverty has halved,
- In all low-income countries the proportion of girls finishing primary school has risen to 40 percent,
- The majority of the world population now live in middle-income countries,
- Average life expectancy across the world is now 70 years,
- According to UN figures there are 2 billion children alive today. They calculate that the 2100 total will be the same,
- The average number of global deaths from natural disasters decreased to less than half,
- 80 percent of the world's children have been vaccinated against at least one disease,
- Worldwide, 30- year-old men have spent ten years at school, women of the same age have spent 9,
- Some 80 percent of the world's population now have access to some form of electricity,
- 1n 1996 tigers, black rhinos and giant pandas were all listed as critically endangered. None now are.

But

- All climate experts worldwide are predicting major climate change, global warning and rising sea levels over the next 100 years,
- Mass migration will continue,

All is most definitely not yet for the best in all possible worlds. However, I still see these global trends encouraging human optimism. And I believe that human creativity and ingenuity will help us develop more humane organisations, despite the desires of all the worlds' autocrats, dictators, and career-politicians to block this. If you seek positive news, you will find it and can build on it.

Ubuntu

I finish this book reviewing some basic governance lessons I have learned, especially when I was way out of my comfort zone in troubled Belfast, China, and South Africa. In each I had to reframe my 'Western' mindset away from media-based, spoon-fed instant 'news', and observe what was happening on the ground, and how local people were designing their own futures despite the huge blockages to them doing so. I noticed that unrealistic expectations offered by political leaders, especially of the supremacy of both individualism, 'hard' capitalism, and socialism were often offered too early and then clung on to for far too long. These prove dangerously destabilising to any society. Seeking always to be 'the best' was often the enemy of seeking 'the good' – the learnable and workable. I learned that any Board can start their move into a more positive future by agreeing simply to do good by doing no harm to their stakeholders. They can build from there.

I found the most helpful mindset for me was to accept Nelson Mandela's concept of *Ubuntu*. Simply stated it is:

> *I am because you are.*

For many westerners raised on an ideology of individualism and self-centredness these five words take some thinking through. Once accepted, mutual commitment and a commitment to action learning show their benefits. It is a return to the notion of individuals only being able to exist in an ecological system of which they are only a minute, humble, part sustained by many others.

I argue that the same is true of boards of directors and effective corporate governance. In future they will have to accept that their organisation is only a fragile part of more powerful ecological systems that can easily do without them. Their survival depends on being able to show to all their stakeholders that they can they continuously prove their worth through the effective use of their scarce financial, environmental, and human capitals for the benefit of humanity. They no longer can assume lazily that they will continue to have Unlimited Licence, Unlimited Size, Unlimited Life, and Unlimited Power.

Accepting this will take us towards a Second Age of Business Enlightenment. So, my second challenge to the Next Generation of directors is: will you use Ubuntu as your future motto for achieving this?

Bob Garratt
London
16 October 2025

References

[1] Hans Rosling, Factfulness, Sceptre Books, London 2018

Index

accidental directors 9, 17, 105
– issues 41–56
– level one boards 17, 35–39
– questions to 39–41
– registered director 56
– scandals 49–50
accountability 18, 42, 44–45, 62, 93–94, 118, 167
– board committee meeting 23
– board decisions 44
– business relationship 127
– community values 156
– competence and 35
– corporate governance 58
– social boundaries 64–65
– stakeholders 148
– strategic thinking and 15
accreditation 18, 25–27, 135, 147
action learning 36, 75, 96, 97, 158, 168, 170
Adams, Douglas 32
appointment 12, 21, 25, 39, 47
artificial intelligence (AI) 9, 75–78, 81, 96, 101, 116, 126, 134, 152, 163
austerity 9, 54, 65

big business 22, 38, 65, 160, 161
board dashboards 62, 77, 80, 91, 93–94, 102–103, 137, 153, 158
board maturity, four stages of 10, 16–17
– level one 17
– level two 17
– level three 17
– level four 18–19
board of directors 3, 6, 13–14, 22, 55, 58, 77, 81, 85, 153, 167
bureaucracy 5, 17, 29
business judgment 12, 108, 143, 148, 149, 151
buzzwords 85–86

Cadbury, Adrian 36–37, 63, 69
Caribbean Corporate Governance Institute 18
Charities Act of 2013 48
chartered director 18, 25, 41
chief executives 21, 23, 28, 89, 100, 131
Churchill, Winston 32
climate change 5, 9, 37, 65–68, 151, 169
Common Law 4, 18–21, 23, 28, 36, 44, 64, 148, 150
Companies Act of 2006 13, 19, 20, 22, 33, 39, 41, 48, 51–52, 57, 68, 108, 146, 166
corporate governance 6, 51–52. *See also* government (corporate governance)
– abstract fields 4
– common language 3
– entrepreneurial purpose 5–6, 15–19, 85, 167
– government and 29–34
– grudgingly compliant directors 58–60
– learning systems 3, 4
– myths 19–29
– next generation directors 3, 6, 25, 35, 67–70
– non-system of directors 8
– private, public, and not-for-profit 7
– public accountabilities 3
– reframing 14–16
– sequential stages of board 9
– US 27–29
Corporate Social Responsibility (CSR) 65–66
Covid-19 pandemic 15, 26, 111, 136, 153, 154
cybernetics 14, 104, 109

dated directors 9, 16, 35, 66, 68, 78, 95, 142
decision-making 11, 13, 42, 46, 55, 70, 75, 129, 139, 168
directoral competence 9, 16, 18, 35, 40, 42, 45, 47, 80, 108
directors 7–8, 19–20. *See also* next generation directors
– appointment 12, 25, 39, 47
– board meeting 23
– classes of 23
– insurance liability 40–42
– oath on joining a board 61, 109, 145, 147
– politicians, regulators, and directors 23
– powers 22
– registration 39–40
– separate employment contract 60–61
– short-term targets 95
– stakeholders and legislators 13
– training 11
– unresolved questions 147–148
directorship 3, 12, 14, 35, 42, 44, 52, 53, 61, 108, 118
due diligence 47, 108

Elkington, John 65
entrepreneurship 37, 46, 59, 82, 132, 167

 | https://doi.org/10.1515/9783112231340-008

- business judgement 12
- corporate governance 63–65
- equality, diversity, and inclusion (EDI) 112
- humanity-enhancing 5–6
- innovation 6–7
- learning organisations 103
- opportunities 96, 97
- polycrises 6
- social consequences 17–18
- state-owned 89
Environmental, Social, Governance (ESG) approach 4, 9, 58, 63, 67, 82–83, 119
equality, diversity, and inclusion (EDI) 59, 112
executive director 23, 60, 81, 146
extra-territoriality 29, 43, 63, 69

Factfulness (Rosling) 169
family firms 15, 38, 45–48, 64, 127, 149
fear of missing out (FOMO) 4, 7, 107, 115, 126, 127, 137
financial stakeholders 149–152
The Financial Times (Tett) 114
first-order change learning cycle 101
Fitzgerald, F Scott 86, 96, 123
free market 22, 29, 148, 151, 164, 168
fund managers 4, 20, 37, 157
- and day traders 108
- as registered directors 44–45
- venture capitalists 43–44

Geertz, Clifford 113
government (corporate governance) 5, 9, 29–31, 43, 51–54, 160–163
- and civil servants 7
- company ownership 146–147
- implementation 31
- market reactions 115
- politicians and 82
- procurement 31
- regulation 31–34
Greenspan, Alan 114, 163
greenwashing 68, 164
Grint, Keith 96–97, 140
grudgingly compliant directors 17, 56–57
- contract 60–61
- corporate governance 58–60
- directoral commitment ceremony 61
- level three board maturity 65–70
- level two to level three board 62–64
- Sections 171 and 172 57–58
- time commitment 61–70
Gulf Co-operation Council 18, 26
Gulliver's Travels (Swift) 32

independent judgement 21, 42, 43, 57, 75, 96, 167
An Inquiry Into the Nature and Causes of The Wealth Of Nations (Smith) 3
integrated learning system 142–143, 159–161
- corporate governance 164–165
- effective corporate governance 156–157
- environmental and community stakeholders 153–155
- financial stakeholders 149–152
- five key corporate governance players 143–144
- future directors 147–148
- 'internal' stakeholders 152–153
- learning approach 158–159
- legislators 145–147
- modern context 161–162
- public learning 157–158
- regulators 155–156
- stakeholders 144–149
- systems-based approach 144
- Western Financial Crisis of 2007–2010 162–163
investors 5, 9, 15, 20, 28, 44, 47, 66, 68, 108, 126, 143, 151

Keynes, John Maynard 86
Kids Company, UK 50–51
King, Mervyn 62, 68, 147
Kubernetes (K8s) 14, 83

learning board 9, 10, 57, 60, 68, 70, 96–97, 101
- artificial intelligence (AI) 78, 81–82
- dated directors 78–79
- decision-making 75
- directoral role 79–80
- five elements 94
- framework 91–93
- intelligence 76–77
- level three board 17
- long-term thinking 93
- naïve intelligence 79–80
- parallel development 80–82
- perspectives 83–88
- polycrises 82–83
- shorter-term thinking 93–95
- techniques 95–105

legal fiction 20, 146
legislators 5, 8, 11, 40, 142, 165–166
- corporate governance 52
- not-for-profits and 131–132
- public relations 30
- and regulators 17, 23, 29, 157
- and senior civil servants 13
- unresolved questions 145–147
Limited Liability Partnerships 53, 147
London Taxi Wars 135–136
long-term learning processes 7, 15, 21, 53, 87, 93, 97, 114–116, 140, 150–152

Mandela, Nelson 5, 70, 170
The Map and The Territory (Greenspan) 114–115
Marshall, Tim 122
mass migration 5, 67, 152, 154, 158, 169
Master's in Business Administration (MBA) 77–78
Mintzberg, Henry 102–105, 125, 132
Mutual Observation Period 39, 80, 88, 109, 110

naïve intelligence 79–80, 85, 89
National Health Service (NHS) 54–56
'net zero' policies 5, 53, 81, 126–128, 137, 154
next generation directors 3, 6, 8, 25, 35, 67–70, 119, 142, 166
NextGens 15, 167, 168
NHS Foundation Trust Boards 54–56
non-executive director 23, 60, 69, 81, 146
not-for-profit organisations 4, 7, 8, 15, 25, 29–31, 48–56, 82, 131, 154, 158

Palmer, Coralie 113
Pandora's box 4
paradox 3, 7, 15, 52, 111, 161, 164
policy formulation and foresight 37, 79, 101, 115–118, 120, 125
politicians 4, 8, 23, 26–27, 50, 52–56, 109, 158
- and corporate governance 144
- and governments 82
- legislators 11, 142
- and regulators 18, 38, 69, 70
- US Presidential model 33
polycrises 6, 11, 75, 77, 80, 81
- demand cooperation 14
- emergence 148
- ESG wars 82–83
- geopolitical environments 145
Porter, Michael 133–134, 137
The Post Office Horizon IT Inquiry 25, 31, 49
PPESTT (Political, Physical environment, Economic, Social, Technological, Trade flows) 62, 84, 86, 88, 94, 120–123, 139–141, 158
P + Q (programmed learning + questioning ability) 126
principles-based approach 27, 29, 70
Prisoners of Geography: Ten Maps That Explain Everything (Marshall) 122
professional board 9, 18–19, 64, 107–108
- agenda 110–111
- culture 112–115
- customer satisfaction 109
- directoral competence 108
- effective strategy 131
- face-to-face team meetings 111
- foresight 115–118
- level 4 boards 109–110
- personal timelines 124
- policy development 118–122
- policy formulation 115–118
- strategic thinking 115–118
- team board strategy 122–141
puzzles 4, 9, 38, 95–96, 107, 123, 137, 146

quantitative easing 63, 108, 115, 163

Reform Act of 1832 161
registered directors 9, 13, 14, 20, 22–25, 35, 36, 44–45, 56, 57, 147
regulators 4, 5, 18, 20, 23, 49, 50–51, 142
- boards of directors 27
- civil-service-based 69
- compliance 37
- due diligence 47
- law and practice 27
- legislators and 29
- politicians 38, 69–70
- unresolved questions 155–156
The Restaurant At the End of The Universe (Adams) 32
Revans, Reg 96, 100, 158
Rhodes, Jerry 87
risk-taking decisions 9, 12, 14, 77, 79, 109, 143, 150, 160
Rosling, Hans 169
Rousseau, Jean Jacques 159
rules-based approach 29, 69

Sarbanes-Oxley Act of 2002 27, 69
Schumacher, Fritz 65
second order change learning cycle 100, 101
Securities Exchange Act of 1934 28
shadow director 41, 42, 44, 45
shareholders 15, 18, 59, 64–65, 79, 82
- control 21–22
- and executives 49
- hard-pressed companies 22
- own the business 20–21
- protection 143
- short-term 44, 152
- supremacy 20, 28, 82
- value 64, 168
Silicon Valley 28, 104, 109, 134
Small Is Beautiful (Schumacher) 65
Smith, Adam 3, 159
The Social Contract (Rousseau) 159
social housing association 121–122
social impacts 15, 18, 28, 29, 37, 70, 79, 140, 143
spin-out companies 41–42
stakeholders 6, 8, 12, 13, 16, 20, 57, 65, 170
- environmental and community 153–155
- hard-pressed companies 22
- internal 152–153
- unresolved questions 144–145, 148–152
Stand And Deliver (Straw) 164–165
Standing Commission on Corporate Governance 164–165
start-ups 41–42, 103, 152
Strategic Responsibilities Grid 129–131
subsidiary boards 42–43
supervising management 93, 116, 118
sustainability 4, 9, 29, 53, 65, 68–69, 107, 127, 158, 163, 168
Swift, Jonathan 32
SWOT (strengths, weaknesses, opportunities, threats) 62, 139

Tett, Gillian 114
Thame, Sue 87
'thinking as seeing' concept 102–105
Thinking Intentions Profile 87
Tricker, Bob 5
trophy director 17, 47

Ubuntu 170–171

value chain 133, 137–140, 152
values washing 68, 112, 164
venture capitalists 20, 21, 23, 38, 40, 43–44, 150
video-assisted refereeing (VAR) 27, 157

Walstam, Gunnar 107
Warren Buffet-style approach 152
The Wealth Of Nations (Smith) 159
Wilson, E. O. 7
Worshipful Company of Management Consultants, London 51–52

www.ingramcontent.com/pod-product-compliance
Lightning Source LLC
LaVergne TN
LVHW081324110826
845149LV00007B/1583

* 9 7 8 3 1 1 2 2 3 1 3 3 3 *